Brazilian Women's Filmmaking

Brazilian Women's Filmmaking

From Dictatorship to Democracy

LESLIE L. MARSH

UNIVERSITY OF ILLINOIS PRESS

Urbana, Chicago, and Springfield

Library of Congress Cataloging-in-Publication Data
Marsh, Leslie L.
Brazilian women's filmmaking : from dictatorship
to democracy / Leslie L. Marsh.
p.   cm.
Includes bibliographical references and index.
ISBN 978-0-252-03725-2 (cloth)
ISBN 978-0-252-07873-6 (pbk.)
ISBN 978-0-252-09437-8 (e-book)
1. Motion pictures—Brazil. 2. Women motion
picture producers and directors—Brazil.
I. Title.
PN1993.5.B6M375   2013
791.43082—dc23   2012017556

Contents

Acknowledgments

Much like a film, this book had a behind-the-scenes crew that offered encouragement and insight over many years. My sincere thanks go to Catherine Benamou, who has been supportive of this project since its beginnings. This book was partially funded by a Foreign Language and Area Studies Fellowship from the International Institute at the University of Michigan. While in Ann Arbor, I received valuable feedback from Lawrence La Fountain Stokes, Sueann Caulfield, Maria Cotera, and Paulina Alberto. I am also thankful for the input offered by Philip Hallman, whose research assistance, knowledge of cinema, and friendship I have deeply appreciated. Rebecca Atencio offered insightful suggestions regarding memory studies. Also, I extend thanks to Ana López for her interest in this project and women's filmmaking in Latin America generally.

The preparation of this text took place over several years, in different states and between continents. Numerous individuals and organizations provided assistance to me while I was in Brazil. Having put the cart before the horse several times during the research and writing of this text, I am very grateful to Eunice Gutman, who kindly met with me in Brazil that first day and whose friendship and support during my time in Brazil was pivotal on several occasions. *Muito obrigada*, Eunice. Ana Pessoa was extraordinarily helpful in the early stages of developing this research project, and I have truly appreciated our conversations. Most certainly, I owe a debt of gratitude to all the women directors who invited me into their homes and offices to talk about their craft and their visions of the world. I am forever grateful for their kindness and willingness to share their experiences with me.

A number of institutions and organizations in Brazil were exceptionally helpful, including the Cinemateca Brasileira (São Paulo), the Cinemateca at the Museu de Arte Moderna (Rio de Janeiro), SOS-Corpo (Recife), TV Viva (Olinda) and an untold number of women's organizations in Recife, João Pessoa, Olinda, Rio de Janeiro, and São Paulo that allowed me to attend meetings and participate in some of their activities. The contact with these organizations helped refine my understanding of Brazil generally as well as feminism and the women's movements of Brazil more specifically.

I have had the great fortune to teach at different institutions during the preparation of this text. I am thankful to my colleagues at Denison University who showed interest in my work on women's filmmaking at a time when supportive voices were much needed. The Department of Modern Languages at Denison made me feel truly welcome and valued. Special thanks to Dosinda García Alvite, Mónica Ayala-Martínez, Bernardita Llanos, Susan Paun de García, Margarita Jácome, and the late Eduardo Jaramillo.

In the final stages of this project, I received generous support from Georgia State University to finish edits to the manuscript. In Atlanta, I have found myself among some of the best colleagues one could ask for. I am especially grateful to Fernando Reati for his sincerity and wisdom. I am thankful for the assistance provided me by Tim Jansa, Deborah Loden, and Melissa Skye and for the fortuitous geography of the "República Independiente," which has afforded numerous thoughtful exchanges with Rudyard Alcocer. I owe a large debt of gratitude to William Nichols for his wise input on "how to publish a book" and his willingness to listen to my queries with or without coffee.

I wish to thank Robert Stam and Zuzana Pick for their insightful comments on this text and for the assistance provided by the editors and staff at the University of Illinois Press. Passages of chapters 1 and 5 previously appeared in "Taking Initiative: Brazilian Women's Film-making before and after the *Retomada*" in *New Trends in Brazilian and Argentine Cinema*, edited by Cacilda Rêgo and Carolina Rocha, 257–70 (London: Intellect, 2010). An earlier version of some sections of chapter 5 also previously appeared in an essay co-authored with Catherine Benamou, "Women Filmmakers and Citizenship in Brazil, from Bossa Nova to the Retomada," in *Hispanic and Lusophone Women Filmmakers: Critical Discourses and Cinematic Practices*, edited by Parvati Nair and Julian Albilla (Manchester: Manchester University Press, 2012).

Finally, I thank Zazie, who will never know how incredibly supportive he has been, bringing a smile to my face and spiritual comfort when needed. As well, my heartfelt thanks to my parents Linda and Larry Marsh, who patiently listened and quietly encouraged me to continue.

Brazilian Women's Filmmaking

Introduction

It was raining the day Dilma Rousseff was sworn in as Brazil's new president. Television commentators noted that the stage before the Planalto (presidential office) was usually open but had to be covered due to the rain. The outgoing president Luiz Inácio Lula da Silva stood before the masses who had gathered to witness the ceremony, removed the one-hundred-year-old presidential *faixa* he was wearing, and placed it over Rousseff, who proudly draped it across her chest. Eight years earlier, on January 1, 2003, Lula (as he was popularly known) received the presidential sash from Fernando Henrique Cardoso, marking the first time in Brazil's history that a democratically elected president peacefully handed over duties to another democratically elected president, who then went on to serve a complete term in office. That Rousseff assumed the highest elected office in Brazil is notable not only for the fact that she is the first woman elected president but also for having been a former Marxist guerilla who had been imprisoned and tortured at the hands of the military during the protracted military dictatorship (1964–85). Brazil has certainly changed since the time of Rousseff's days as a political activist. Indeed, just shy of three decades earlier, the open space of the Praça dos Tres Poderes had been the sight of people waving banners, demanding the democratic right to vote for government officials. Despite the rain that day, large crowds—including a significant number of women— had gathered to celebrate.

Commentators did not fail to notice that among the twelve federal police officers who escorted Rousseff (and her daughter, Paula) that day, six were women. The Rousseff administration has unavoidably brought increased attention to women and their vital contributions to Brazilian society. After taking the oath of office, President Rousseff made quick note of her unique status as the first woman president of Brazil. Among her first publicly stated goals as president, she declared she had come to open doors for other women and draw attention to the lives of Brazilian women while governing for all and continuing the social and political advances begun by her predecessor. Indeed, during her first months in office, Rousseff appointed nine women to ministry positions, representing 25 percent of her administration. Notably, Rousseff has also brought attention to women's contributions to the arts. As part of the commemorations of Women's History Month in March 2011, President Rousseff spearheaded the "Mostra das Artistas Brasileiras," an art exhibit that paid homage to renowned twentieth-century Brazilian women painters. Clearly, President Rousseff finds herself in a unique historic position to redirect the conversation on gender and equality in Brazil.

In addition to the art exhibit, Rousseff has given a nod to the increasing number of women in the Brazilian film industry, setting aside a special event to meet with Brazilian actresses and women directors. Perhaps because it is a new development for a (female) president of Brazil to bring such attention to Brazilian women's cultural production, the gathering lends itself to possible misinterpretation of sudden "arrivals." On the contrary, the moment is a long-awaited opportunity in the making, and it is remarkable that only two decades earlier this snapshot would have seemed unlikely, given that at the time the political system seemed a failure (for example, the first democratically elected president Fernando Affonso Collor de Mello was on the verge of being impeached, and inflation was crippling the economy), and filmmaking in Brazil had come to a virtual standstill after Collor's dismantling of the state film agency, Embrafilme.

Among the women filmmakers joining President Rousseff are several directors who were active during the 1970s and 1980s and continue to produce and direct today. While they are known artists being recognized for their work, what is not known is how they managed to break into the industry decades earlier. What is more, little attention has been paid to the philosophical challenges their works have posed. The contemporary successes of women in political life and the increasing numbers of women directors in Brazil can be attributed in part to the broad, sweeping changes in political policies and ideologies that feminism and the second-wave women's movement in Brazil called for starting in the 1960s. In the case of the latter movement, which emerged in the midst of an authoritarian military regime, fighting for full citizenship rights and privileges was a key rallying point. Whether affiliated or not with feminist organizations, the work of Brazilian women filmmakers of the 1970s and 1980s greatly paralleled the country's women's movement and the irrepressible activities of civil society demanding the return to democracy and the expansion of full membership in Brazilian society.

If Rosalind Gill is correct that a great deal of feminist activity in the West now happens in the media,[1] then it seems wholly beneficial to explore how women's film and videomaking in Brazil has served as an arena for feminist ideology and practice. In the 1970s and 1980s, women cultural producers working in audiovisual media challenged authoritarian institutions, questioned women's exclusion, and promoted new understandings of gender, sexuality, and *brasilidade* (Brazilian cultural identity). It is remarkable that women working in film and video demanded rights and privileges as citizens of Brazil at a time when fundamental democratic freedoms did not even exist. Thus, a key concern for this project is how women's film and video concomitantly challenged institutional limitations on Brazil's female citizens and promoted new understandings of gender, sexuality, and women's roles in Brazilian society at a time when their civil and political rights were markedly restricted.

This work presents a study of Brazilian women's audiovisual production from the mid-1970s to the current era. In my discussion of key women's films, documentaries, and independent videos, I argue that Brazilian women's audiovisual production during the authoritarian military regime (1964–85) up to the ratification of a new democratic constitution in 1988 contributed to the reformulation of sexual, cultural, and political citizenship in Brazil. The demands for democracy, or the fight for the return and expansion of civil rights during the 1970s and 1980s, has shifted to a questioning of the quality of democracy in the 1990s and the first decade of this century. Although production contexts have dramatically changed, more recent Brazilian women's films have continued debates regarding citizenship and democracy that were raised by women filmmakers in the 1970s and 1980s. In sum, the central aims of this book are to offer a unique view of how women's audiovisual production has intersected with the reconfigurations of gender and female sexuality put forth by the women's movements in Brazil and to show that women's filmmaking continues to make demands for women's greater social, cultural, and political inclusion.

Filmmaking in Brazil has received international acclaim since the emergence of Cinema Novo in the 1960s, when filmmakers such as Glauber Rocha, Carlos Diegues, and Nelson Pereira dos Santos rose to prominence and were seen as revolutionizing filmmaking in Latin America. Film historians have taken note, publishing several critical works on Brazilian cinema.[2] These texts have laid the fundamental groundwork in the study of Brazilian cinema and, in addition to interpretive works, they have provided much-needed statistical data on film production, the laws and provisional government measures that affect the film industry, and the direction of institutions and agencies dedicated to Brazilian cinema.

However, no study has adequately addressed the role of women in the Brazilian film industry during the last decades of the twentieth century. Randal Johnson and Robert Stam briefly acknowledge women's filmmaking in their co-edited text *Brazilian Cinema* (1982), translating and adapting the article by Elice Munerato and Maria Helena Darcy de Oliveira, "When Women Film."[3] Under the direction of Heloisa Buarque de Hollanda, the text *Quase catálogo: Realizadoras de cinema no Brasil (1930/1988)* provides the most complete index of women filmmakers in Brazil. In addition to the titles of films directed by these women and their formats (in other words, 16 mm, 35 mm, super-8, or Betacam), the catalog provides key production information for each work. As well, in 2002, historian Ana Pessoa published her text *Carmen Santos: O cinema dos anos 20*, focusing on the actress, film director, and producer Carmen Santos (1904–52), who established her own film studio, Brasil Vox Film, in 1934.[4]

Brazilian women have been channeling through cinema their visions of politics and society throughout the twentieth century. From the beginnings of sound cinema to the close of the studio era, pioneer Brazilian women filmmakers sought out their own opportunities from within the structures of the film industry.[5] They often began as actresses who learned the craft of filmmaking and influenced a film's production while on set. Others relied on their personal finances to produce their own films, referred to as *cavação*—a staple of production practices in Brazil during the early twentieth century. In 1930, Cleo de Verberena produced, directed, and starred in the film *O Mistério do Dominó Preto* (The Mystery of the Black Domino). The multitalented Carmen Santos, who began acting at age fifteen, starred in many roles and produced films before taking a role behind the cameras. Her self-financed 1948 film *Inconfidência Mineira* (Minas Conspiracy) was surprisingly the only film Santos completed and released. Another actress, Gilda de Abreu, is said to have intervened decisively in several sequences of the film *Bonequinha de Seda* (Silk Doll, 1936), directed by Oduvaldo Vianna. Years later, Abreu wrote and directed the film *O ébrio* (The Drunk, 1946), which was produced by the newly founded film studio, Cinédia.

As it modeled itself after the Hollywood studio system, the increasing industrialization of Brazilian cinema during the 1950s resulted in more clearly defined roles in film production, which subsequently resulted in a decrease in the number of women participating behind the cameras as directors. In sum, more well-defined roles in production meant women became less likely to make informal directorial contributions. Meanwhile, positions were made available to women as script girls and editors.[6] International sociopolitical crises resulted in a number of technicians from Italy moving to Brazil to perform various duties in the growing Brazilian film industry. Notable among those who arrived are Maria Basaglia and Carla Civelli, both of whom went on to direct feature-length films.[7]

It was on the heels of the international success of Cinema Novo that women began gaining a more solid foothold in filmmaking in Brazil. And, given its hegemonic orientation, the military also contributed to women's emergence into the film industry when it established agencies dedicated to the moving image shortly after the coup d'etat of 1964 (discussed further in chapter 1). During the years following General Ernesto Geisel's declaration of *distensão* (political relaxation) in 1974, the door to democratic freedoms opened and closed on several occasions. Artists pushed against the limits placed on the process leading toward democracy and sometimes found themselves in a room before government censors. Both political and economic censorship were key issues during the second half of the 1970s. Prior to 1974, women who were interested in directing films had to draw from their own savings or seek out private investors to fund their independent short or feature-length film projects.

After 1974, cultural policy in Brazil shifted significantly. Embrafilme, previously dedicated to film distribution, began programs to fund independent film production and provide technical assistance. Young women filmmakers were able to take advantage of Embrafilme's new programs and its generally proactive role in the Brazilian film industry. However, economic difficulties, increasing production costs, and a general failure to establish policies to consolidate the Brazilian film as an industry during the 1980s led to a crisis in Embrafilme and the eventual decision by newly elected president Collor to dissolve Embrafilme in 1990.

The closure of Embrafilme dealt a significant blow to Brazilian cinema and resulted in the virtual standstill of filmmaking in the early 1990s. Fortunately, new cultural policies were quickly put into place, and by the mid 1990s film production crews were back to work. But the contours of filmmaking in Brazil had once again changed considerably. Between 1994 and 1998, critical years of the Retomada (or, "rebirth" of filmmaking in Brazil), a total of twenty films directed by seventeen different women were released, which has resulted in increased attention to the presence of women in filmmaking in Brazil. The number of women participating in all facets of filmmaking in Brazil continues to rise.

❑ ❑ ❑

Among the official photographs of the swearing-in ceremony, Dilma Rousseff is captured at one point sitting next to José Sarney, the current president of the senate and a former president of Brazil during the periods of redemocratization and democratic transition (1985–90). This curious juxtaposition of past and present prompts reflection on the remarkable sociopolitical changes Brazil has undergone in recent decades.

The redefinition of citizenship in Brazil has been one of the most important processes taking place in the past five decades. Since the 1960s, Brazil has transitioned from a bifurcated system of social rights that has produced and reproduced subaltern groups,[8] through a period of repressive authoritarian military rule and subsequent transition to democracy to become a prosperous, vibrant nation. Since 1990, democratic elections have taken place regularly, and concerns about Brazil's governability have waned. Having joined the Southern Common Market (Mercosur/Mercosul) in 1991 and successfully campaigned to host the 2014 World Cup and the 2016 Summer Olympics, Brazil is well on its way toward shedding its image as an exotic, poor Latin American nation and becoming a significant player on the global stage. A founding member of the United Nations, Brazil has campaigned for a permanent seat on the U.N. Security Council, having been elected along with Japan more times to the council than any other member state. Not long ago, Brazil was a country affected by periodic economic crises and intractable foreign debt. Recently, Lula became the first president in Brazil's history to lend money to the International Monetary Fund. Brazil has recently proved to be a socially progressive nation as well. While the United States makes slow, lumbering gestures toward the expansion of civil rights for LGBTQ citizens, Brazil's supreme court unanimously affirmed on May 5, 2011, that stable homosexual couples possessed the same rights as heterosexual married couples. This recent extension of civil and legal rights to Brazil's LGBTQ community is part of a concerted effort over the past decades to extend full citizenship to all men, women, and children in Brazil.

According to Evelina Dagnino, a renewed concept of citizenship through-out Latin America was a "fundamental instrument used by social movements in the struggle for democratization" in the 1970s and 1980s.[9] In the case of the women's movement in Brazil, the concept of citizenship became a rally-ing point for a multifaceted struggle for liberation, including feminine (for example, militant motherhood, protesting rising costs of living, access to public education, and so on) and feminist (for example, gender-role change, female sexuality, women in the workforce) lines of activism. During transition politics, the women's movement saw important successes in the democrati-zation of public and private life, including the creation of "women's institu-tions" such as the state and federal councils focused on women (Conselho Estadual da Condição Feminina, Conselho Nacional da Mulher). Women's groups were particularly successful in areas of daycare, combatting violence against women, and, in 1987, creating the government-backed, feminist-inspired women's health and family planning program (PAISM). With these successes came some shortcomings. Under economic and political pressure from traditionalist lobbies, the final draft of the Constitution of 1988 upheld gender role equity but deleted provisions that promoted gender-role change.[10]

But citizenship involves more than the conquest of rights. Theoretical discussion of citizenship tends to depart from the groundbreaking work of T. H. Marshall, who first suggested a multifaceted understanding of citi-zenship as composed of social, civil, and political phases.[11] Building on this, scholars have suggested that citizenship be thought of less as a status and more as an institutionalized process or a set of relational practices.[12] Nira Yuval-Davis warns that citizenship cannot include all dimensions of social life, but studying citizenship does cast a light on "some of the major issues which are involved in the complex relationships between individuals, col-lectives, and the state, and the ways gender relations (as well as other social divisions) affect and are affected by them."[13] Though the concept of citizen-ship has been frequently framed in legal and political terms and often refers to larger debates regarding inclusion and exclusion, a number of scholars (James Holston and Janice Perlman are two) have argued that citizenship in Brazil should be further theorized in cultural terms. Thus, the important work to undertake at this juncture is to examine how understandings of eth-nicity, race, gender, sexuality, and other factors have shaped the unevenness of democratic citizenship and the experience of belonging.

❏ ❏ ❏

To begin my study, I investigate the role of the Brazilian state in women's filmmaking. Working with extensive oral interviews of women filmmakers I conducted in Brazil, I address several questions regarding Brazilian women's film practice: How and to what degree were new women filmmakers able to negotiate with the military government and Embrafilme (Brazil's state-led film agency) during the 1970s and 1980s? What access points for film production financing were available to them and to what degree were they able to take advantage of them? Second, I consider the changing social and political landscape. How did these women filmmakers position themselves in the context of a society undergoing significant political and cultural change? The history of contemporary Brazilian women's filmmaking offered here is a compilation of published documentation and extensive oral interviews with the filmmakers. These directors provide insights into their film practice, experiences with censorship, and challenges they overcame to produce and direct their own works. This historiographic information is vital for understanding women's filmmaking in the 1970s and 1980s and allows us to appreciate differences and continuities during the resumption of filmmaking in the mid-1990s. Given that an exclusive reliance on textual evidence can greatly limit understanding of the past, chapter 1 takes a cue from Paul Thompson, who asserts that oral histories allow for understanding the experience of others outside the central power structures. What is more, oral histories illuminate "official" history by providing key insights into social, political, and economic processes where the course of events as they are understood and experienced by a range of individuals are juxtaposed with documented dates, names, and places.[14]

Of the women who began directing films during the dictatorship, Ana Carolina,[15] who trained with Cinema Novo directors, is considered a groundbreaking auteur female director. Though she directed nearly a dozen politically oriented documentary films during the late 1960s and early 1970s, my discussion of her work in chapter 2 centers on the trilogy *Mar de Rosas* (Sea of Roses, 1977), *Das Tripas Coração* (Heart and Guts, 1982), and *Sonho de Valsa* (Dream Waltz, 1987). At a time when it was untenable to express her feminist views by way of a realist register, all three films develop a surrealist mode of expression. What is particularly interesting about these works is the overall development from an aesthetics of late Cinema Novo (Marginal Cinema) in the case of *Mar de Rosas* to a surrealist meditation on the masculine imaginary in *Das Tripas Coração* and the eventual move into a surrealist-informed melodramatic story of liberation in *Sonho de Valsa*. As envisioned primarily by male artists of the early twentieth century, surrealism sought the emancipation of the psyche and freedom from material repression. I assert that Ana Carolina's films adapt a surrealist mode of representation to critique repressive ideological constructions of femininity and seek the emancipation of the female psyche. Ultimately, her trilogy critiques those institutions and established beliefs through which presumably good, moral citizens are manufactured—the family, education, religion, romantic love, honoring the father, and the like—and reflects a desire for a new sociability and a new political system in which women are full, equal members. The gesture toward freedom in these films resonates with the second-wave women's movements and the larger struggle to escape a repressive authoritarian regime in the 1970s and 1980s.

Whereas Ana Carolina's films took a psychoanalytical approach to the cultural imaginary, other women directors such as Tereza Trautman, Suzana Amaral, Norma Bengell, and Tizuka Yamasaki drew on the melodramatic mode to offer feminist interventions in the reconstruction of Brazilian politics and cultural identity. After briefly addressing the work of her peers, chapter 3 focuses on Tizuka Yamasaki, another "offspring" of Cinema Novo directors and one of the first women filmmakers, alongside Ana Carolina, to establish a continuous career trajectory in filmmaking. Yamasaki, who claims she inaugurated a "cinema of emotion" in the 1980s, strategically turned to melodrama to comment on Brazil's past in an effort not only to address lacunae in official versions of Brazil's history but also to contribute discursively to a process of redefining citizenship during the years of political opening before the official end of the military dictatorship. And although her career spans four decades, I am interested in her first, highly acclaimed films from the 1980s, including *Gaijin: Os Caminhos da Liberdade* (Gaijin: Paths to Freedom, 1980), *Parahyba, Mulher Macho* (Parahyba, Manly Woman, 1983), and *Patriamada* (Sing, the Beloved Country, 1984). Against a production backdrop in which the military government openly sponsored the production of certain types of historical films that would maintain its hegemony and censored others that criticized contemporary events and authoritarian policies, I explore how Yamasaki's first two works draw on the melodramatic mode to represent iconoclastic, defiant women of the early twentieth century and suture the political milieu of the past to the contemporary push for redemocratization in Brazil. Reflecting an easing of government control in the mid-1980s, one finds in *Patriamada* a blending of melodrama and documentary modes that engage directly with feminist discourse of the time and the struggle for a return to democratic elections in 1984. Her last film is notable in that it reflects a desire for direct engagement with political life, a spirit that is developed further in women's independent and alternative film and video projects.

This project takes a cue from contemporary feminist film studies and extends its study of moving image production beyond feature-length films to include audiovisual works by women that were produced, distributed, and exhibited outside mainstream channels. To that end, chapter 4 offers a historiography of a select group of Brazilian women's independent, alternative film and video production during the 1980s. In addition to exploring funding and production practices, I address how women's independent, alternative film and video contributed to the politicization of gender, race, class, and sexuality at a new political and cultural crossroads during the final days of the military regime and during the period of redemocratization from 1985 to 1988. By opening the discussion to film and video production, my analysis moves to the Northeast of Brazil. In the metropolitan region of Rio de Janeiro, I consider works by independent film- and videomaker Eunice Gutman, whose work has shifted from 35 mm to video over the decades. In the metropolitan region of São Paulo, I address work by the Lilith Video Collective, a group of three women who, like Gutman, dedicated themselves to bringing greater awareness to women's issues as the Brazilian constitution was being rewritten. In the northeastern state of Pernambuco, the feminist nongovernmental organization SOS-Corpo drew on the communicative possibilities afforded by video to contribute to the developing feminist discourse in the metropolitan region of Recife, the state capital of Pernambuco and one of Brazil's largest cities. In the case of SOS-Corpo, my discussion considers women's audiovisual production within an internationally funded women's group and how video became a vital avenue to address the most pressing concerns for feminist activism in the region. This treatment of women's independent, alternative film and video production draws attention to a significant yet understudied area of women's media production that has existed outside the mainstream channels of production, distribution, and exhibition but has greatly contributed to reformulating citizenship in Brazil.

The years encompassing the transition from an autocratic regime to a new democracy did not progress without challenges, but, relative to the past, Brazilians have new understandings of what being a *cidadão* (citizen) signifies and with this has come an increasing awareness of their ability to put pressure on government officials and a decreasing tolerance for the unevenness of citizenship that persists. Concomitant with these changes in society, the film industry in Brazil underwent dramatic reorganization after the closure of Embrafilme (1989/90). Perhaps owing to the emergence in the mid-1990s of several new women directors, critics suggested that women were at the forefront of the Retomada. Furthermore, while it is true that from 1990 to 2010, no fewer than forty-five women directed feature-length films for which they have received numerous awards, female directors have hardly dominated the field. They continue to face a general film production context in which it is increasingly difficult to realize aesthetically and ideologically challenging works, let alone count on continued access to production funds. Thus, in chapter 5, I close my discussion of Brazilian women's filmmaking with an overview of the current shape of filmmaking and how women directors have positioned themselves in this new context. In addition to an analysis of production, distribution, and exhibition, I address questions regarding contemporary women's filmmaking: What distinguishes women's filmmaking in the current context? To what degree do feminist discourses exist in women's filmmaking today, and how are these discourses framed? How do more recent women's films address questions of feminine agency? The majority of films directed by women that take up the feminine condition focus on the experiences of adult women. However, as I argue, the most critical explorations of gendered relations, sexuality, and the unevenness of democracy are found in contemporary cinematic representations of female youth in works such as Sandra Werneck's *Meninas* (Teen Mothers, 2005) and *Sonhos Roubados* (Stolen Dreams, 2010), Tata Amaral's *Antônia* (2006), and Denise Garcia's *Sou Feia Mas Tô Na Moda* (I'm Ugly but I'm Trendy, 2005). Indeed, it is in the representations of youth where one finds the most marked differences between mainstream, masculinist cinema and women's cinematic contributions to debates surrounding femininity, citizenship, and Brazilian cultural identity.

Brazilian Women's Filmmaking and the State during the 1970s and 1980s

Despite a long history in filmmaking and increasing visibility, women's contribution to Brazilian cinema has only recently begun to gain greater attention from scholars of Latin American film. In the preface to the article they include in their volume on women's filmmaking in Brazil, Randal Johnson and Robert Stam refer to the presence of women filmmakers in world cinema as a strong but subterranean current.[1] Thus, this chapter aims to fill a void in Brazilian film historiography and bring women's activity in Brazilian film to the surface. By drawing on both published materials as well as oral interviews, I aim to place an important group of women filmmakers on the cultural map of contemporary Brazilian cinema.

A considerable amount of historiographical work on Brazilian cinema has been undertaken, but it has overlooked or only tangentially included women's participation. Although textual documentation may often form the basis for historiographical work, textual evidence should not be considered the only source for understanding what has unfolded in the past. Paul Thompson provides a foundational account of how oral testimony holds a central role in the charting of history. He asserts that, as a methodology, oral histories offer several advantages for historical research in that they allow for understanding the experience of others outside central power structures. They illuminate "official" history by providing key insights into social, political, and economic processes where the course of events as they are understood and experienced by a range of individuals are juxtaposed with documented dates, names, and places. Calling on participants' experiences then allows the cultural historian to explore alternative angles of established history and consider the viewpoints of "minor" figures. Oral histories allow researchers to cross the public-private divide to consider those participants in political processes that have not held an elected office or other public position. In addition, oral histories offer an advantage in that they serve as a key mode of research for investigating firsthand the lives of women and how they have "unofficially" participated in political processes.[2]

Taking into account the key processes taking place in Brazilian cinema during military dictatorship and the transition to democracy, I first investigate the role of the state in women's filmmaking. How and to what degree were new women filmmakers able to negotiate with the state and the state-led film agency Embrafilme during the 1970s and 1980s? What access points were available to them and to what degree were they able to take advantage of them? Second, I take into consideration the changing social and political landscape. How did these women filmmakers position themselves in the context of a society undergoing significant political and social change? Once the government took on a more supportive role in the film industry, contemporary women filmmakers began participating in filmmaking; however, women filmmakers in Brazil have conflicting opinions about the state-led agency and its role in supporting their careers as directors.

Before Embrafilme

Prior to the military coup d'état of 1964, the Brazilian film industry received little assistance from government agencies. Ongoing discussions at this time regarding the role of the state in the film industry led to the creation of GEICINE[3] in 1961 at the beginning of the administration of Jânio Quadros. Generally speaking, GEICINE successfully articulated the concerns of the film industry to ministries and government agencies, but its programs largely benefited large production companies and foreign distributors.[4] Independent filmmakers were at a great economic disadvantage, as there were few funding options available to filmmakers who were starting out in the late 1950s and early 1960s. Concurrently, Cinema Novo filmmakers, taking inspiration from the production practices of postwar Italian neorealist directors and the French notion of the auteur, introduced their own understanding of filmmaking in an economically disadvantaged context, became a reference point for contemporary Brazilian cinema, and greatly influenced Latin American Cinema generally.

Some financial relief came to independent directors in 1963 when Guanabara governor Carlos Lacerda decreed the formation of the Comissão de

Auxílio à Indústria Cinematográfica (CAIC, Commission for Aid to the Film Industry). This agency, charged with administering two programs of financial assistance to the film industry, is notable for becoming a major source of funding for filmmakers in and near Rio de Janeiro, including Cinema Novo directors, and was the first state agency to provide money to a woman filmmaker. Helena Solberg received funds from the CAIC to produce her groundbreaking short film *A Entrevista* (The Interview) in 1966, a film in which Solberg offers a critique of female social values of her own upper-class Rio de Janeiro.[5] The CAIC brings about another important "first" involving the state and the film industry in Brazil in that it exerted ideological control over the film projects that would receive its financial assistance. Monies were denied to any film that attacked the democratic system through the use of violence, racial or class prejudice, or propaganda. These early signs of economic and political censorship proved to be a multifaceted problem during the 1970s and into the early 1980s during the authoritarian military regime.

Despite its neoliberal economic stance, the military regime began investing in and taking control of the cultural sector soon after assuming power. In 1966, The Instituto Nacional de Cinema (INC, the National Film Institute) came into being by decree. During its existence from 1966 to 1975, the INC was responsible for increasing film production in Brazil by 157 percent.[6] The institute passed a number of resolutions that provided funds for the importation of expensive filmmaking equipment, provided cash awards and subsidies for film production, and established an increase in compulsory exhibition of national films.

In retrospect, the INC effected some positive changes in the national film industry. However, the nature of those successes needs to be evaluated more closely. Starting in 1967, the INC sponsored three key programs to provide production assistance to Brazilian filmmakers: an awards program based on quality, a subsidy program based on box-office receipts, and a co-production program drawing from income taxes of foreign distributors. While these programs became important sources of funding for Brazilian filmmakers, especially the members of the Cinema Novo group,[7] the INC policies did not benefit newcomers. Notwithstanding that few women were in a position at this time to take advantage of the funding made available, the INC measures largely assisted already-established filmmakers and production companies, which would prove to be a trend in later years. From 1965 to 1969, no women working in 16 mm or 35 mm film received funds from the INC. From 1970 to 1974, the INC funded no feature-length film projects by women directors but did fund seven out of a total of seventy-one short film projects, representing approximately 9.85 percent of women's short film production during this period.[8] While the INC was in existence, most women continued to draw from their own finances or from private investors to help fund their short or feature-length film projects.

Women who began their careers in film in the mid- to late 1960s were entering a profession that had not been truly open to them previously. In Brazil at the time, filmmaking was a mode of expression open to few individuals. This, in part, explains why women took different paths to learn the craft of filmmaking. A few decided to go abroad to study filmmaking. Suzana Amaral and Helena Solberg both went to the United States in the late 1970s.[9] Sandra Werneck completed a one-year practical course in Holland, and Eunice Gutman studied in Brussels, Belgium, where she completed a degree at the National Institute of Art, Spectacle, and Techniques of Diffusion (INSAS). Others took less conventional routes. Tereza Trautman explains that she became interested in cinema in her teenage years but when she wanted to learn how to make films, she was aware of only one private school in São Paulo, which was not an economic option for her. Instead, she learned by reading books on her own, borrowing materials, and working with friends who contributed supplies or their labor.[10]

This sort of cooperative work Trautman describes is common to many of these women filmmakers and has been central to the development of their careers. Tata Amaral explains that she learned to make films by collaborating with an informal group of people in São Paulo and by assisting her husband at the time, who was involved in filmmaking.[11] Amaral's experience also resembles that of Lúcia Murat, who was dating a man involved in cinema and journalism. Murat, an experienced journalist, notes that her involvement in cinema came about organically since the two fields were closely linked in the 1960s and 1970s.[12] Sandra Werneck reflects on her own experience selling a family cow to get supplies to make her first film and working in a context where, lacking a commercial structure, "tudo era co-operativado" (everything was cooperative).[13] Julia Lesage has discussed different modes of media production by women, noting that a collective approach such as the one described by Sandra Werneck, allows for (in addition to sharing economic resources) skill sharing and nonhierarchical, collective scripting, editing, and filming.[14] Werneck notes that her daughter, who is trying to break into the field in the Retomada period, has to come up with a lot more money to complete her first film. Werneck asserts that the collaborative environment she experienced no longer exists.[15]

Some followed the path that women directors such as Carmen Santos, Gilda de Abreu, and Cleo de Verberena took in the early years of cinema. Ana Maria Magalhães worked behind the scenes on films in which she also acted. Under the direction of Glauber Rocha and Nelson Pereira dos Santos, Magalhães learned to edit film, the discourse of film, and the professional rigors of being a director. She notes, however, that her proximity to production as an actress did not translate into an easier entrance into the field. Actresses who showed interest in the technical realms of the profession were not always taken seriously.[16] Ana Carolina and Tizuka Yamasaki combined their formal study of cinema with practical experience. While Ana Carolina studied at the Escola de São Luiz in São Paulo, Tizuka Yamasaki began her studies at the Universidade de Brasília before transferring to Rio de Janeiro upon the closure of her program in the capital. In addition to their formal training, both worked on film sets with established Cinema Novo directors such as Walter Hugo Khouri, Glauber Rocha, and Nelson Pereira dos Santos.[17]

The contact Ana Carolina and Tizuka Yamasaki had with these respected male filmmakers provided them with invaluable experience and gave them additional credibility years later when they needed to apply for production funding with Embrafilme and private investors in order to direct their first feature-length films. Revealing the importance of her experience working with Cinema Novo directors, Yamasaki declares that during her years of learning the trade, the most important thing for her "era ter conseguido ficar perto do Nelson (Pereira dos Santos) que era uma ponte para o mercado de trabalho" (was to have managed to stay close to Nelson [Pereira dos Santos], who was a bridge to the labor market).[18] The influence of Cinema Novo filmmakers was as much a benefit as it was a detriment to aspiring women directors. In short, they appreciated the training they received and the insights into filmmaking they learned when working with these filmmakers, but they certainly do not feel they owe their success to Cinema Novo predecessors.

In 1969, the Empresa Brasileiro de Filmes (Embrafilme) came into being during the most repressive years of the military regime. Originally created to promote and distribute Brazilian films abroad, Embrafilme was charged to oversee commercial and noncommercial film activities such as film festivals, the publication of film journals, and training of technicians. As an *autarquia*, Embrafilme was an independent enterprise that operated with funds from the state. Although the organization was self-governing, the state could still exert a great deal of influence.

Embrafilme held relatively few powers during the first years of its existence, but by 1974 it had grown into a national distributor and a significant source of film-production financing. The agency began a low-interest (10 percent) loan program in 1970, which made funds available to production companies based on a ranking system. Each company was placed into three categories according to its production history. The vast majority of available funds went to well-established firms, and a small percentage went to less experienced or beginning producers. Beyond production history, Embrafilme did not presumably make qualitative or ideological judgments about proposed film projects, which explains why some producers of *pornochanchadas*, a genre of film produced in the 1970s that combined soft-core porn and comedy, were able to take advantage of some state financial assistance.[19]

With little to no production history, Embrafilme's loan program did not benefit many women filmmakers. From 1970 to 1974, only one woman, Lenita Perroy, received production assistance from Embrafilme to produce her second feature-length 35 mm film, *A Noiva da Noite* (The Night Bride, 1974). In contrast, women received most of their support from funds they were able to come up with on their own and, to a limited degree, from private investors, programs still in effect in the INC, and regional and local sources of support of filmmaking. From 1965 to 1974, no regional or state entity funded a woman's 16 mm or 35 mm feature-length film.[20] During the same period, regional or state entities assisted with the production of nine (or 12.7 percent) short films made from 16 mm or 35 mm film stock.[21] Ana Carolina, as a case in point, was able to direct a 35 mm short film *Indústria* (1969) after winning a prize from the Secretary of Culture in the State of São Paulo.[22] Other novice women directors received financial support to make films while they were enrolled in university programs that were opening up in the late 1960s and early 1970s.[23] These awards and university programs were an important source of local and regional funding for women's filmmaking.

As discussed further on, women's participation in filmmaking in Brazil took firm root in the 1980s on the heels of a period of significant expansion of Brazilian cinema in its own market[24] and at the intersection of second-wave women's movement and a slow return to democracy. By the early 1980s, Embrafilme had become a vital source for independent, auteur cinema in Brazil and helped secure (but not sustain) women's place in the Brazilian film industry.

(Re)entering the Frame

The 1970s can be defined as the years when women were beginning to appear in the contemporary film industry as directors, and they were entering a context that was not entirely prepared for them or what they had to express. Tereza Trautman describes her experiences in the early 1970s that are illustrative of the context many women directors faced. Lacking mechanisms of support for film production, Trautman took on several roles in film production, relied on loaned equipment, bought expired film stock, and solicited the help of many friends to complete her first film *Fantástico* in 1970.[25] She signed a contract with a small distributor, which has long since gone out of business. Once in the hands of the exhibitors, the film was given the subtitle *Os Deuses do Sexo* (The Gods of Sex), but the film, she states, had nothing to do with sex at all.[26] The title of Trautman's film had been altered to attract spectators. A government censor stopped the film and demanded scenes be cut, which she did before the distributor put the scenes back in a week later.[27]

Aware of her need to build a curriculum to submit for future proposals and concerned about the future of her film, she entered one of the nation's most respected newspapers, *A Folha de São Paulo*, to announce the release of her first film. Here she was met with shock, disbelief, and comments such as "uma mulher fazendo filme, aqui no Brasil?" (a woman making movies, here in Brazil?) and "eu não tinha nem idéia de nada disso" (I had no idea about any of this).[28] Shortly thereafter, exhibitors and distributors asked about her next film, which she would complete three years later.[29] The film, *Os Homens Que Eu Tive* (All The Men I Had, 1973), contested the objectification of women in Brazilian society and marked a significant point in women's production when women sought to make a shift from being discursive objects to being discursive subjects.[30] The female protagonist, Pity, questions her happiness in her marriage and engages in an extramarital affair, with her husband's consent. Trautman's second feature-length film entered a context when the military government exercised strict control over all forms of mass media. Charged with denigrating the Brazilian woman, the film was hypocritically banned until 1983[31] while *pornochanchadas* became a staple in the Brazilian film industry. In contrast and perhaps because it features a widowed female protagonist who takes on a younger lover, Carlos Reichenbach's *O Império do Desejo* was released in 1981.

What is clear from the experiences Trautman describes is that women began to gain access to film expression but they entered a context in which they had little to no production assistance and a very limited infrastructure to support independent filmmaking. If their points of view were not accepted, they were vulnerable to censorship and the ruining of their careers. Years later, many of the multiple roles Trautman took on to produce, direct, market, and distribute her own film would be overseen by units within Embrafilme.

For women, the struggle to gain access to film as a means of expression would not truly take off until the mid-1970s at the confluence of Embrafilme's reorganization and the redirection of the state in 1974. On the heels of rising social protest following an economic boom, which created greater social divides between the wealthy elite and the working classes, General Ernesto Geisel assumed the office of president in 1974. As indicated previously, one of his first declarations was the slow, gradual return to democratic rule. Geisel's political position was not met with unanimous support, and the period is marked with tensions and contradictions within the military regime. Nonetheless, the nation entered a period of political decompression (or, *distensão*) that lasted until approximately 1979, when the regime declared general amnesty.

Parallel to these political events, Embrafilme took over many of the duties previously held by the INC, and filmmaker Roberto Farias was chosen as the agency's new general director. Many members of the Cinema Novo group joined him and eventually secured a place within the state apparatus. During Farias's tenure, state policy shifted away from what had been a relatively neutral, technical, and supportive role regarding the film industry to a selective, market-driven approach. The original loan program Embrafilme instituted in 1970 was restructured to further benefit stable production companies. Only those producers with moderately established capital could apply; thus, new or beginning producers (including women directors) were not eligible for financing. Second, Farias expanded an existing coproduction program. The maximum amount Embrafilme would contribute to a film's production cost rose from 30 percent to 100 percent. To be eligible for coproduction financing, producers were ranked according to a point system based on prior experience, awards received, and activity in the industry. These guidelines clearly favored Cinema Novo producers and directors who had a history in filmmaking and more awards to their credit. In his assessment of the film industry in Brazil, Randal Johnson notes that these new policies, combined with the arbitrary exercise of censorship, ultimately resulted in the state's becoming the primary source of funding for independent film production.[32]

In contrast to the experiences of Trautman, Ana Carolina reflects on the important transition in production practices that took place in the mid- to late 1970s, when she started her first feature-length fiction film. For her as well as for veteran filmmakers, Embrafilme was a vital source for funding. Ana Carolina notes that when she began making films, the Cinema Novo directors had firmly established their presence in Brazilian cinema. When asked if she feels that their aesthetic proposals or their strategies for production influenced her, she highlights her similarities and differences from Cinema Novo filmmakers:

> When I arrived in cinema, the Cinema Novo directors they were already established, consolidated. And they had created a production strategy that we all absorbed completely. This type of inexpensive production with a lot of people in the same film, several individuals—one got a camera, then another got sound, and another got access to a lab and whatever. One gave a little bit of money. Another gave another little bit. A very little bit. That there, I assimilated that completely. The difference is that when I got to feature-length filmmaking in '74 or '75, Embrafilme was already functioning, it already existed. And I with my first fiction film went off to make it with Embrafilme—which is a substantial change from Cinema Novo. I'm an offspring of Cinema Novo. I'm not a legitimate representative of Cinema Novo. When I got to filmmaking they were already grown. And the first offspring of Cinema Novo, in which I'm included, they all went running for Embrafilme.[33]

Here, Ana Carolina makes the keen observation that she and her generation of filmmakers bridged two different modes of production. A cooperative, inexpensive form of production came into contact with the support structures of the state-led agency, Embrafilme. In addition to aesthetic and thematic differences, these women entered into a new era of film production in Brazil after the creation of Embrafilme in 1969 and its reorientation in 1974. New filmmakers could take advantage of new procedures put into place. Next, I discuss how they got their foot in the door.

Working with Embrafilme

The response from women filmmakers was to establish their own production companies, to produce their own projects with or without government assistance and, if possible, to become eligible for production funding according to new requirements set forth by Embrafilme. A notable example is that of Tizuka Yamasaki. While working on film sets in the mid-1970s, Yamasaki developed the idea for her first feature-length fiction film. But, as a student, a newcomer, and without a family that could support her, she didn't know how she would be able to make her first film. It was at this point, she states, that she realized she needed to form her own production company. With two friends (Cacá Diniz and Lael Rodrigues), she established the Centro de Produção e Comunicação (CPC, Production and Communication Center) in 1976, two years after Embrafilme was reorganized.[34]

In order to request funds from Embrafilme, new filmmakers needed to develop a curriculum. Specifically, Yamasaki explains that she needed to produce one film with funds from Embrafilme and one film made outside Embrafilme.[35] Yamasaki and her partners in the CPC worked with a mutual friend to produce a very inexpensive film called *J. S. Brown: O Último Herói* (directed by José Frazão, 1977). At this time, Glauber Rocha was looking for a producer for his film *A Idade da Terra* (1980) and, according to Yamasaki, Rocha liked the idea of a group of young people producing his film, as it would allow him to make the film as he wished.[36] Since Rocha's project was funded by Embrafilme and her friend's was not, Yamasaki explains that when both films were completed they had the right to request funds from Embrafilme. The CPC was to act as the producer and she would be the novice director. In this way she was able to make her first feature-length film, *Gaijin: Os Caminhos da Liberdade* (1980). It bears noting that at this time the CPC was also the executive producer of *Eles Não Usam Black-Tie* (directed by Leon Hirszman, 1980), *Eu Te Amo* (directed by Arnaldo Jabor, 1981), *Rio Babilônia* (directed by Neville D'Almeida, 1981) and *Bar Esperança* (directed by Hugo Carvana, 1982).

Embrafilme played an important role in helping many women finish their first feature-length fiction film. Rare, however, are the cases in which women received full or continuous support from the state agency. By contrast, those who had consolidated their careers as directors within the Cinema Novo group had much greater financial support from the state. In his analysis of the film industry in Brazil, Randal Johnson characterizes the Cinema Novo group as forming a hegemony in the state apparatus, which is perhaps most evident in the fact that nearly all films by Cinema Novo participants were coproduced by Embrafilme.[37] The three films not coproduced were ultimately distributed by Embrafilme and, in this way, still benefited from state support. Indeed, filmmaker Glauber Rocha unsuccessfully presented his film *A Idade da Terra* to producers in five different countries over the course of five years but was only able to obtain production funding from Embrafilme in Brazil.[38] In fact, Embrafilme financed 100 percent of Rocha's film.[39] This further reveals the degree to which Embrafilme was an important resource for Cinema Novo.

Unlike the Cinema Novo group, women filmmakers did not hold a privileged position within the state apparatus and did not bank on continued production support from the state. In addition to Ana Carolina and Tizuka Yamasaki, Ana Maria Magalhães (*Mulheres de Cinema*, 1976), Suzana Amaral (*A Hora da Estrela*, 1985), Norma Bengell (*Eternamente Pagú*, 1987), Lúcia Murat (*Que Bom Te Ver Viva*, 1989), Tereza Trautman (*Sonhos de Menina Moça*, 1988), and Maria do Rosário (*As Pequenas Taras*, 1980) utilized funds from Embrafilme to produce and direct their own works. Of the fifteen feature-length films directed by women from 1975 to 1989 in 16 mm or 35 mm format, twelve (or 80 percent) were made with some financial support from Embrafilme.

Despite its perceived deficiencies, the agency is noted for helping and allowing new people to enter the film industry. Lúcia Murat, who arrived on the filmmaking scene toward the end of Embrafilme's existence, expresses mixed feelings about a centralized agency: "If you have a centralized agency that has the conditions to define support for a project, it permits, on the one hand, distortions such as using influential contacts—like any bureaucratic society in the name of equality—but it also permits that new people can begin, so they can function in some manner. It still is, I think, a way for people to get a start in these things."[40] As a relatively new film director, Murat received help from Embrafilme to produce her first widely distributed film, *Que Bom Te Ver Viva* (How Nice to See You Alive, 1989), which treated state-sponsored torture and repression of women during the military dictatorship. She explains that the project took off after she won a prize sponsored by Embrafilme for *media-metragens* (medium-length films). In the end, she credits Embrafilme for providing up to 70 percent of the production funding for her film. With this money and the contributions of four additional coproducers, she completed what she refers to as a very inexpensive film.[41] It is important to note that Murat emphasizes that it was "a very inexpensive film," thus putting the amount of funding into perspective. Although Embrafilme provided a substantial percentage of production funding, it was nevertheless a relatively small sum.

As indicated earlier, women may have started with Embrafilme, but they did not count on continued production support. After releasing her first film *Gaijin: Os Caminhos da Liberdade* (Gaijin: Paths to Freedom, 1980) with assistance from Embrafilme, Tizuka Yamasaki went on to establish herself as a director of award-winning, feature-length films. With CPC, she produced and directed *Parahyba, Mulher Macho* (Parahyba, Manly Woman, 1983) and *Patriamada* (Sing, the Beloved Country, 1984) with monies from private investors.

All three films were distributed by Embrafilme and, in this way, benefited from the state film agency. Yet her memory of this period in the late 1970s and early 1980s, when she produced and directed her first feature-length fiction films, reveals a particular frustration: "I joke a lot about this—I see it like this: Cinema Novo took a long time to accept me, to give me a certain credibility as a director. I made a film but this wasn't enough. I'm a daughter of Cinema Novo."[42] Despite the close working relationships that Yamasaki developed with Cinema Novo filmmakers Nelson Pereira dos Santos and Glauber Rocha, she does not feel she was considered a true colleague. She further states that she does not describe her experience as having been admitted to the inner power structures of the Brazilian film industry: "I was never called upon by those in power in Brazilian cinema, which for many years was in the hands of Cinema Novo. Cinema Novo never admitted me into their group. . . . We were never very well received. For many years, we weren't—I wasn't included in Brazilian Cinema. My activities were always isolated, parallel, because I wanted to know what was happening."[43] Although it is impossible to specify when or how this underlying social and political marginalization within the power structures of Brazilian cinema expressed itself overtly, it is reasonable to believe that it was manifest in some concrete fashion. I will explore this issue further in a discussion of the effects of political and economic censorship.

Ana Carolina has unambiguous opinions regarding how power was exercised inside Embrafilme when she reflects on her experiences producing and directing films in the 1970s and 1980s. She directed three films regarded as forming a feminist trilogy: *Mar de Rosas* (Sea of Roses, 1977), *Das Tripas Coração* (Heart and Guts, 1982), and *Sonho de Valsa* (Dream Waltz, 1987). Emphasizing that she received limited help from the state film agency, she reveals that with regard to these films she "only had help from Embrafilme with *Mar de Rosas*, which had Embrafilme and four other producers, one with a crew, another with the lab—everything, like a group of people." Ana Carolina further reveals that her first feature-length documentary film, *Getúlio* was completed in 1974 and had no support from the INC or Embrafilme. In a rare gesture of cooperation between film producers and exhibitors, she reveals that Severino Ribeiro, the owner of a chain of movie theaters in Rio de Janeiro and São Paulo entered in the final stages and helped with the promotion of the film.[44] Her comments suggest that Embrafilme was far from being a neutral government agency charged with overseeing the Brazilian film industry:

I think Embrafilme was an extraordinary creation with a great percentage of perversion. Because, at the same time that it came along to bring together, to unite directors and give them shelter, it came with something else very perverse because it began to choose: "You yes, him no. You yes, him no. You yes, him no." Who is the darling chosen one of Embrafilme? There, you, you are the darling of Embrafilme. And then you have the damned one who is out of Embrafilme. There was never any course correction in Embrafilme. It didn't need to be demolished in the way that it was. It was demolished very quickly and with a lot of rage. There's something strange in that. It came to represent something like a horrible stepmother, a perverse mother that gave food to some and killed others. It's all complicated. This was the total absence of cinema policy.[45]

However, Ana Carolina does not reveal specific moments of having felt she was excluded from the privileges afforded by Embrafilme. Similar to Tizuka Yamasaki's experience, her next two films, *Das Tripas Coração* (1982) and *Sonho de Valsa* (1987), were produced with private funding and then distributed by Embrafilme. Notably, both films were completed many years apart due to difficulties in amassing the necessary production funds.

Regardless of the degree to which they feel they were or were not integrated into the inner circle of power controlling the film industry in Brazil, Tizuka Yamasaki and Ana Carolina were both able to establish contacts with the necessary financial networks to produce and direct their films. For this they should be commended but also seen as holding a particularly privileged position vis-á-vis other women who were equally interested in and motivated to produce and direct films during the 1970s and 1980s.

Their critiques need to be balanced with praise for the state agency. Independent efforts to improve filmmaking in Brazil were supported by the state through its film agencies. In fact, Embrafilme provided much-needed assistance to the film industry, which is all too often overlooked. In addition to its financial assistance to produce films, Embrafilme developed a legal discourse to protect and promote Brazilian films. One of the most important laws affecting women's filmmaking was the *Lei do Curta* (Short Film Law), first ratified in 1975. This law stipulated showing a short Brazilian film before every foreign film shown in the Brazilian market. The vast majority of films produced and directed by women are, in fact, short films.

São Paulo filmmaker Tata Amaral notes that, in addition to the *Lei do Curta*, regional financial support of short filmmaking has been a vital resource. Since the 1970s the state of São Paulo has offered an annual "Prêmio de Estímulo á Produção de Curta Metragens" (Prize to Stimulate Production of Short Films).[46] Other states started to hold a similar annual award program in the mid-1990s.[47] While some disparagingly refer to short films as *cartões de visita* (calling cards), short films require less funding and are therefore more accessible than feature-length projects. Moreover, short films have served a vital role in training new filmmakers and certainly comprise an artistic format in its own right.

Eunice Gutman describes taking advantage of the opportunities provided by the *Lei do Curta*. She explains how she and colleague Regina Veiga would produce their short films in 35 mm, and then Embrafilme would give them an advance on the distribution. If she hadn't spent much on the short film's production, she would recoup her capital and make another one.[48] In this way, she and other young women filmmakers were able to break into the film industry and, perhaps more important, short films became a viable outlet for their work. Because their films were produced with 35 mm film stock, they could enter the mainstream theater circuits and be distributed throughout Brazil. The full potential of the short film program was not realized, unfortunately, as exhibitors would produce low-quality short films and randomly include them with the feature-length film. Spectators became disgruntled, and there were few measures to enforce compliance with the statute.[49]

Gutman describes a number of services Embrafilme offered to filmmakers that she found highly beneficial, and which the current filmmaking context lacks. First, there were projection rooms for 16 mm and 35 mm film available for showing films: parties interested in the film or its progress would sometimes like to view a work in progress, and at that time, it was impossible to screen a work without access to a 16 mm or 35 mm projector. A press service would spread news about a film's release. Assistance was available to mail films abroad to festivals without cost to the producers. Moreover, if a film were accepted in a film festival, Embrafilme would pay for part of the travel expenses for the director.

Gutman also underscores the importance of Embrafilme's physical existence. Because Embrafilme was a public facility, the average person had the right to go there to see films made by fellow Brazilians.[50] With the vast majority of Brazilians living in poverty, this democratized access to cultural works. As well, Embrafilme established a supportive environment for filmmakers. Gutman notes that Embrafilme's existence benefited filmmakers as a community. Although situated in Rio de Janeiro, Embrafilme was a location where people could meet, talk about their projects, and perhaps find work. That is to say, the existence of Embrafilme led to a richer dialogue among filmmakers in Brazil.[51] Gutman emphasizes the importance of being able to meet with other members of the profession to solidify their professional demands vis-á-vis the state and in conjunction with state-sponsored agencies such as Embrafilme and Concine. In contrast, she finds today's context to be much less organized, more fragmented:

> People were in contact with one another then more than now. The filmmaking sector today is very dispersed. The big hit, one of the big hits to cinema, was the disappearance of Embrafilme. [. . .] Then people had a really active life, the filmmaking sector, because we had representation in government conferences. I'm not saying that this doesn't exist today. It does, but just not in the same way.[52]

Similarly, Sandra Werneck holds some praise for the past and critique of the current situation. Active in short-film production during Embrafilme's existence, Werneck commends the ways in which selection committees assisted new filmmakers. As a new filmmaker, she says she would submit her project proposals to a selection committee that would then provide her with an evaluation. She feels this process greatly contributed to her learning the craft but, unfortunately, she does not believe the current landscape provides this form of support for novice filmmakers. Werneck notes that this selection process was truly democratic, a description that stands in contrast to what occurred during the years of the Retomada when committees composed of trained film professionals were replaced by marketing executives of companies that transferred a portion of their tax income to the state for cultural production.[53] When asked to reflect on the current funding situation in light of the past, Werneck feels there are now few film awards such that most people work on others' projects and gain experience that way rather than develop their own projects.[54] For those starting out now, she has two words: "Puxa vida!" (Gosh!).

Despite the technical and financial assistance with production, distribution, and, to a limited extent, exhibition, few women filmmakers miss Embrafilme. A common critique these women launch against the agency is the traffic of influence within it. These women's comments on Embrafilme need to be put in context, however. They are now distanced greatly from the years of Embrafilme and are in the midst of their own production difficulties. Some women filmmakers see the absence of a centralized state film agency as positive; several claim they enjoy a certain degree of freedom now. Others see a film agency as something that is really beneficial if it works effectively. Still others feel that they have been squeezed out of the film industry altogether.

At the Crossroads of Censorship

Shortly after Roberto Farias took over the position as general director of Embrafilme in 1974, the organization shifted to a market-driven approach. This continued orientation indirectly altered the formats and modes of production for several women filmmakers. Increased pressure for films to be commercially successful resulted in a decreased share of the market for documentary films and a decisive shift away from less expensive, cooperative film productions. While this would have certainly had an effect on all filmmakers in Brazil, the consequences for this shift hold specific significance when we consider women's filmmaking, which was effectively emerging at the crossroads of economic and political censorship.

When women started taking roles in film production, they were keenly interested in gaining access to a mode of audiovisual communication to which they had not previously had access. Once they arrived, they were interested in developing new modes of expression.[55] One of the challenges women filmmakers faced was distancing themselves from prevailing aesthetics while competing for their own place in movie theaters. Tizuka Yamasaki explains that when she was starting out, Cinema Novo was such a strong point of reference that if your work was not in a similar vein, then it was considered inferior.[56] However, these women did not wish to follow established modes and styles of filmmaking.

Cinema Novo aesthetics had gained a dominant position in the Brazilian film industry in part because of the international attention it received and in part because Cinema Novo filmmakers were able to work within the political and economic system. As Randal Johnson suggests, the most important factors contributing to the dominance of the Cinema Novo group were their relationship to the state and their highly pragmatic approach to filmmaking.[57] Johnson and Stam note that directors associated with Cinema Novo initially rejected commercial cinema and Hollywood-style aesthetics and sought to produce films that contributed to a struggle against neocolonialism. In time, Cinema Novo directors began to see greater advantage in making films that combined popular appeal with a left-leaning vision of Brazilian society. Having solidified a presence within Embrafilme, their works continued to seek popular appeal but were critiqued for seeking commercial success over political perseverance.[58]

There were two significant problems with Cinema Novo discourses as seen through a feminist lens. Despite her praise and respect for her predecessors and mentors, Yamasaki expresses mixed feelings about the discourses advanced by the Cinema Novo group:

> I had the privilege of having two—two great cineastes in my formation. But at the same time this close connection with the two left me very frustrated, very deceived. The discourses of Cinema Novo were marvelous in terms of politics, in terms of social questions, in terms of thinking about Brazil. But they were very, very chauvinistic in their daily lives. Not so much in their work, but it's an observation of them with their families. It was just an observation. In that time I still didn't have a clear understanding of things. Much later yes.[59]

While it is difficult to believe these filmmakers would not have expressed chauvinist beliefs on their film sets, Yamasaki did not sense that they expressed these attitudes while working. I would argue that, in fact, they did express their bias in their work. Yamasaki, regarding this very issue, touches on one critical shortcoming of Cinema Novo discourses. The representation of women was relatively nonexistent, and scant consideration is paid to issues affecting women. Few female figures appear in Cinema Novo films and, when they do, they are not developed characters. As we will see in chapter 2, a second fault with Cinema Novo discourses had to do with allegorical representation. Allegories, by definition, provide generalizations about human experience on a literal and figurative level. The tendency toward generalization in allegorical representation may contradict a more feminist goal to speak to difference and specificity. In the case of the Cinema Novo directors, their use of allegory, as Ismail Xavier has observed, tended to provide totalizing visions of the nation and contemporary society.[60] And, as noted above, these visions failed to include women.

The first women directors to emerge in the contemporary film industry did not follow the aesthetic and political proposals of those who came before them. Ana Carolina feels her work proposes a significant thematic departure from Cinema Novo filmmaking. Her first feature-length film, *Mar de Rosas*, discusses psychoanalytic and political questions, such as female sexuality and the state's role in limiting women's political enfranchisement, taken to an extreme that did not exist at that time in Brazilian cinema.[61] Yamasaki feels that her work proposes a rupture from prior film aesthetics and treated themes, stating that her first film (*Gaijin: Os Caminhos da Liberdade*) inaugurated a new "cinema of emotion" in Brazil.[62] Prior to this, Yamasaki explains, there was no middle ground between doing "political" cinema—meaning work that was similar to Cinema Novo—and *pornochanchadas*.[63]

By contrast, women filmmakers were interested in exploring subject matter that affected them personally as well as held ties to the political and social context of the time. They shifted away from allegory and introduced psychological and emotional experiences to reveal the effects of social, political, and cultural marginalization. Overall, the women filmmakers I interviewed revealed a concern with particularity.

These women drew on personal experience and emotion to talk about the nation. Tata Amaral advocates representing women's emotion and sees such focus as having a political role as a great harmonizing force: "Many times we live in the world of men, and these are the values that are known. Feminine emotion isn't known publicly. It isn't put on the screen. When you make something really strong from a feminine point of view and put this up on a screen, it is really surprising for men, too. And it's a new vision of things. It's the revelation of something that was always there. None of that is new. It just wasn't seen."[64] Her assessment suggests a close tie between revelation and participation. As Amaral points out, concealed female emotion harmonizes or balances out predominant male values. It's important to put her words into context here and state that she does not essentialize the feminine or masculine. In other words, feminine emotion does not counter masculine rationality. Rather, she refers to the political potential of acknowledging female experience. The representation of emotion was a way to intervene in society.

Instead of receiving praise for their aesthetic and thematic innovations, women filmmakers paid for it in the form of censorship of their films. Responding to increasing public protests, the military regime declared the Fifth Institutional Act (AI-5, Ato Institucional Número 5) in 1968. A coup within a coup, the AI-5 called for the censorship of print and audiovisual media, led to the torture of political dissidents, and resulted in the voluntary and involuntary exile of hundreds of Brazilian citizens. From the declaration of the AI-5 in December 1968 until the first direct, free elections held in 1984, the military regime actively and arbitrarily censored mass media. It is important to note that no woman I spoke with, who was directing films at this time, reports having felt pressured to not express herself in a particular way for fear of being censored. For those whose films were targeted by the authorities, they had to negotiate with the censors to prevent having scenes and dialogue edited out of their films. The egregious case of Tereza Trautman's *Os Homens Que Eu Tive* has been described above. Yet she is not alone. Ana Carolina reflects on her own experience with censorship, stoically listing the films that have come under attack: "I always had experiences with censorship. *Pantanal* did. *Guerra do Paraguai* did. *Getúlio* did. *Mar de Rosas* did. *Das Tripas* did. I really had years and years—*Sonho de Valsa* didn't. The *Abertura* had already arrived. So, the censorship ended with *Das Tripas*. Really harsh censorship."[65] Ana Carolina was able to free her films from the censors but only after a great deal of effort on her part. In the case of *Mar de Rosas*, the film was banned for six months, during which time she successfully argued with the censors in Brasília to keep all scenes intact.[66]

Ana Carolina's second film, *Das Tripas Coração* (1982), was banned for ten months and released under unusual circumstances. A Canadian Catholic priest came to the film's defense, claiming that it was a manifestation of God. She reveals that he accompanied her to Brasília on several occasions to help defend the film, and they both participated in open debates where they discussed sexuality in general, homosexuality, family, religion, and other controversial issues of the day.[67] In exchange for having no scenes deleted, Ana Carolina was forced to include a statement at the beginning of the film taking responsibility for and completely discrediting her work:

> I had to sign a statement of responsibility for *Das Tripas* and include a warning in it before the film. I thought it was great. I said to myself, "That, that I will go for. That there, I'll go for. Either that, or nothing." The warning said that it was a delirious film that didn't treat any reality and that I assumed complete responsibility for that madness. I said, perfect. I thought that was cool because it was so crazy for someone to do that—a person to make someone else do that—so crazy, that I said that it's good that it be seen. That was the government. So, I signed it. I put that text in the very beginning and signed my name to it. It was as if I promised to never speak any nonsense again. As if everything were just my own madness. It doesn't exist. That doesn't exist. It was the military government. I thought, "It's clear that this, how is it that this doesn't exist!"[68]

Clearly the declaration of amnesty in 1979 and the move toward direct, free elections had not translated into greater expressive freedom in the cinema. This, as Ana Carolina states, was the government in Brazil at this time, a government that censored people and ideas in a perversely mobile and undefined way. Ana Carolina notes that censorship was not limited to Brazil alone. When she participated in a film festival in Portugal, she says the festival director demanded that she rise in front of the audience to apologize for having made *Das Tripas Coração*. She rose to present herself to the crowd but refused to apologize.[69]

Despite official declarations moving toward greater political freedoms, filmmakers continued to experience censorship. For example, the 1976 film *Iracema: Uma Transa Amazônica*, directed by Jorge Bodanzky and Orlando Senna, was detained by government censors. Although the film was critiqued for denigrating a native Amazonian woman, Randal Johnson notes that the film was not screened until 1980 for technical reasons. The film stock had not been processed in Brazil and, therefore, did not qualify for industry protections offered to Brazilian films.[70] The process toward greater freedom of expression was quite slow and cultural producers were under much greater scrutiny than might be expected. No individual was free from the possibility of censure, even on the eve of redemocratization. Although political parties could start forming in the early 1980s, materials of a politically sensitive nature were still censored. Embrafilme chose not to distribute Sílvio Tendler's 1984 documentary *Jango* for fear of political consequences.[71] The case of former Embrafilme director Roberto Farias stands out: in 1982, his film *Pra Frente, Brasil* (Onward Brazil) was banned for showing acts of torture that had taken place during the 1970s. Despite the fact that censorship was waning, the cases of these films by Farias and Tendler in particular illustrate that discussions attacking the foundations of the conservative, neoliberal bases of the military regime were not allowed.

During the period of redemocratization from 1984 to 1988, censorship was lifted and filmmakers could develop projects related to more controversial topics with greater freedom in feature-length fiction films and notably in nonfiction film. In addition to the documentary film *Que Bom Te Ver Viva* by Lúcia Murat, Tetê Moraes directed *Terra para Rose* (Land for Rose, 1987), which follows a young wife and mother who fights for land reform before she is mysteriously killed. The film denounces the authoritarian repression of poor, rural sectors of Brazilian society who bore a particularly harsh brunt of political violence before and during the years of the military regime. Political openings met advances in technology, paving the way for the rise of popular and alternative video production at this time. (The development of alternative and independent film and video is discussed in chapter 4.)

Women filmmakers reveal that economic censorship, not political censorship, has been a more daunting problem affecting their film practice. There are several consequences of economic censorship. Women have moved from less expensive, cooperative filmmaking to more expensive, commercially viable filmmaking. Some left documentary filmmaking and moved to fictional filmmaking for economic as well as personal reasons. Others eventually left their work in film completely and began working with (Betacam) video. The term "economic censorship" is one that these women introduced during their interviews. From their comments, the concept can best be defined as a feeling that one has not been allowed access to production funds to make a film project based on criteria related to predictions regarding the film's potential success in the marketplace.

During the military regime, economic censorship ran alongside political censorship. Ana Carolina and Tereza Trautman reflect on their experiences having their films banned for extended periods; they note that this translated into a form of economic censorship. There are concrete economic consequences of having a film banned. If the film is not released, then, as an independent producer and director, your production company can go bankrupt along with your reputation. Ana Carolina notes that having one film censored did not prevent her from getting to do subsequent films but that she is certain she was put on a sort of list of the *malditos* (damned).[72] Tereza Trautman states she was told by the general director of Embrafilme that she wasn't going to receive more funds because she would just end up making one more banned film.[73] Trautman asserts that an official in Embrafilme said that her film *Os Homens Que Eu Tive* was going to be nominated to compete for the Coruja de Ouro (a prestigious film award in Brazil). But, since her film was banned, it was not eligible for the award.[74]

Perhaps the most insidious factor characterizing political censorship in Brazil is the way in which it diverted attention away from the realities of economic censorship. Ana Maria Magalhães reveals they all knew political censorship would end one day but they did not have an adequate plan to address structural changes when this became reality.[75] Once redemocratization began in 1984, she says the situation for artists turned into a violent form of economic censorship in which you had to "matar um leão por dia para conseguir trabalhar dignamente, fazer teu filme" (kill a lion a day to be able to work with dignity, to make your film).[76] Suggesting favoritism described earlier by Ana Carolina, Ana Maria goes on to explain that this context of economic censorship is a rigid system and operates from within: "[In this context] many injustices are committed against artists. Among them, between them. You have an artist with more status. You have another with less. This is all very tied to economic power. . . . You have economic censorship from those in power tied to the filmmaking sector, and this is something that's very sad."[77] Ana Maria Magalhães believes that the main difference between the type of censorship people experienced under the military regime until the mid-1980s and the type of economic censorship experienced since then is that there is no light at the end of the tunnel with regard to economic censorship.[78] Comments by other filmmakers suggest they concur with Magalhães' assessment but they do not go into details. Clearly, complaints about the inner workings of a system in which they still wished to work would not advance their careers.

Partly as a response to the changing economic landscape, these women filmmakers changed their film practices. Many left documentary filmmaking to direct fictional films. The reasons for this shift can also be understood as a continuation of a learning process. Novice filmmakers often start by directing shorter works and less expensive documentary films before taking on more expensive, feature-length fiction films. The move to fiction filmmaking was also a result of women being able to secure production funding—from private as well as public resources. Some women began working in fiction for personal reasons. And some women left documentary filmmaking because there was simply no market for it. Embrafilme provided indirect support for documentary film in the form of distribution. But the exhibition sector was not interested in screening documentary films, and the orientation of Embrafilme from the mid-1970s on supported feature-length fiction filmmaking to compete with imported foreign films (in other words, American and European films).

Although there was a shift to fictional filmmaking as a result of Embrafilme's focus on the market and competing with Hollywood films, these women gave individual reasons for moving into fictional filmmaking, often reflecting a desire to talk about the nation from a personal, intimate perspective as opposed to a distant, intellectual approach. Sandra Werneck, who produced and directed many short documentary films, decided that documentary film was not an effective tool for her. She says she felt that denouncing social ills didn't help and, for this reason, decided to focus on human beings and their feelings as a possible outlet for her concerns about politics and society.[79] Others surmised that documentary filmmaking was, in fact, an effective tool for intervening in social and political issues. Lúcia Murat indicates that the structure of her film *Que Bom Te Ver Viva* was directly related to the politics at the time. At a point when there was a strong general desire to move beyond the years of the dictatorship, Murat felt that the combination of documentary-style testimonies and fictional scenes would be the most effective way to discuss the long-term effects of torture, political repression, and survival.[80] Murat states that she thought her strategy of representation was effective in that the testimonies would provide the information and the fictional scenes with the actress would provide the emotional response.[81] Ana Carolina describes her departure from documentary to fiction film as a highly personal endeavor related to a change in her curiosity:

> The documentaries already have a great concern for "what is this here?" But with the documentaries, I was still worried about being an intellectual and analyzing issues. I was apt to make a lot of errors in the role of a sociologist, which I'm not. But when I went off to make fiction films, I completely abandoned my high heels and said, "I'm going to talk about my concerns, what I'm feeling regarding my inclusion in Brazilian cultural identity, of my disgruntledess about being or not being Brazilian."[82]

For Ana Carolina, the shift to fiction filmmaking represented an opportunity to talk about highly personal experiences. As she indicates, she was greatly concerned with Brazil, Brazilian identity, and how she fit into the prevailing concepts of *brasilidade* (Brazilian cultural identity). The shift to fiction filmmaking, for her, represented a way of making herself the subject and object of the discussion.

However, independent, auteur filmmaking came under attack as being detrimental to the success of the Brazilian film industry. Considered a highly personal manner of expression, auteur film was central to women's filmmaking.[83] The ability to maintain an independent, auteur film practice was extremely difficult and led to unfair criticisms of both groundbreaking filmmakers. Whereas the auteur visions of the Cinema Novo filmmakers were lauded and seen as the gemstone of Brazilian filmmaking, by the time women filmmakers starting directing their own films, they faced a context that did not necessarily welcome aesthetically challenging, thoughtful films. A balance needed to be struck between these projects and films that were commercially successful so that money from the latter category could be reinvested into those projects that were socially and culturally significant.[84]

The successes these women filmmakers have had as both directors and producers belie the presence women have in Brazilian cinema. Countering the assertion that Brazilian women had confirmed their place in the film industry, Gutman asserts: "The space for women was restricted—the space as a producer and as a director, of course. As technicians, people were already getting some victories. But that's not the problem. When it comes to the area of production and direction, it was much more complicated."[85] She explains that the process became more complicated when it came to matters of handling large sums of money. Women (historically) have lacked access to and control of financial networks and, thus, were at a distinct disadvantage when they wanted to direct their own films.

On Being Women and Filmmakers

Organizing and fighting for a spot in the Brazilian film industry as women filmmakers posed a challenge. Women held very different opinions about their work, how they had or had not been integrated into the film industry, how they had or had not suffered from gender discrimination or the same forms of oppression that other women claimed to have experienced. Some questioned the term "women filmmakers," doubting the significance of being female and directing a film. They also questioned the role of the state.

Not everyone believes that state support led to women's success as filmmakers. Some would place less importance on financial support and argue that women filmmakers in Brazil made their way to the director's chair as a result of larger shifts in society. Ana Maria Magalhães, who worked as a film and television actress in the 1970s and 1980s, produced and directed the 1976 film *Mulheres de Cinema*, which treats the participation of women as actresses and members of production crews since the introduction of the art form in Brazil. When she reflects on women as directors, she states: "In the '70s, at the time when I made this film, it wasn't so common for a woman to be directing films. . . . There were a few people making movies. But it wasn't so common."[86] She notes that she associated the emergence of women filmmakers such as Ana Carolina with an emerging feminism and that "already in that period women were starting to invade cinema by working in the crew. They were only allowed to be script girls—because they only had script *girls*—and they began to stop only doing this to work a little more in production, assistant director, working a little here, a little there. And this went about forming a generation of women directors."[87] Magalhães makes an important connection between the increased presence of women in cinema, this being associated with an emerging feminism, and the broadened opportunities afforded to women at this time. Her reflection on this period suggests that there was an awakening of possibilities and that the success of one woman led to others' wanting to gain access to filmmaking as well, most notably by participating in film production crews in technical positions. She reveals that she considered Ana Carolina to be a role model as a woman director because she was serious, highly skilled, knew cinema very well, and put her personal vision into her films.[88]

Magalhães's comment that there was an invasion or sudden presence of women filmmakers suggests that a structural shift took place that brought about their participation. As indicated previously, film production in Brazil increased dramatically under direction of the INC (Instituto Nacional de Cinema). This increase in the number of films being produced translated into an increased number of opportunities for women to fill positions in film crews. This experience became a vital step in developing the skills and connections women needed to direct feature-length films during the era of Embrafilme. However, when asked if she felt that Embrafilme played a role in helping women enter the film industry as directors, Magalhães emphasized women's desire to express themselves and gain greater social acceptance over state support:

> I think Brazilian society absorbed women's liberation and its manifestation in this way. Because audiovisual form, the mode of audiovisual expression, was up until then a highly masculine mode of expression with few exceptions. . . . After women's liberation and significant production—filmmaking in Brazil, in the 1970s, was significant—one thing led to another, and I think that women began to occupy this space in the production of films in crews, in all areas. I think that this was a response from Brazilian women and by women in relation to this liberation. I mean, it was a practical response. It wasn't something that was coordinated. It wasn't something thought out. It wasn't a formal movement. [89]

Magalhães's comments indicate that tangible and intangible factors came together and led to more women directing films in Brazil. The observation that "one thing joined another" reflects on the gradual creation of access points and establishing a context that was more hospitable to newcomers, women included. Although clearly not a coordinated movement or a result entirely attributable to one or two specific measures, there are a few salient forces that helped restructure filmmaking in Brazil, which, in turn, facilitated women's progress toward becoming film directors. It is curious that state film agencies did not figure into Magalhães's memory as having provided specific benefits to women and filmmaking. This indicates some difficulty in defining what it meant to be a woman and a filmmaker in the 1970s and early 1980s as well as conflicting opinions of Embrafilme and its role in supporting filmmaking in Brazil.

The appearance of several young women film directors coincided with the rise of the international women's movement in the mid-1970s. Not surprisingly, this group of young Brazilian women filmmakers found themselves and their work interlinked with larger questions about the changing roles of women in society and politics. Being women and entering a profession that had been dominated by men led to discussions of how women filmmakers had inserted themselves into the profession. In what ways, if any, did they differ from dominant, male models of producing and directing films?

When I asked women filmmakers to reflect on the idea of a specifically women's cinema or films by women, differing opinions arose. Although most state that filmmaking in Brazil had been dominated by men and had been a highly masculine mode of expression for years prior to their arrival, few explicitly agree that a category of "films by women" or "women's cinema" exists.[90] Most vocal in her rejection of the category, Ana Carolina views the concept as nothing more than a chauvinist maneuver to marginalize women filmmakers.[91] Rejection or uncertainty regarding the category may stem from difficulties in defining what specifically characterizes films made by women other than the fact that there is a woman making the final decisions behind the cameras. Another explanation may rest with the idea that these women do not feel they have been oppressed in any significant way or that being female prevented them from advancing in their careers. Illustrating this point of view, Tizuka Yamasaki highlights that she grew up in a household with three generations of independent women and, because of this, did not feel that she experienced the same forms of oppression that others may have.[92]

One characteristic used to define films directed by women or women's cinema was the notion of a particular way of seeing—a gaze—or a particularly female mode of communicating that could be attributed to the filmmaker. In feminist film studies, the issue has largely fallen out of favor but it was a controversial issue women faced when they first started directing films and one that resurfaces on occasion. The main theme of the São Paulo Short Film Festival held in August 2001 was women in cinema. A plenary session was held where several generations of women gathered to discuss the notion of an "olhar feminino" (a female gaze). Eunice Gutman reveals that women gathered to discuss these same issues in the 1970s and 1980s.[93]

These women film directors generally reject the concept of the "gaze" as theorized by Laura Mulvey. They do not embrace the voyeuristic-scopophilic ways of seeing as described by Mulvey in her essay "Visual Pleasure and Narrative Cinema," originally published by *Screen* in 1975. More specifically, they do not embrace the concept of the gaze as informed by psychoanalytical theory aimed at providing a conceptually grounded critique of the representation of women in Hollywood cinema.[94] The concern over whether or not a woman sees the world in a way differently from a man stems from anxious joy. On the one hand, some women directors embrace the communicative potential, resistance, and liberation of holding firm to the notion that women see the world in a way differently from men arising from their biological sex and subsequent social conditioning. On the other hand, some women directors are wary that the potential to challenge prevailing understandings of gender and society may be jeopardized if the message and the message maker are positioned as belonging to a separate context. For these women, embracing the notion of the "female gaze" may only serve to short-circuit the goal to participate fully in social dialogue. In short, these women do not embrace the notion of a female gaze tied to the female body. Uninterested in essentialist notions of representation, these directors seek to work on issues that pique their curiosity or affect them or the worlds in which they live.

Gutman most clearly defends her position. She supports the idea of women's cinema but denies the idea of a particularly female way of representing. Instead, she maintains there is one cinematic language that is used differently by different filmmakers depending on their background: "There's one cinematographic language, it's technical . . . how you use an establishing shot, how you use a close-up, how you use a medium shot. This is one language, it's universal. There exists *auteur* filmmaking, there exist various tendencies— but within this language. Now, logically, if you are going to interpret a story, you are going to interpret it according to the upbringing that you received. So, everything comes from there."[95] What matters fundamentally, according to Gutman, are the experiences you have had and how you have been shaped as an individual. In addition, Magalhães asserts that, as a director, you have to develop a complex vision of the world. She warns against "uma visão compartimentada" (a compartmentalized vision) and emphasizes that you have to move beyond yourself when directing.[96]

Alongside Social Movements

Today, it is unlikely these women would be asked to reflect on the fact that they are female and directing films. Their work would most likely not be analyzed with the surprise or curiosity that a woman directed a film. However, these questions arose from a context in which many social shifts were taking place. In 1964, the military regime took power with the goal to effectively silence social and economic reform movements. The state punished trade unionists and labor activists in the south and sought to crush land and economic reform movements in the northeast. The "economic miracle" of 1968 to 1973 exacerbated social inequities and brought union leaders and mothers into the streets to protest for change despite potential state repression. Out of this initial phase in which women were making demands on the government in the name of motherhood arose fervent discussions of women's rights and their changing roles in society. In 1975, the United Nations announced the Decade of the Woman and, effectively, solidified a new international women's movement.

A few women active in filmmaking at this time were also politically active. Tetê Moraes took a keen interest in land reform movements in the south. In 1987, she completed the documentary *Terra para Rose*, in which she focused on one woman and her family's struggle for land reform during the occupation of an abandoned farm in Rio Grande do Sul. Prior to this, Moraes had studied law and worked as a journalist. Because of her close connections to individuals who had been captured and tortured by the regime and her work as a journalist, she was arrested and held for three months in 1970. Fearing she would be arrested again under a program called "preso preventivo," (preemptive imprisonment) she fled the country and remained in exile for ten years.[97] For Moraes, filmmaking has been an extension of her training in the law, her work as a journalist, and an expression of her political concerns.

Political activism was not the safest or necessarily the most viable option to express one's opinions during the military dictatorship. Filmmaker Lúcia Murat was arrested for her participation in the leftist guerrilla movement. In the text *Brasil: Nunca Mais* (Brazil: Never Again) Murat denounces the torture to which she was subjected while imprisoned.[98] When asked if she participated in any social movements or political groups, Ana Carolina states she participated in a great deal of political militancy starting in 1964 and almost entered into the political group *Ação Popular* (Popular Action). However, she describes her experience as highly frustrating:

I almost entered the AP [*Ação Popular*]. I fought. I flirted with the Communist party and I detested it. I hated the people. I always left upset with the people. And all of the—at that time—masculine and feminine behaviors were very different than today. The men from the Communist Party were something awful. The comrades. The comrades—they had a way of discriminating against women. . . . They were men, better than us. They were capable men. We were just women. At the meetings, they would leave. They went someplace else to talk. Including other film directors! They would tell me to leave so they could talk. I almost entered the AP but I didn't. I particpated in a really serious militant group, the VPR [*Vanguarda Popular Revolucionária*/Popular Revolutionary Front]. Then I got out because in 1970 and '71 I was arrested twice.

So, I said, I'm going to stop with this. Later I attended the formation of the PT [*Partido dos Trabalhadores*/Worker's Party]. . . . But I made very political films but I didn't participate in any political party. . . . My militance was in the cinema. It wasn't in feminism and it wasn't in leftist political parties. It was in cinema. It was through cultural expression.[99]

In addition to the dangers of imprisonment, Ana Carolina's account suggests that it was particularly difficult for women to participate in political activity due to internal discrimination against women members. While it may be upsetting to hear her account of gender discrimination, the important point to extract from Ana Carolina's accounts is that film was a viable outlet to express her political views and a form of political activism.

Tizuka Yamasaki shares a similar perspective on her filmmaking practice and political activism. Like Ana Carolina, Yamasaki reports that she was not welcomed to political conversations with other (male) filmmakers. When asked to explain why, she simply states that politics was an "assunto de macho" (a male matter).[100] Although she did not participate in political parties, Yamasaki was invited to participate in the Conselho Nacional das Mulheres (National Council of Women) in Brasilia in 1985, which oversaw the creation of the women's police delegacies, maternity leave, and other issues that affect women's ability to join the workforce. Overall, she sees her film practice as her best weapon to defend an issue she feels strongly about, and cinema has always been her best tool for manifesting her role as a citizen.[101]

Each woman I spoke with expressed her particular views on society and the issues she prioritizes. Despite their differences, these women share concerns for Brazilian identity, or *brasilidade*, Brazil as a nation, and communication between disparate groups. The women I interviewed were concerned with and advocated for the quotidian needs of women. As discussed briefly in the introduction, the women's movement in Brazil was composed of those who advocated for feminist causes and those who fought for what have been termed "feminine" needs. The majority share a common rejection of "feminism." Although they do not define themselves as having feminist perspectives, they acknowledge that feminist readings of their works can result. It is interesting to note that when the subject of feminism was broached, some filmmakers started shaking their heads, or quietly stated "no" at the first mention of the word "feminism." Many women filmmakers who did not embrace feminist thought as introduced in Brazil suggest that European- and North American–based concepts of gender do not fit within the Brazilian context. Although they are unable to specify why they do not and did not embrace feminism, their comments suggest that they associate feminist thought with essentialist ideas and an antagonism between classes, races, and cultures.

Crisis and Renewal

In his study of the Brazilian film industry in the 1980s, Randal Johnson notes that general economic difficulties and increasing production costs combined with failure to establish policies that would consolidate the Brazilian cinema as an industry were leading toward a significant crisis in Embrafilme.[102] By the end of the 1980s, the crisis had come to a tipping point, and in March 1990, newly elected president Fernando Collor de Mello announced his Plano Collor, which, among other acts, extinguished fiscal incentive laws for cultural production, demoted the Ministry of Culture by replacing it with a Secretary of Culture, eliminated public companies and foundations such as the Fundação do Cinema Brasileiro (FCB, Brazilian Film Foundation), and dissolved *autarquias* such as Embrafilme. Having transitioned from a regional distributor of Brazilian films to become a significant player in Brazilian cinema and serving as a key funding agency for Brazilian directors, the closure of Embrafilme dealt a significant blow to Brazilian cinema and resulted in the near standstill of filmmaking in the early 1990s. The closure of Embrafilme meant that film projects were immediately suspended, production funds were lost, and contracts were broken.[103]

But the standstill was short lived. New cultural policies were passed quickly, starting with the 1991 Federal Cultural Incentive Law (or, *Lei Rouanet*) and the 1993 Audiovisual Law (or, *Lei do Audiovisual*), which were aimed at bolstering audiovisual production. Both laws allowed Brazilian companies to contribute portions of their yearly tax liabilities toward cultural projects, providing much-needed funds for cultural producers. After a few years, Brazilian filmmaking began to pick up, which brought forth optimistic claims that the industry was experiencing a rebirth, or a Retomada. Between 1994 and 1998, critical years in the redevelopment of Brazilian cinema, twenty films directed by seventeen different women directors were released in Brazil. This historically high number—combined with the facts that Ana Maria Magalhães was one of only seven directors to release a film in 1994 (*Erotique*, co-directed with Monika Treut, Clara Law, and Lizzie Borden), that Carla Camurati's 1995 film *Carlota Joaquina: Princesa do Brasil* was a box-office success, and that the films *Terra Estrangeira*, co-directed by Daniela Thomas and Walter Salles, and *Um Céu de Estrelas*, directed by Tatá Amaral, received critical acclaim nationally and internationally—prompted the problematic assertion that women directors were at the forefront of the Retomada. Taking note of these events, critics resuscitated discussion of the category of "films by women," an area of film studies that had been addressed extensively in the 1970s and 1980s. From an optimistic vantage point of the late 1990s, film critic Susana Schild predicted a slow, gradual increase in the number of Brazilian women directing feature-length films.[104] In many respects, Schild's prediction was correct: at most recent count, there are no fewer than forty-five women in Brazil directing or co-directing feature-length fiction or documentary films. However, in terms of overall film production from Brazil, women still very much occupy a minority status. From 1990 to 2009, films directed by women represent approximately 14 percent of all short, medium-, and feature-length fiction and documentary films produced in Brazil.[105] The initial feeling of joy and relief at the start of the Retomada has passed, and women I spoke with were tentative about the current context of production financing, distribution, and exhibition.

Despite the successes that Embrafilme had consolidated during the nearly two decades it operated, many welcomed the "creative destruction" that newly elected president Fernando Collor instituted in 1990. As indicated earlier, few women filmmakers are nostalgic for the days of Embrafilme. Their critiques rest less with the existence of a state agency to assist independent filmmaking in Brazil and more with the orientation of Embrafilme during the 1980s, when Embrafilme was driven by a concern for the market and producing films that could compete with American ("Hollywood") cinema. For some the closure of Embrafilme resulted in positive changes. Specifically, they note greater aesthetic freedoms and a break from old patterns. Lúcia Murat feels that because film really is not an industry in Brazil, there are greater opportunities for personal expression. Murat also believes that the closure of Embrafilme has allowed filmmaking to emerge in other parts of Brazil. She suggests that independent cinema is quite strong now and will become stronger when ANCINE (Agência Nacional do Cinema, National Cinema Agency) develops a pro-cinema discourse. Tizuka Yamasaki agrees with Lúcia Murat's assertion that there are greater freedoms after the closure of Embrafilme, but she differs from Murat in that she feels that independent, auteur cinema suffers in the current context.

When asked to reflect on filmmaking in Brazil today vis-á-vis the era of Embrafilme, Sandra Werneck concurs with Murat and Yamasaki and believes that there is greater diversity now in Brazilian film, noting that there are more genres and a greater variety of cinematic languages. Werneck also observes that now productions are larger, and filmmaking has become more glamorous and more polished; as well, there are big contracts, large crews, and a lot more money involved. I believe her description points to the increasing market orientation of Brazilian cinema. A balance needs to be achieved such that smaller, independent, auteur films are as valid a contribution to Brazilian cinema as large, glamorous productions. The problem with the current context is that independent, auteur cinema has been largely squeezed out. Ana Carolina notes that as an independent filmmaker she has had great difficulty producing. She cites that the only aesthetic that has been able to take root in Brazil is a banal, superficial, polished language promoted by TV Globo. Ana Maria Magalhães agrees, adding that Brazilian cinema began copying TV in the 1980s, which resulted in a horrible superficiality. In the current context, Magalhães feels that people do not develop their own models to represent their reality in TV or in cinema.

The current system of film financing is certainly imperfect. At the time of my interview with Ana Carolina, the Audiovisual Law was set to expire. Although she believed (at the time) that it would be renewed, she clearly states that if it isn't, she does not know how she will be able to produce films. Overall, she feels that she has been forced out and the market has taken over. Independent cinema, in her mind, was far more independent in the past. It is difficult to disagree with her when large corporations in the current context are able to establish foundations, call themselves independent producers, and acquire funding to produce films. For example, TV Globo has spawned Globo Filmes Independente. Technically an independent film producer, it is in a position to take advantage of the Audiovisual Law intended to assist (truly) independent film producers. (The difficulties independent women producers and directors face in the current context are addressed further in chapter 5.)

The case of Globo Filmes Independente speaks to a neoliberal trend in Brazilian cultural policies starting in the early 1990s. Film projects are now selected and funded by private industries. In the past, recall, Sandra Werneck noted that the selection process under Embrafilme was very democratic. While she makes no direct critique of the current system of funding, her choice of words to describe the past context as very "democratic" suggests that the current situation may very well lack this characteristic and what prevails is a new mode of economic censorship against artistically challenging, politically charged, socially relevant works. Although she says she has not had any problems lately, Tizuka Yamasaki notes that there are certain obligations to associate yourself with the companies that support your film.

She also notes that companies may choose not to support your film because they do not like the "cara" (look) that it may have.[106]

What has been shown is that state support, direct or indirect, is a vital source for independent filmmaking in Brazil. Financial assistance to filmmaking and political policies that promote independent cultural productions are absolute necessities for the continued existence of independent filmmaking. Without proactive legal backing and state orientation favorable to Brazilian cultural production, access to participate in the cultural development of the nation will continue to be limited to the privileged few, creating an entirely anticitizen, antidemocratic context.

2

Contesting the Boundaries of Belonging in the Films of Ana Carolina Teixeira Soares

Having begun her career in filmmaking in the 1960s and continued into the new millennium, Ana Carolina is a foundational woman director of twentieth-century Brazilian cinema. Before directing her first feature-length fiction film (*Mar de Rosas*) in 1977, Ana Carolina directed numerous documentaries in which she demonstrated a keen interest in artists and their artistic practice (*Três Desenhos*, 1970; *Monteiro Lobato*, 1970; *A Fiandeira*, 1970; *Nelson Pereira dos Santos Saúda o Povo e Pede Passagem*, 1978). Her early films also reveal a keen political eye. She offers sympathetic explorations of labor in *Lavrador* (1968), a poetic analysis of unions in São Paulo; *Pantanal* (1971), the life of *mateiros* (lumberjacks) in Mato Grosso; and in *Indústria* (1969), an examination of economic policies during the administrations of Juscelino Kubitschek and General Costa e Silva. Her early works also reveal a keen interest in exploring history and historical figures, as demonstrated in *Guerra do Paraguay* (1970) and also in a biographical exposé of Brazil's former dictator Getúlio Vargas (1933–1945) in an eponymously titled documentary. As noted in chapter 1, several of these documentaries resulted in Ana Carolina's being called before censors during the military dictatorship. Although she establishes important differences from her predecessors, she shares with Cinema Novo directors a vision of her film as part of a political praxis. As a key transitional filmmaker whose work emerges at the intersection of numerous shifting paradigms (political, cultural, aesthetic, and others), and as the first female director in the contemporary era to have established a continuous career trajectory in filmmaking in Brazil, it is unfortunate that her work has been generally neglected in studies of Brazilian cinema.

This chapter aims to fill this historiographic lacuna by exploring Ana Carolina's feminist trilogy: *Mar de Rosas* (1977), *Das Tripas Coração* (1982), and *Sonho de Valsa* (1987). After offering an overview of the cultural, social, political, and economic factors that have shaped Ana Carolina's film practice, the discussion here of the filmmaker's work offers a close analysis of her groundbreaking trilogy with references to concurrent film practices and styles found in Brazil. Although Ana Carolina does not self-identify with any specific philosophical position, her trilogy clearly offers a feminist critique of the female condition and women's rights most notably through a refusal to collaborate with a masculine imaginary. The female characters who populate her works are confused by and in continual confrontation with their surroundings. In their attempts to escape confinement, they move through space and time, pressing against the subjective boundaries of cultural and sexual citizenship. Ana Carolina's work places the female body at the interstices of social relations and explores the experience of female alienation from society and from herself. Hence, the critiques of politics and society offered in these films are not direct. Rather, they radiate outward from the interactions between female characters and the characters and worlds in which they find themselves, manifesting a feminist discontent with authoritarian, patriarchal politics and repressive gender relations. The three films touch on the key phases of a woman's life—adolescence, youth, and maturity.[1] And the popular press in Brazil referred to the three films as a search for female identity, three steps in the same direction,[2] and marked by a transgressive, "anarquic style."[3] Ultimately, her trilogy critiques those institutions and established beliefs through which presumably good, moral citizens are manufactured—the family, education, religion, romantic love, honoring the father, and so on—and reflects a desire for a new sociability and a new political system in which women are full, equal members.

What is particularly interesting about these works is the overall development from an aesthetics of Marginal Cinema (*Mar de Rosas*) to a surrealist meditation on the masculine imaginary (*Das Tripas Coração*) and the eventual move into a surrealist-informed melodramatic story of liberation (*Sonho de Valsa*). Thematically, these films move toward reclaiming and redefining female subjectivity and women's participation in Brazilian culture and society. Whereas the Tropicália countercultural movement and late Cinema Novo offered mostly ironic critiques of state-sponsored patriarchal ideology in the 1960s and 1970s, Ana Carolina's films are far more trenchant in their analysis, probing the psychological and physical dimensions of women's social and political repression.

Perhaps the most notable auteurist trait of Ana Carolina's trilogy is a refusal to offer up easily digestible audiovisual texts. Her films challenge and confuse as much as they engage their audience. In her trilogy, one finds acting that pushes the edges of sanity and decorum, frequent moments of baroque visual excess, and a refusal to develop clear narrative lines. While a disjointed structure found in *Mar de Rosas* takes a cue from Marginal Cinema aesthetics and the road-movie genre, the exploration of the subconscious in *Das Tripas Coração* and *Sonho de Valsa* does not lend itself to a straightforward plot with traditional narrative tensions and resolutions. By eschewing neatly developed narratives, Ana Carolina's work holds great political valence in that her work challenges the ostensibly logical discourses that have been used to subjugate and marginalize women.

In a context where very few women film directors move beyond their first feature-length fiction film, Ana Carolina's trilogy is of particular importance to Brazilian Cinema as well as women's filmmaking in Latin America in general. Although all three films received production assistance from Embrafilme, several years passed before Ana Carolina was able to amass the funds necessary to produce and direct the third film in this series. (This delay may be due, in part, to the experiences she had with censorship of her second film, *Das Tripas Coração*, discussed herewith in chapter 1.) Notwithstanding that her trilogy extends over nearly ten years, the three films show great coherence. A number of actors reappear in these works, which, in turn, evidence similarities in terms of aesthetic style. In terms of thematics, the trilogy focuses on a nexus of concerns during the military regime and emerges out of a sociopolitical context of the 1970s, often referred to as a period of "vazio cultural" (cultural vacuum) and the "anos de sufoco" (years of suffocation) by those individuals who sought to practice their artistic craft at that time. This is also an era when the second-wave women's movement was raising vital questions about the feminine condition and female subjectivity.

❑ ❑ ❑

Though the first years of the military regime are not known for extreme forms of cultural repression, the 1969 Lei de Segurança (doctrine of national security) motivated increasing control of cultural production and society at large. In the late 1960s, student and labor unions vociferously protested the government's austerity programs and the loss of civil liberties. The military regime responded with a harsh crackdown, declaring the Fifth Institutional Act (AI-5, Ato Institucional Número 5) in 1968. A coup within a coup, the AI-5 called for the censorship of print and audiovisual media, led to the torture of political dissidents, and resulted in the voluntary and involuntary exile of hundreds of Brazilian citizens. In 1970, the military established the Department of Internal Operations—Operation Center for Internal Defense (DOI-CODI, Departamento de Operações Internas—Centro de Operações de Defesa Interna), an organization which illegally held and tortured political dissidents. It is the mandate of General Médici (1969–1974) that is known as the most violent and repressive period of the military dictatorship in Brazil.

Starting in the mid-1970s, the sociopolitical landscape began to shift, consequently allowing for greater vocal participation of civil society and for women in particular. Three key developments took place in Brazilian politics. The hard-line position of the military regime was attenuated when General Ernesto Geisel assumed power in 1974 and declared *distensão* (a slow period of political relaxation). Shortly thereafter, women gained international support when the United Nations declared the International Decade of the Woman in 1975. Third, the Catholic Church in Brazil gradually adopted a new message in the 1970s that women should be treated as equals in society. Despite these openings, a place for women in the public realm was hard fought and not without its vicissitudes.

The period of *distensão*, from 1974 to 1979, is characterized by tensions between a democratically leaning leadership, recalcitrant military leaders who did not wish to give up their power, and a reinvigorated populace eager to restore and reclaim their civil, political, and social rights. Although some progress was made toward redemocratizing the nation at this time, the specter of violence and repression loomed. Wladimir Herzog, journalist and director of TV Cultura, died as a result of state-sanctioned torture in the DOI-CODI in São Paulo in 1975.[4] Herzog's death reverberated throughout the country. Thousands occupied the Praça da Sé, a plaza in the heart of São Paulo, to attend a Catholic Mass for Herzog. The public protest, which heralded fervent discussion of human rights in Brazil and future protests, was the first public act widely covered in the news media since the coup d'état of 1964.[5] Approximately one year later the metalworker Manoel Fiel Filho was also found dead in his cell from torture, prompting additional public outcry. By 1978, students returned to the streets to demand change, and emboldened union workers went on strike in São Paulo. Repressive politics may not have changed by the mid- to late 1970s, but a re-empowered Brazilian public's expectations for their government had.

Motivated by the United Nations declaration of the Decade of the Woman and the political liberalization that came with the Geisel government, the second-wave women's movement greatly expanded in the mid-1970s.[6] Newspapers such as *Brasil Mulher* (1975) and *Nós Mulheres* (1976) began publication, and women mobilized in favor of general political amnesty (Movimento Feminino pela Anistia) and protested the rising costs of living (Movimento do Custo de Vida). Advances were made in women's civil and legal status. In 1975, a proposal was drafted for a new Civil Code, which included some suggested measures to reduce the inferior, subaltern status of women. The revisions removed stipulations that a woman's virginity prior to entering into a marriage could be a factor in determining the validity of the union if the husband so chose to contest it, and a "dishonest daughter" could no longer be disinherited by her father. However, the proposal for a new civil code retained language that gave the male partner in a heterosexual union primary authority in deciding questions essential to the couple and any children they may have.[7] In 1977, a law permitting divorce went into effect. And, as the decade progressed, women protested the "legitimate defense of honor" (legítima defesa da honra) used in Brazilian courts to exonerate men who had killed their wives or female companions for presumed infidelities.[8] It was not until 1980 that the women's movement organized around violence against women, or so-called "crimes of passion," which is suggestive of great silence surrounding the issue of domestic violence as well as the difficulties that organizations encountered in pursuing social justice for women prior to the declaration of political amnesty in 1979.[9] In sum, these years represent a somewhat undefined mode of feminism in which a tension can be found regarding how and in what directions the women's movement should proceed—general struggles vis-á-vis specific demands (*as lutas gerais* versus *as lutas específicas*).[10] Until the end of the decade, the second-wave women's movement in Brazil can be considered relatively unified but on the verge of splintering as groups focused increasingly on more specific objectives.

In the early years of the women's movement, problems faced by women with work, daycare, and political participation were foregrounded. Feminist challenges to gender ideology became more developed in the late 1970s after the declaration of Amnesty (1979) and when women, who had gone into exile in Europe and North America (voluntarily or otherwise), returned to Brazil with ideas from different feminist movements abroad. Indeed, historian Sonia E. Alvarez reports that female sexuality was not openly discussed in the Brazilian women's movement until 1979.[11]

The lack of overt challenges to traditional notions of women's roles in society and gender identities may be a consequence of the actions of state censors at the time, which kept a repressive vigilance for sexually subversive material. Tereza Trautman's film *Os Homens Que Eu Tive* (All the Men I Had,

1973) provides a measure of the body politics of the early and mid-1970s. The film stars Darlene Glória[12] in the role of Pity, a woman who, in agreement with her husband, engages in several extramarital affairs. When none of these relationships satisfies her, she comes to the realization that the problem resides with her. Trautman's film was first exhibited at a time when the dictatorship justified its existence as protector of the Brazilian family and defender of Catholic morality, and, given the provocative discussion of female sexual liberation, the film was subsequently banned until 1983.

Although Trautman's film was censored for ostensibly denigrating Brazilian women, more sexually explicit but nonsubversive material suffered far fewer restrictions. The state was generally tolerant of the numerous *pornochanchadas* (light erotic comedies) released during the 1970s. The highly successful *A Dama do Lotação* (directed by Neville d'Almeida, 1978) stars Sônia Braga and, taking an apparent cue from Luis Buñuel's 1967 film *Belle de Jour*, follows the female protagonist Solange, who in an effort to prove she is not frigid and unable to be satisfied by her husband, engages in anonymous sexual encounters with men she meets on a mass transit bus. Yet another film with great box-office success from the period that celebrates but does not fully advance more progressive views of female sexuality is *Xica da Silva* (directed by Carlos Diegues, 1976). With Zezé Motta in the lead role, the film's narrative is a fictional recreation of the history of an eighteenth-century freed slave woman who, through unique sexual prowess, ascends to a position of authority in the state of Minas Gerais. That Trautman's and not these films were censored speaks less to the hypocrisy of the state ideology at the time and more to the fact that neither the vast output of *pornochanchadas* nor *A Dama do Lotação*, nor *Xica da Silva*, challenged sexual norms and gender hierarchies. In fact, they ultimately upheld traditionally defined gender roles of power (coded as masculine) and passivity (coded as feminine).

Patriarchal authority, however, did come under attack starting in the late 1960s. Ismail Xavier notes that the counterculture movement Tropicalism took aim at patriarchy as it had been employed to legitimize a repressive politics of the military regime.[13] A number of films from this period also reflected on patriarchal authority. As will be discussed further herewith, Xavier observes that Cinema Novo filmmakers in the late 1960s turned their cameras—in melodramatic fashion—to reflect on private life and sexual morality as the basis for a critique of the military regime's program of conservative modernization.[14] These late Cinema Novo films may have connected private dramas with public crises, but they also failed to advance a progressive gendered vision of society. More often than not, they mourned the debilitation of a traditional patriarchal order while female figures remained largely un-developed. In contrast, Ana Carolina's work does not lament the usurping of authority from a formerly powerful figure. Rather, her work challenges patriarchal power dynamics while questioning women's roles in society and demanding new understandings of female sexuality and political subjectivity.

From the late 1960s to the early 1970s, an aesthetic division emerged among Brazilian filmmakers. While late Cinema Novo directors sought to connect with popular audiences by producing more polished productions, others who aligned themselves with an underground aesthetics, becoming known as Marginal Cinema, opposed making compromises to the market. These directors promoted a radical auteur cinema and an aggressive aesthetics of violence in which ironic juxtapositions and disjunctive narratives would provoke spectators' discomfort and deconstruct state-defined notions of the nation and preconceived social illusions.[15] It is with the aesthetics of Marginal Cinema that Ana Carolina closely coincides in her first film.

Manifesting Feminist Discontent in *Mar de Rosas* (1978)

While it takes into account the gender and body politics of the 1960s and 1970s described above, Ana Carolina's first fiction film, *Mar de Rosas*, estab-lishes a highly avant-garde, sarcastic tone, which is sustained in the trilogy. All three titles are idiomatic expressions in Brazilian Portuguese and, in the case of the first work, is an idiom that means "everything is fine." However, the narrative structure and aesthetics of the film could not be further from this. When the first two films were screened in Brazil, critics labeled them as "corrosive," "disconcerting," "uncomfortable," and "disordered."[16] The general sentiment expressed in this and the other films is a refusal of that which is taken for granted in everyday life. What is found in *Mar de Rosas* is a complex aesthetic blend of irony and the absurd to critique the experience of extreme alienation within a traditional family and the breakdown of intersubjective democratic political process. What is more, Ana Carolina's *Mar de Rosas* makes manifest a feminist discontent with authoritarian, patriarchal politics and repressive gender relations.

After having explored Brazil, its people, and the dynamics of power in her documentary films, Ana Carolina's first feature-length fiction film draws on the road-movie genre and her own quotidian experiences to discuss Brazil-ian culture and identity. At its core, *Mar de Rosas* deals with control and persecution: a woman argues with her husband in a car, believes she kills him in a hotel bathroom, and escapes with her daughter. The woman and her daughter are then followed by a man who is out to capture the woman. In turn, the woman chases after her daughter, who employs a number of tricks to free herself from her mother. A series of absurd situations culminates in the daughter's final escape and radical rejection of authority.

The first images link the film to the road-movie genre. Automobile headlights breaking through the darkness of night while vehicles navigate a curving, hilly road constitutes the opening shot in *Mar de Rosas*. Then there is a cut to a close-up shot of an adolescent girl in early-morning light squatting down to urinate along side a car that has pulled over to the edge of a highway. The girl, Betinha (Cristina Pereira), stands up, stretches, scratches herself, looks out over the landscape, and then unceremoniously gets into the car to rejoin her parents, Felicidade (Norma Bengell) and Sérgio (Hugo Carvana), and they continue on their way toward Rio de Janeiro. This opening image is a crass rejection of Brazil's geologic beauty and bounty—much touted by the military regime while it ignored social inequality. It is also a rejection of a physical propriety demanded of women. The opening scenes also establish that Ana Carolina draws on the narrative structures and aesthetic devices frequently found in road movies. In his work on the genre, David Laderman asserts that at the core of the road-movie genre rests a rebellion against social norms. What is more, the journey undertaken in a typical road movie allows for development of a cultural critique in that characters move outside society, which seems lacking or oppressive in some way. A distancing from the familiar frequently leads to profound revelations as main characters search for happiness or escape toward freedom.[17] In what may be a response to or a sign of influence by her predecessors, Ana Carolina coincides with several directors of Marginal Cinema who adapted elements of the road movie genre to launch critiques of Brazilian society during the late 1960s and early 1970s.

But Ana Carolina does not borrow from all the genre's features. Whereas a traditional road movie tends to liberally employ traveling shots and privilege a male point of view, Ana Carolina's work reveals a preference for mounted cameras that look in on the bodies framed by car windows and front windshield. *Mar de Rosas* thus grants slightly less prominence to the outside world and more to the interpersonal tensions that develop between individuals in a nomadic, in-between space. One of the effects of this technical preference is an emphasis placed on the notion that how one regards the world emerges from more personal, intimate experiences. While she does place a couple behind the wheel of an automobile—prevalent in a traditional road movie, Ana Carolina draws on the physical proximity of characters in order

Figure 2.1. At the first "pit stop," Betinha looking at the landscape in *Mar de Rosas*.

to engage in a conversation about marital tensions and a dysfunctional family dynamic. After a series of shot and reverse-shot images of Felicidade and Sérgio looking at one another sideways, suggesting contempt and mistrust, Felicidade—whose name ironically means happiness in Portuguese—breaks the silence reigning in the car to tell Sérgio she would like to talk. Specifically, she wishes to discuss their relationship and wants her husband to help save their marriage. By measure of physical gestures and tone of voice, they are clearly not a happy couple, and her question is met with a threat from Sérgio to get out the civil code and tell her exactly what their marriage is. Effectively, she should be quiet and do what he says. By referring to the Brazilian civil code, the dialogue here reveals the infiltration of the state into private relationships between individuals. More important, that Felicidade expresses her desires for greater equality in her marriage speaks to Brazilian women's growing sense of empowerment in the late 1970s and offers a critique of the military government's gender policies that consistently failed to grant women full rights as citizens of Brazil.

It is important to note that not all countries have civil codes, but for those that do, it is a code intended to orient the creation of laws that regulate social relations. As well, behind the creation of a civil code rests positivist ideals of order, progress, and civilization. In 1975, just two years before the release of *Mar de Rosas*, a project for a new civil code had been introduced in the Brazilian legislature.[18] In the to-be-revised civil code, not all individuals were equal. Women, in particular, were inscribed as being under the tutelage of their husbands and categorized as incapable beings next to minors, the mentally deficient, beggars, and indigenous peoples. Meanwhile, husbands were the defined heads of families to make all legal and social decisions.[19] Thus, when Sérgio threatens to get out the civil code in this scene, a connection is made between the marital tensions between Felicidade and Sérgio and the inferior sociopolitical status of women at the time in Brazil and the belief that a civil code should and can regulate interpersonal relationships.

In addition to women's legal status as defined in the civil code, this opening sequence brings forth the specific question of divorce. During the heated exchange between Sérgio and Felicidade, she states that she wants things to be better for her daughter. She says she wishes to establish a new way of being, and, despite her desire to salvage her marriage with Sérgio, she says that she has considered leaving him: "Consigo aceitar uma separação" (I even manage to accept a separation). Although the struggle for divorce in Brazil dates to the country's independence from Portugal, the legalization of divorce was being considered at the time by the state and was a hot-button topic within the Brazilian women's movement.[20] Given that civil codes pass between generations and give rise to the laws that shape a culture, the exchange between Felicidade and her husband targets long-standing, culturally defined narratives on family law and the regulation of interpersonal relationships.

From the initial exchange in the car between Felicidade and Sérgio, the episodic narrative of the film consists of attempts on the part of Felicidade to escape and her subsequent capture with no clear ending. Felicidade's first attempt to flee takes place shortly after the opening exchange in the car. The three travelers arrive at a hotel where Felicidade and Sérgio continue to argue about their relationship in the bathroom leading to a physical altercation in which they slap and hit each other. There is a cut to a close-up shot of Felicidade's hand at the bathroom sink and she picks up a razor. There is another cut to a medium shot showing the couple. Felicidade turns from the sink and swipes the blade across the back of Sergio's head. He grabs at the back of his neck, looks in horror at his bloodied hands as he falls in agony to his knees. When he hits the floor and falls silent, Felicidade, in voiceover, simply and calmly says, "Matei" (I killed him). Off-key, nondiegetic musical outbursts punctuate the action of this scene, characteristic of avant-garde, experimental film. The scene possesses a kitschy feel in which violent acts are as abrupt as they are absurd. If the familial violence erupting without apparent warning is reminiscent of *Matou a Família e Foi ao Cinema* (Killed the Family and Went to the Movies, directed by Júlio Bressane, 1969), then the nonsensical chase of an outlaw figure recalls *Bang, Bang* (directed by Andrea Tonacci, 1970), both films that exemplify the aesthetics of violence and the absurd in Marginal Cinema. Immediately assuming she has killed her husband, Felicidade looks at herself briefly in the bathroom mirror and calmly pulls her hair back. Ostensibly liberated through this act of violence, Felicidade leaves the bathroom, grabs her belongings, and pulls Betinha by the arm to get into the car.

A quest for happiness and marital reconciliation pivots to a narrative of escape as Felicidade becomes an "outlaw" figure. Thus, the first escape attempt begins, and the "corrosive" style of Ana Carolina's film is revealed. In the next scene, a disheveled Felicidade sits behind the wheel of the car, driving out of a large city while singing a song about the absurdity of love originally written by the Brazilian musician Noel de Medeiros Rosa (1910–1937): "O que você bem sabe / é que você é um ente / que mente inconscientemente / gosto de você imensamente" (what you don't know / is that you are a being / that lies unconsciously / I like you immensely). The tune has a nursery rhyme quality to it—limited notes with rhyming, repetitive lyrics—and seems particularly incongruent with the previous violent scene. Indeed, the ironic juxtaposition of this scene and the nondiegetic music of the previous scene are again consonant with an aesthetic found in Marginal Cinema. As Felicidade and Betinha drive out of Rio de Janeiro, there is a shot of people gathered, looking down on a car that has crashed over a guardrail and fallen into a drainage channel. A closer shot reveals a bloodied woman's hand floating in the water, and Felicidade learns from another motorist that it was a couple that fell into the waterway, creating a metaphorical link with Felicidade's own relationship that has been overturned. Seasoned with off-key musical outbursts, the image of the car wreck cues a surrealist rupture with rational boundaries and suggests metaphorically that the narrative to come will literally go "off course."

Mar de Rosas develops out of aesthetic trends in place in Brazilian cinema and countercultural expression from the late 1960s to the late 1970s. Given that the tempestuous marriage between Sérgio and Felicidade could certainly be interpreted as a violent, authoritarian regime from which Felicidade wants to escape and that one may see the series of escape attempts as referring to a woman's desire to escape patriarchal authority or a more general desire of

Brazilian society to shed dictatorial repression, *Mar de Rosas* could be seen as developing out of a broader allegorical tradition in contemporary Brazilian cultural expression.

In the case of film, Ismail Xavier has discussed the extensive use of allegory in Cinema Novo from the 1960s to the late 1970s. While allegory served as a way for artists to avoid the censors in dictatorial Brazil, it was also a mode that allowed filmmakers to reflect on issues of national identity and its crisis in an uneven process of modernization.[21] In his study, Xavier notes an evolution of allegory from the messianic hope of early Cinema Novo to a more caustic, ironic, disjointed mode of representation found in Marginal Cinema. Films such as *Matou a Família e Foi ao Cinema* (1969), *Bang, Bang* (1971), *O Anjo Nasceu* (directed by Julio Bressane, 1969), and *O Bandido da Luz Vermelha* (directed by Rogério Sganzerla, 1968) illustrate an "aesthetic of violence," alienation or radical disenchantment in which territorial displacement and a traveler on a pointless journey are significant tropes.[22]

It is with the aesthetic style of Marginal Cinema that the above scenes most clearly resonate. But despite its aesthetic and thematic similarities, Ana Carolina's first film does differ from the films of (male) Marginal Cinema filmmakers in several key ways. Primarily, she includes a feminist imprint on her films: female characters in her films are integral to the plot rather than bystanders or targets of violence. Second, in *Mar de Rosas*, the concept of the nation is not the "central meditation for understanding human experience."[23] Rather, the experience of the female characters in interaction with their sociopolitical milieu is the point of departure. Also, *Mar de Rosas* poses a critique of power relationships in (heterosexual) marriage as an institution and the role of the state in supporting the patriarchal oppression of women.

What is more, Ana Carolina's work clearly differs from her filmmaking cohort with regard to the way she discusses the family and marital relations. Ismail Xavier has noted that the family frequently served as a microcosm of the nation in Brazilian cinema of the 1970s.[24] Indeed, a critique of the family as a symbol of society at large was a salient feature of the literary works of Nelson Rodrigues published in the 1960s and subsequent film adaptations in the 1970s and 1980s.[25] Of the filmmakers from this period, Arnaldo Jabor stands out as a director who consistently engaged in discussions of gender, sexuality, and sociopolitical impotence. In the 1970s, he directed two adaptations of Rodrigues's work *Toda Nudez Será Castigada* (1972) and *O Casamento* (1975), followed by *Tudo Bem* (1978). In these three films, we follow debilitated male father figures. The plot of *Toda Nudez* centers on the suffering of the film's protagonist Herculano, who marries Geni, a prostitute with whom he had a brief affair after the death of his first wife. Meanwhile, his castrating son, Serginho, engages in a love affair with his father's new wife, before she eventually commits suicide. In *O Casamento*, an adaptation of a novel by Rodrigues, the male protagonist Sabino struggles with his own identity as he incestuously obsesses over his daughter on the eve of her wedding to a reportedly homosexual man. And, in *Tudo Bem*, a bourgeois couple hires construction workers to renovate their apartment. After maids, the workers, and migrants from northeast Brazil take over their home, the male head of household becomes aware that he is no longer the king of his domain. These portrayals of father figures in Jabor's films are conservative responses to military ideology and state-led economic shifts that ultimately debilitated a patriarchal system it ostensibly supported. In this, these films are more ironic than subversive, failing to challenge patriarchy as a system that in itself can be held responsible for familial conflicts and individual suffering. Ana Carolina's *Mar de Rosas* clearly differs from films by Jabor: while he is ultimately concerned with the crisis of male figures confronted by a shifting sociopolitical landscape, Ana Carolina investigates the perspective of the female figure in crisis. *Mar de Rosas* critiques patriarchal authority in the family, taking into account the sociopolitical debates of the day regarding gender policy. Despite an evident concern for sexuality and its intersection with sociopolitical identity, Ana Carolina's work offers a depiction of what had been largely absent in Brazilian cinema prior to the release of *Mar de Rosas*: a critical reflection on the status of women in Brazil vis-á-vis an authoritarian, patriarchal state.

Despite her desires for happiness and freedom, Felicidade does not manage to escape. In each unsuccessful attempt and subsequent recapture, one finds increasingly more trenchant critiques of the effects of patriarchal, authoritarian control and the extent of the violence it promotes. Betinha, who voices allegiance to her father, is not pleased that she has been forced on this trip with her mother. Irritated, she draws on Felicidade's face from the back seat with black marker before finding a safety pin with which she pokes her mother in the neck, drawing blood and causing Felicidade to scream out in pain. Initially, Betinha's desire to harm her mother could be interpreted as a replaying of an Electra complex, which Jung defines as a mother-daughter psychosexual conflict in which the daughter competes with the mother for possession of the father.[26] In this scenario, Betinha wishes to get rid of her mother so she may return to reestablish her bond with her father.

The injury Felicidade sustains and the need to fill the car with fuel occasions a second pit stop. While Felicidade waits for the tank to be filled,

Figure 2.2. Orlando helping Felicidade after Betinha
set a fire near her mother in *Mar de Rosas*.

Betinha grabs a container of gasoline and pours it on the ground and near
her mother's feet. She then lights a match, causing the fuel to ignite and
burn her mother's legs. As Felicidade cries out in pain, a mysterious man
appears: Orlando (Otávio Augusto), who had been following them in a black
Volkswagon Beetle—a symbol of the military regime.[27] As if chivalry were
his objective, Orlando swoops in, attends to Felicidade's injury and, since she
is in no shape to drive, charms Felicidade and Betinha into accepting a ride
with him to São Paulo. That we later learn he is an associate of Felicidade's
husband, Sérgio, makes Orlando, by extension, a patriarchal agent of the
state sent to uphold a repressive social order.

The three continue en route to São Paulo, and Orlando engages in what
initially seems to be casual conversation. Similar to the opening scene, a
mounted camera predominates to focus on the characters and their dialogue.
Orlando shares his thoughts regarding family, work, the importance of obey-
ing laws, and his belief that cities are not a good place to raise his family.
It should be noted that his comments echo important aspects of Brazilian
military doctrine drafted shortly after the military coup of 1964. The family

was a unit to be protected and defended, while curtailing civil liberties in the name of public safety was crucial to national development. Orlando also asserts a belief in authority and hierarchies, which he apparently believes rest on the body as his comments begin to mix themes of body and pleasure with punishment and control. He shares with Betinha and Felicidade that all the women in his family have names that begin with "Cli-" and proceeds to list them all. Betinha, sitting in the back seat of the car, ends the list of women's names by blurting out "Cli-toris!" For Orlando, the female is equivalent to the physical and evidently that which needs to be controlled as he punctuates the conversation by abruptly grabbing Felicidade's arm with a menacing look on his face. The shifting tone of the scene from pleasant and trivial conversation to threatening gestures and looks reflects the political moment of the mid- to late 1970s when state-sponsored violence loomed over and occasionally surfaced unexpectedly during the slow process of reclaiming civil and political rights.

Orlando's call for control, hierarchies, and order is juxtaposed by slightly absurd, incongruent remarks. After Orlando seizes Felicidade's arm, there is a moment of calm before Felicidade suddenly shouts out, in English, "Oh what a beautiful country. I just love Brazil!" To which Orlando responds by nodding and simply repeating in English, "Yes. Yes. You know, why not?" in a manner giving the impression that he does not know what he is saying. Again, the effect here is strikingly similar to the ironic juxtapositions characteristic of Marginal Cinema, with the sarcasm found here serving to destabilize accepted notions of order.[28] The outburst in English combines with the song "Isn't She Lovely" (a 1976 hit by U.S. singer and songwriter Stevie Wonder) playing on the radio—a sarcastic touch, given Felicidade's appearance—and constitutes a decidedly tropicalist-udigrudi (tropicalist-underground) turn here, where the perspective and expression of Brazilian reality are seen through a caustic melding of native and foreign influence.

In a broader sense, this sequence introduces a critique of what Brazilian sociologist Marilena Chauí has referred to as the "discurso competente" (competent discourse). In her discussion of culture and democracy, Chauí takes up larger questions of intersubjective communication and reveals a concern for a disconnection between ideas, people, and places. One process she observes in the Brazilian context is the development of a "discurso competente," which she defines as a form of discourse that comes to be accepted as true or authorized because it has lost its connections to specific places and moments, is instituted and suffers particular restrictions first because "não é qualquer um que pode dizer a qualquer outro qualquer coisa em qualquer

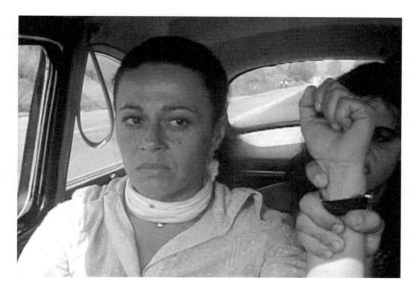

Figure 2.3. Felicidade threatened by Orlando as Betinha looks on from the back seat in *Mar de Rosas*.

lugar e em qualquer circunstância" (it isn't just anybody who can say anything to anybody else at any time and under any circumstances) and second because only an authorized or institutionally permitted language can be used.[29] Chauí argues that one result from the proliferation of this competent discourse is the conversion of an individual as a political subject into an individual as a political object whose personal experiences with the world are no longer a factor in determining her or his subjectivity.[30]

What becomes clear, then, is that Felicidade's obliviousness to Betinha writing on her, the outburst in English, and Orlando's non sequitur response underscore a particular disconnect between people, places, and ideas in the 1970s. Praising the beauty of Brazil (in English) is not consonant with the actions taking place before or after the exclamation. What is more, the ex-claimed praise for Brazil resonates more with the ideology of a nation sup-ported by the military regime, which sought to unify the nation and erase contradictions and ideological conflicts in the name of security and prog-ress. Military doctrine was particularly interested in national security that sought to eliminate antagonisms and social integration aimed toward an instituted sense of common good (*o Bem Comum*).[31] But what is truly at stake here, reflected in the outburst by Felicidade, is the inability to dialogue with others and offer concrete critiques based on one's individual experience which would, in fact, be an *instituting* discourse rather than an imposed, *instituted* discourse. It is this "competent discourse" and the ideology that supports it that Felicidade wishes to escape from.

As the film takes a turn to the incongruent and the sarcastic, it is imperative to ask what is at stake here for feminist filmmaking. Despite important debates raised in feminist film theory in the 1970s regarding realist versus avant-garde aesthetics,[32] for feminist-oriented artists, employing realist strategies was not necessarily an effective option in 1970s Brazil, as this mode of representation had been appropriated by the state. As Flora Süssekind has pointed out in her discussion of literature from this period, the military-state-sponsored representations portrayed Brazil and Brazilian nationality in a naturalist manner that failed to recognize important social and political divisions.[33] By contrast, an experimental approach serves as a particular mode of resistance in Brazil during the 1970s (and early 1980s) that avoided censors and hegemonic realist portrayals. (See the discussion herewith of Marginal Cinema and late Cinema Novo's cannibalist-tropicalist tendencies.) In the case of *Mar de Rosas*, the "chaotic" or "corrosive" style employed has to do with introducing fractures and differences into assumed social unities. The chaotic style found in *Mar de Rosas* disrupts preconceived unities in order to make a space for the individual experience of the female protagonist. In this film, the subjective experience of the female protagonist is taken as a point of departure to talk about gendered oppression and what this means for society at large. In this way, Ana Carolina's film contests a state-sponsored vision of the nation that excluded and repressed Brazilian women.

As stated previously, (male) directors of the late 1960s and early 1970s Brazilian cinema may have taken up representation of the family as a way to discuss the nation, but their works rarely posed disruptive challenges to traditional patriarchal family relations. Ana Carolina temporarily suspends her characters' journey to delve into dramas in a domestic space. Whereas the road-movie genre has been noted for its "disintegration of the concept of home,"[34] the disintegration found in *Mar de Rosas* differs in the sense that one does not find a leaving behind of a home but, rather, a tracing back into the nucleus of society where a process of disintegration has already taken place. In this deconstructed space, *Mar de Rosas* furthers Ana Carolina's critique of power and violence as means for social control. Unlike the chaotic domestic space of Jabor's *Tudo Bem* (1981), the domestic space represented here is a site of death, destruction, and abuse where the female protagonist can offer neither body nor rational argument to secure her freedom and happiness.

It is in the next sequences that Ana Carolina furthers a critique of (heteronormative) marriage and its disintegration. Upon arriving in a small town somewhere between Rio de Janeiro and São Paulo, the three travelers stop so Orlando can make a phone call. Felicidade remains in the car where she finds evidence—documents and a gun—that Orlando is an agent associated with her husband, who did not die in the hotel bathroom attack. At this location, Betinha escapes and joins a Carnival troupe dancing through the streets. Betinha's brief moment of freedom ends when Felicidade catches up to her. As if a political subversive being detained by the police for secret interrogation, Felicidade sneaks up from behind Betinha while she frolics with the troupe, pulls a gunnysack over her head, and drags her back into Orlando's car. With a smile on her face, Felicidade seems to enjoy her dominating role as she tells Betinha that this is the eternal price for freedom. The scene also suggests how easily the victim (or pursued) can become the victimizer (or pursuer).

Moments later, Felicidade pushes Betinha out of the moving car and attempts her own escape through the streets of the town. With Orlando chasing after them, Felicidade doesn't notice the bus heading straight for her. She is hit, falls to the ground, and Orlando catches up with her. Several onlookers appear; among them is a concerned woman named Niobi. She convinces Felicidade, Betinha, and Orlando to come into her house where they can make sure Felicidade is not injured. It is in the home of Niobi (Miriam Muniz) and her husband Dirceu (Ary Fontoura) that nearly forty minutes of the film take place.

All three enter the home and meet Dirceu, a dentist by profession. It becomes quickly apparent that Niobi and Dirceu do not have a harmonious relationship. Although they do not physically hit one another, comments and gestures clearly indicate they barely manage to tolerate one another. This second example of conjugal misery reignites the critique of marriage. Making her point very clear, Niobi critiques marriage as a space that you may enter but never exit, warning, "Quem está dentro não deve, não pode sair. Quem est>á fora, não deve entrar" (Whoever is in a marriage should not, cannot leave. Whoever is not married, should stay out of it).

Niobi and Dirceu try to make their guests comfortable, offering them a homemade liqueur and making casual conversation in their living room. The direction of the conversation, although seemingly nonsensical, again points toward a common feeling of disconnection from each other and their environment. Niobi talks about a recipe for potatoes and enters into a sort of religious ecstasy examining the possible greater significance of mundane observations. She believes for example that Betinha has appeared to her as an angel on the street. The word "coletivo" (collective) is mentioned at one moment. And, as if stunned by the word, Niobi shares: "Quando penso na palavra coletivo, penso na morte. Eu não posso deixar de pensar na morte" (When I think of the word collective, I think about death. I cannot stop thinking about death). For his part, Dirceu is obsessed with blood and death, seen at one point experiencing a moment of ecstasy when he sees blood on his hands after cutting himself in the bathroom with a razor that Betinha had buried in a bar of soap. The obsession with death and Niobi's comment suggest that a collective, cohesive society cannot thrive under current authoritarian, patriarchal conditions—created and supported by the military regime. The interaction that does take place between the individuals in Dirceu and Niobi's living room consists of isolated co-existence and occasionally slapping each other.

The lack of connection between the characters is underscored by few close-ups, minimal camera movement, and the positioning of the characters in the living room. With significant exceptions, the majority of the action that takes place in this domestic space is filmed with long takes, and characters are framed within three walls, as if they were on a theatrical stage. The physical arrangement of the characters in the on-screen space of the living room shows Felicidade between Niobi and Dirceu on one side and Betinha and Orlando on the other. Sitting in the middle, Felicidade is the one character that is most unengaged in the "conversation," making minimal eye contact, looking forward, and smoking a cigarette. She does not participate in the nonsensical dialogue, being the one character who claims a (coherent) right to speak and be free, and whose words reject the situation in which she finds herself. The relatively immobile camerawork in this scene draws attention to the act of watching, and the spectator observes the performance of social breakdown on a domestic stage framed by living room walls. Although the characters do talk, Niobi being the one who speaks the most, the general absence of a more conventional shot and reverse-shot structure while they speak signifies a fundamental disconnection between these people, as if to confirm the death of the collective or the possibility for rational communication.

In terms of the visual representation of the dramatic space and the acting, the scene possesses a Brechtian spirit, particularly the notion of gesture detached from language and the concept of alienation.[35] Notably, estrangement effects were common in Marginal Cinema to create discomfort for the spectator and destabilize established modes of representing and understanding the nation.[36] Alienation, whether understood as a state of being alienated or

Figure 2.4. In Niobi and Dirceu's living room in *Mar de Rosas*.

estranged (*Entfremdung*), the device or act of alienation (*Verfremdung*), or the moment of bewilderment on the part of spectators (*Befremdung*),[37] can be understood as an experience as well as an aesthetic device. Although there is no one particular acting style that can bring about a sense of alienation, the lack of coherence in the dialogue and the absence of cohesive interaction among these characters in the scene are notable. The characters' bodies are physically close yet emotionally distanced from one another, revealing people disconnected from their physical space and others within it. This is so much the case in *Mar de Rosas* that at one point Dirceu leans back and rubs his feet against the chest and abdomen of his wife Niobi, who either doesn't mind or doesn't notice. Meanwhile, Betinha shifts around uncomfortably on the sofa and Orlando looks off into space, engrossed in his own thoughts.

The characters' estrangement from one another, and especially Felicidade's disconnection from the others, becomes most pronounced in the subsequent "dirt pile" scene. In an attempt to punish her mother as well as create a diversion that would allow her to escape and return to her father, Betinha manages to lock Felicidade inside Dirceu's dental exam office and then cues a dump truck driver to unload several tons of red dirt through the window. As the dirt flows in and threatens to smother Felicidade, Betinha states nonchalantly, "Terra ésempre terra" (Earth is just earth). The simplicity of the statement belies the significance of the act and the image of what has happened. While Betinha's previous efforts to harm her mother were successful, here she does not succeed in burying her mother alive.

The others gather on the mound of dirt in Dirceu's office as if it were a sacred hill on which to meet. Indeed, the scene recalls messianic moments found in Glauber Rocha's *Deus e o Diabo na Terra do Sol* (Black God, White Devil [English title], 1964) but also invokes Marginal Cinema's radical rejection of Cinema Novo, which it felt had become too middle class and tame in its aesthetics.[38] This scene in Ana Carolina's film mocks the bourgeois intellectualism that one finds in later Cinema Novo films. This sentiment is underscored with the religiously ecstatic proclamation by Niobi at a high point in the dialogue, wherein she urges people to raise their eyes up and just realize that "o imóvel fica fixo. O iníquo fica inócuo. O histérico fica histórico" (what is unmovable becomes fixed. What is wicked becomes innocuous. What is hysterical becomes historical). Niobi's comments speak to the perverse mutation of social values and political processes. The scene rehearses the style Glauber Rocha frequently employed in his films, such as *Deus e o Diabo na Terra do Sol* and his last film *A Idade da Terra* (1980), in which documentary hand-held camera work records highly theatrical performances.[39] Ana Carolina may employ similar techniques here but, unlike Rocha's style, the scene undermines an allegorical condensation of national history and cultural identity. Rather, the enraptured Niobi's fervor and radically opposing concepts amounts to a zero-sum game and serves as a rejection of the possibility of offering a unified understanding of Brazilian culture and society—especially while many citizens, including women, are socially and politically excluded. For her part, Felicidade wants to have nothing to do with the absurd dialogue; she is not mesmerized by the "histérico" discourse. In disgust, Felicidade fervently critiques women's limited roles in society, exclaiming, "Eu quero viver de algúm outro jeito!" (I want to live some other way).

What can we make of these two scenes in the domestic space of the living room scene and on top of a dirt pile? What are these two scenes saying about society and politics of the late 1970s? In addition to the acerbic critique of women's roles within the heteronormative family, these two scenes underscore the absence of relational subjectivity that forms the foundation for civil, democratic society. Noëlle McAfee proposes an understanding of the modern political subject that brings much to bear on Ana Carolina's representation of these disconnected, alienated characters. Following a poststructuralist, Kristevan concept of the subject that is constantly being constituted, McAfee

Figure 2.5. A gathering on a dirt pile in Dirceu's office in *Mar de Rosas*.

proposes the notion of the relational, political subject. In her formulation, an intrasubjective tension leads to intersubjective deliberation. What is more, individuals are most democratic when they are "inclined" toward one another.[40] What Ana Carolina's representation here reveals is the absence of this "inclination" toward one another, which precludes intersubjective deliberation and democratic process. What we see in the living room scene and the dirt pile scene is a portrayal of people who have been dulled, made incapable of intersubjective deliberation by an absurd, autocratic regime.

The final scene of this film poses a question as much as it demonstrates an abrupt rejection of authority. The chase continues and Betinha and Felicidade find themselves on a train headed to São Paulo. Orlando catches up to them and seizes Felicidade's arm as she stands on the back platform of the train. As a functionary of the state and patriarchal power, Orlando states that he has orders to follow. Betinha agrees, "Ninguém pode desobedecer as ordens" (Nobody can disobey orders) and then pauses before she questions her own statement, "Ou pode?" (Or can they?). In that instant, Betinha, who had earlier shown an adherence to authority and was upset when her father was harmed, comes to an abrupt realization that rules can be broken. Once outside on the back platform of the rail car, she pushes her mother and Or-

Figure 2.6. Betinha's final rejection of authority in *Mar de Rosas*.

lando from the train and flips off the spectator, riding into the sunset as if she were the ultimate antiheroine of a perverse Hollywood Western. Whereas Cinema Novo developed a convention of closing its films with an image of a road or straight visual line, intended to represent a new consciousness, Marginal Cinema directors tended to oppose this teleological stance on the nation and history.[41] Ana Carolina's *Mar de Rosas* coincides here again with the disjunctive strategies of Marginal Cinema. It is notable, however, that Betinha moves away from the spectator and the adult figures she has tossed aside, underscoring a radical rejection of previous role models and modes of authority and places the potential for significant social change in the hands of a wily, rebellious female youth. Thus, the film ends with the claim that a new female political subjectivity must be radically and dramatically assumed.

Surrealist Disruptions in *Das Tripas Coração* (1982) and *Sonho de Valsa* (1987)

While *Das Tripas Coração* retains several characteristics from *Mar de Rosas*— specifically an episodic structure that refuses a clear narrative line and an aggressive rejection of "civil" behavior—it differs in that it further develops a surrealist foray into the masculine imaginary and associated psychophysical dimensions of the feminine condition. If the surrealist touches found in *Mar de Rosas* were a few drops of ink on a cloth, then in *Das Tripas Coração* the surrealist ink has fully saturated the fabric. Film scholar Laura Podalsky, who offers an insightful analysis of "carnavalesque strategies" employed by Ana Carolina to subvert patriarchal order in *Das Tripas Coração*, reports that critics identified the surrealist nature of Ana Carolina's films but were "stymied" at the time, since linkages between surrealist aesthetics to political or historical significance fell outside paradigmatic approaches to Latin American cinema.[42] However, drawing on surrealist practices was not new at this historical juncture in Brazil. It should be noted that surrealist tendencies may be found in avant-garde Brazilian cinema in the tropicalist-underground period of the late 1960s and early 1970s. Robert Stam observes that the first underground film, *A Margem* (directed by Ozualdo Candeia, 1967) includes surrealist characteristics, the preface-manifesto to dramatist José Celso Martínez Corrêa's play *O Rei da Vela* (1967) called for a theater of deliberate bad taste as an ideal expression of Brazilian surrealism, and the tropicalists of the late 1960s and early 1970s took inspiration in the early twentieth-century avant-garde, including the surrealist movement.[43]

However, if Ana Carolina coincides with others in the employ of surrealist representational strategies, the political attitude in *Das Tripas Coração* does not. The title of her second feature-length fiction film is an idiomatic expression that can be translated to English as "grin and bear it," which suggests accepting a situation that is not justified or fair. However, the sentiment here is highly sarcastic. A representation of extreme otherness short-circuits conservative, codified ideas regarding women and the female body. Whereas *Mar de Rosas* draws from the destructive impulse developed in Marginal Cinema, in *Das Tripas Coração* we find a surrealist disruption of rational boundaries that unbinds female sexuality from patriarchal authority.

The opening and closing scenes establish that the film delves into the realm of the imagination. With a military-style march—referring to the dictatorial state—playing in off-screen space, the camera tracks behind a young woman wearing a Catholic-school uniform who tries to speak with a man (Antônio Fagundes) who identifies himself as a federal administrator. In what can be seen partly as a critique of thoughtless neoliberal developmentalism promoted during the dictatorship, we learn that he has come to inform the school directors that the institution will be closed and the land will be sold off to developers. Having arrived a few minutes early, the man enters the school and then sits down in a conference room to wait for the start of a meeting with the school's teachers and supervisors. He asks a cleaning lady who serves him some water if the teachers are pretty, and then puts his head down to take a short nap. The camera, which has remained positioned behind the federal administrator the entire time (and has also added a sense of anonymity), identifies the mind from which misogynist thoughts later proceed. In the final scene of the film, there is a knock at the door of the conference room. The camera, again positioned behind the head of the federal administrator, captures him lifting his head up, looking at the clock in the room, and realizing that he had fallen asleep for a few minutes. The school director, Muniza (Miriam Muniz), and two teachers, Renata (Dina Sfat) and Miriam (Xuxa Lopes), walk in orderly fashion into the conference room to begin the meeting, and the administrator signs the papers closing the school. Although a shot of a head nodding off to sleep or waking up was once an avant-garde technique to suggest and introduce a dream state (such as that found in Maya Deren's *Meshes of the Afternoon* (1943) or in Luis Buñuel's *Un Chien Andalou* (1929), Ana Carolina employs this convention in a manner suggesting less an homage to avant-garde directors and, given the persistence of the camera behind the head of the male figure the entire time, establishes a hyperbolic, mocking tone. Thus, the sequences that take place between the opening and closing scenes constitute a dream or, more specifically, a figment of one man's absurd imagination.

The dream-like structure of the film aligns *Das Tripas Coração* with a surrealist artistic practice, albeit with some feminist divergences. As a cultural movement with its own philosophy most vocally developed by André Breton, surrealism was a highly political movement, dedicated to psychic emancipation and freedom from material repression. In terms of historical periods, surrealism is not bracketed by the years following World War I and up to the death of its most visible leader, André Breton, in 1966. Beyond the group led by Breton, other artists engaged in surrealist practices. Indeed, a number of women artists were affiliated with the historical surrealists,[44] and international exhibitions introduced surrealist works to publics throughout Europe, the Americas, and Asia.

In terms of political practice, surrealism was seen to consist of a two-part political strategy. After first unmasking the depths of alienation in modern life, the surrealists sought a reintegrated life through the fusion of the conscious mind and the unconscious mind.[45] Thus, discussion of surrealism as an artistic practice frequently refers to the emancipation of the psyche developed outward in automatic texts, dream narratives, and fragmented visions. However, Michael Richardson asserts that there is no one style or

Figure 2.7. The administrator moments before nodding off in the opening scenes of *Das Tripas Coração*.

list of defining characteristics to check off, underscoring the importance of ascertaining marks of the practice of surrealism or evidence of surrealist intentions. With regard to the use of dreams, perhaps a trait most commonly associated with surrealist aesthetics, Richardson further explains that the employ of dreams has been largely misunderstood as simply making manifest what lies dormant within a collective consciousness. Rather, Richardson asserts that for the surrealists, the dream afforded an experience of otherness that, in turn, would allow for exploring conjunctions or points of contact between different realms of existence.[46]

In an exploration of otherness, the female body frequently became a central focus of the surrealists. For male surrealists, woman was muse, her body was fetishized, and female hysteria was celebrated. Although erotic desire was seen as having a disruptive and creative potential, the erotic drive was located in the masculine libido. In her discussion of a feminist employ of surrealist practices, Whitney Chadwick notes that women surrealists frequently repositioned desire and employed a surrealist disruption of rational boundaries in works that explore the female body and femininity as "a taut web of social expectations, historical assumptions, and ideological constructions."[47] Similarly, critic Rosalind Krauss asserts that the deconstructive logic of surrealism was able to lead to a deeply antipatriarchal opening up of the question of "woman." Indeed, some female artists were drawn to surrealist practice as a way to call attention to the construction of identity and gender, and as a way to explore female subjectivity.[48] Latin American artists (Frida Kahlo, Tarsila do Amaral) as well as European-born surrealist women artists who went into exile in Mexico (Kati Horna, Remedios Varo, Leonora Carrington) have demonstrated a similar reclaiming of the female body in their works. What is more, Francine Masiello, referring specifically to the works of writers Norah Lange, Teresa de la Parra, and María Luisa Bombal, asserts that the representation of the female body in Latin American women's writing of the 1920s speaks to "fragmentation and exuberant disorder" as a way to "refuse to collaborate with the demands of the masculine imagination."[49]

It is with a feminist appropriation of surrealism that Ana Carolina's film most closely overlaps. Whereas the historical (mostly male) surrealists were concerned with woman as a mediator or an Other through which man could achieve liberation, Ana Carolina's films develop an iconography based on women's experiences that rejects a presumably male psychology and a misogynist concept of woman. Generally speaking, in masculinist surrealist practice, woman was not an independent, active subject, and the female body was often presented as fragmented. This has led art critic Rudolf E. Kuenzli to argue for an investigation of power relations in surrealism in the construction of surrealist images, asking, "Who has the power, who dominates and who is disfigured by whose power?"[50] In *Das Tripas Coração*, fetishizing and erotic exaggeration are employed to disrupt ideological constructions that have shaped women's roles in society and the female condition more generally. *Das Tripas Coração* focuses on repressed erotic desire and places the female body at the center of analysis to take aim at patriarchal understandings of women in education, religion, and political ideology. But, again, Ana Carolina may draw from surrealist representational strategies, yet her political perspective differs. Robert J. Belton offers the observation that women surrealist artists frequently "spoke with forked tongues" in that they entered surrealist discourse but exposed it for its shortcomings.[51] Ana Carolina enacts a similar gesture. The female characters in her film appear sexually aroused in seemingly uncontrollable fashion, and their bodies are fetishized, but these representations are then thrown back against those institutions that have oppressed and repressed women. Indeed, the female characters' uncontrollable, exuberant physicality is presented as a central challenge for the church and the educational system in *Das Tripas Coração*. Extreme close-ups capture feet in high-heeled shoes, a (male) school doctor examining a student's "butt crack" to verify her lung capacity, and a male janitor distributing playing cards with images of women posing erotically and engaged in fellatio. Ana Carolina develops a surrealist exploration of the masculine imaginary, presenting an exuberant, disordered female body that, in the end, refuses to collaborate with patriarchal codes.

As part of the opening sequences that establish the surrealist nature of the film, Miriam talks with her colleague Renata, reflecting on how strange "that day" was and mentions how Guido (also played by Antonio Fagundes), their colleague, was just starting his first class. The scene is shot partly out of focus, suggesting the "fog" of remembering. With Miriam's reflective statement, one finds a destructuring of space and time that leads to the disrupting of rational boundaries. For the female characters in the film who embody the man's imagination, the time frame consists of one day (or less than twenty-four hours), which contrasts with the male inspector's dream of only a few minutes and the spectator's experience of watching the film for nearly two hours. A piano, which reappears at the end of the film, suddenly crashes through a window and into an office where the two teachers, Renata and Miriam, are talking. Both this first image of the piano crashing through a window and the image of a piano flying out of a window in slow motion at the end of *Das Tripas Coração* echo Buñuel's surrealist films, making visual reference to the pianos dragged through a living room in *Un Chien Andalou*, and the closing images of *L'Age d'Or*, when objects (including a burning tree, a priest, and farm implement) are tossed from a window. The piano's first appearance here sets off a series of chaotic episodes that make up the man's dream. The sequences that follow are relatively independent of one another and show little linear arrangement of action, which is the kind of fractured texture one finds in a subconscious dream. Disregarding the conventions of film continuity and aiming for a baroque dramatic intensity over narrative development, this film seems designed to fulfill the pronouncement made by Niobi in the film *Mar de Rosas* that the hysterical becomes historical. Indeed, in *Das Tripas Coração*, Ana Carolina investigates what is hysterical and subversively makes this the story.

There is a cut from the hallway to a classroom where Guido, who appears to be an incarnation of the federal administrator himself, lectures about the general inferiority of women. If the opening static shot of the man's head as he nods off to sleep establishes a mocking tone of the masculine imagination, Guido's introductory, self-ridiculing remarks confirm it. During his pontificating, he simultaneously claims and questions: "Does any one of you know of my madness better than I? Madness is the best way to praise oneself. Here, today, I am going to set off my madness and you are

Figure 2.8. Muniza and Nair next to the disruptive,
surrealist piano in *Das Tripas Coração*.

going to represent it."[52] Acknowledging that the subsequent portrayal of the
more than seventy female students and teachers stems from his own madness undermines those very portrayals. The film clearly aims to address the
unconscious mind and, by extension, the way women are incorporated into
a patriarchal social imaginary. The representation that follows—from the
madness of the man's imagination—questions the logic that has shaped the
concept of woman and female sexuality.

What subsequently takes place during the dream narrative is a frenetic
exposé of embodied chaos. Young female students toss instruments around
in chemistry class, make phallic symbols with their erasers during lectures,
kiss and caress one another in bathroom stalls, and dance in circles singing
erotic songs while masturbating en masse.[53] The young women's uncivilized
behavior reaches an apogee during the celebration of Mass in the school's
chapel. Recalling the opening shot of *Mar de Rosas*, a young woman gets up,
walks to the front of the pews, and urinates in the middle of the aisle during
the priests' homily in order to win a bet. As the young woman who won the
bet is taken away, the priest, rather than being outraged by the sign of disre-
spect, becomes sexually excited and must be carried away by his assistants.

Such "anti-social" behavior serves as a physical rejection of bourgeois values and repressive social conventions promoted by conservative educational and religious institutions.

The exaggerated portrayal of the female body extends as well to adult women characters in *Das Tripas Coração*. Two younger teachers, Renata and Miriam, represent stereotypes of women as vengeful, competitive, and petty. The development of their characters manages to include some humor. At one point, after the two have attempted to kill one another, pulling at each other's hair and tearing off each other's clothes, they appear walking nude together down a hallway. One casually (and ironically) comments that she sometimes just feels completely exposed.

Two older women who work at the school, Muniza and Nair (Nair Bello), embody stereotypes about older women. The two wear conservative clothing and express puritanical values. At one point, Muniza claims she pities women of her age that still have sexual desire. In addition to age, class differences between women are represented by the group of cleaning ladies; Almindra (Cristina Pereira) stands out among these. The women are portrayed as unsophisticated, undisciplined, and generally simple minded. Nonetheless, it is the frank observation by Almindra—"O homem é corajoso com aquilo que ve; a mulher é corajosa com aquilo que não ve" (Man is courageous with what he sees; woman is courageous with what she does not see)—that recalls a surrealist encounter with difference between a masculine imaginary and female lived experience and implies that women have to rebel against unconscious obstacles.

The scene of public urination during the school Mass is one example of taking aim at the Church. A number of venerated symbols of the Catholic Church are also called into question. Indeed, the repressive nature of Christianity surfaces several times in the course of the dream narrative. Before she begins her day, one of the female teachers, Miriam, stops to read a banner painted in the auditorium that offers the female students and other women who work at the school a daily reminder that they are the source of original sin. In addition to the "urination scene" described above, other scenes portray the Catholic priest as a pederast who can be sexually aroused very easily. After an apparently cross-dressed student raises his/her skirt, showing that "she" in fact is a "he," the priest squeezes the student's thigh assuring that they are going to be "very good friends," suggesting that an inappropriate sexual encounter will take place. Toward the end of the film, the priest walks with a female student, suggesting in their conversation that they are going to go have sex as they enter a private area.

In addition to its treatment of the agents of Christianity, the film takes aim at the figure of Christ. In several sequences, a Christ figure is portrayed as coming to life as a real man standing on a cross platform. In one instance, the school directors, Muniza and Nair, take a group of girls to an isolated area as a form of punishment. Rather than contemplate their misbehavior, the girls kiss and caress one another in front of the living Christ who looks down over them longingly. In another scene, the three schoolteachers, Miriam, Renata, and Guido, are engaged in a steamy ménage á trois. The living Christ, who has been watching them from above, descends from the cross structure, leans over the three, and pleads, "Let me lick." The humanized representation of Christ as a voyeuristic man of flesh with sexual desires suggests that sexual pleasure is not a sin. *Das Tripas Coração*, like films of the historical surrealists and reminiscent specifically of the final sequence in *L'Age d'Or*, when a Christ figure emerges from a cave-like dwelling after four months of debauchery, attacks sexual repression instituted by "civilized" society and religion.[54] Her approach takes aim specifically at the patriarchal hypocrisy associated with conservative Christian beliefs that espouse female chastity, fidelity, and eternal dedication and veneration of a male figure.

Alongside religion and education, ostensibly liberating leftist politics are not immune from critique. At a rehearsal for a concert to celebrate the end of the school year, a male professor from the University of São Paulo shows up and sits down next to the school directors. However, he is particularly interested in two young cleaning ladies. He leans over and asks one of them if she has had the chance to read the "pamphlet" he had prepared for her. His voice and gestures suggest that this is not a work of political enlightenment but something more along the lines of the Kama Sutra. Two of the cleaning ladies and the professor leave the rehearsal hall to go clean the boiler room. There, he asks one cleaning lady, Almindra, about her education. She says she is enrolled in the first course of MOBRAL (Movimento Brasileiro de Alfabetização, the Brazilian Literacy Movement). Generously, he offers her private lessons in "coito" (coitus). Laying on top of her in the boiler room while she squirms and cackles underneath, he ecstatically cries out various names for cleaning ladies: "mucama," "faixineira," "doméstica," and "criada." In a metaphoric critique, the professor finds himself impotent and unable to "conquer" the young cleaning lady. As she leaves, thinking that she must have done something wrong, the professor asks her if she has read Engels— an absurd question given her earlier statement that she was just learning to read. The scene mocks the ostensibly progressive, left-wing intelligentsia that views the poor as an abstract "object of desire" but is incapacitated and unable to address the material realities of the poor and working class.

While it might seem incongruous to relate a surrealist film to the question of citizenship, it is important to recall the fundamental, revolutionary, liberating goals of surrealist thought. A surrealist mode of representation, in fact, speaks very much to the question of citizenship in Brazil. In one sense, the choice to develop this mode of representation serves as a rebuttal to the years of authoritarian rule that began even prior to the military coup d'état of 1964. Although surrealism was an international phenomenon, it was generally rejected by Latin American elites who wished to overcome the perceived incivility of its populations and espoused more positivist ideals of rationality, order, and progress. During the dictatorship, positivist notions of order and progress were called upon and functioned to repress the most disadvantaged sectors of Brazilian society (in other words, rural and urban poor) who had begun making demands for change.

To the degree that surrealism is about sexuality and social norms, it is also about citizenship. Recent discussions of citizenship have focused on the cultural aspects that shape the boundaries of belonging. Defined and demarcated by cultural values and expectations, sex and sexuality clearly contribute to the cultural and legal boundaries of citizenship. In other words, citizenship is not defined exclusively by discourses of rights, legal obligations, and duties. Rather, scholars have taken up the question of culture and sexuality, seeing these as key discourses on social and political inclusion and exclusion.

For some scholars, citizenship has always been about sex. Diane Richardson discusses the ways in which sexuality, and heterosexuality more specifically, has encoded dominant social and political participation. She calls for examining the relationship between the sexual and the social "to raise questions about the relationship between . . . the body and social membership."[55] In a similar vein, David T. Evans asserts that the entire history of citizenship is "a history of fundamental formal heterosexist patriarchal principles and practices" that has served "to effect unequal differentiation."[56]

Both female sexuality and citizenship were gaining attention in Brazil after the declaration of amnesty in 1979. The film *Das Tripas Coração* appears at a time when female sexuality was becoming a more openly debated topic in the Brazilian women's movement. If notions about women's sexuality and the female body give shape to the very laws and government policies that regulate them, then Ana Carolina's surrealist exposé is certainly a highly political work. Consonant with the political precepts put forth by André

Breton, *Das Tripas Coração* seeks the emancipation of women (their bodies, sexuality, and subjectivity) through an examination of a misogynist male psyche. Ultimately, the film engages with the female body and questions of inclusion. The hysteria and chaotic female physicality are defined in the film as the way women are positioned in a patriarchal social imaginary; in turn, this mode of inclusion is roundly rejected. As the film returns to its starting point and the federal administrator wakes up, a bridge is made between the unconscious beliefs about the female body, sexuality, and female identity, and experiences in the material world.

Whereas *Das Tripas Coração* focuses on the masculine imagination and prohibitions of the female body, *Sonho de Valsa* investigates the female imagination and the myths that sustain it; and the film promotes a rupture from past models of gender and female sexuality. In this last film of the trilogy we find a number of elements of style apparent in the previous two films, such as an episodic structure, recasting actresses (Xuxa Lopes, Cristina Pereira), and a surrealist disruption of space and time to further a psychophysical exploration of the female condition, tying inner beliefs to outer material experiences. Indeed, throughout the film it is difficult to assess clearly on what experiential plan a scene occurs—as a dream, a dream within a dream, or diegetic reality. This blurring of existential states arises from plays on words, from Tereza's (Xuxa Lopes) referring to the dreams she has had, and from the reappearance of actors in more than one role. Highly disparate sequences are linked by sound bridges and match-on-action continuity editing. As if two pieces of a puzzle fitting together, the theme of romantic love and its effects on lived female experience (a subject which Miriam [Dina Sfat] and Renata [Xuxa Lopes] discussed at one point in *Das Tripas Coração*) is readdressed in this final film. However, as a film released in 1987 after the official end of the military dictatorship and during the first years of the redemocratization process, *Sonho de Valsa* bares the marks of a new political era. Given the narrative fragmentation found in Ana Carolina's first two films, the fact that the episodes in *Sonho de Valsa* show greater narrative coherence can be interpreted as an inclination toward believing in the development of a new female subjectivity and, concomitantly, in the possibility of a new sociopolitical story.

In this film, one follows the female protagonist's development from childhood to maturity in an examination of how the concept of love has shaped her subjectivity. While debates surrounding the female condition continued to be waged in the women's movements in Brazil, *Sonho de Valsa* offers up a vital message on how women are positioned (and position themselves) ideologically and with regard to their sense of belonging in the world. The film follows the female protagonist, Tereza, who has visions of Prince Charming in full medieval garb and lives out vivid dreams as she miraculously crosses through space and time. Tereza's movement is loosely organized around the evolving romantic relationships she has had with male figures in her life from youth to maturity.

Cinema is certainly no stranger to love stories. Romantic notions of love have thematically contextualized narrative tensions in countless cinematic melodramas in Latin America. Indeed, film critic Silvia Oroz asserts that melodramas have offered a sentimental education, teaching generations of Latin Americans that "love can conquer all."[57] In *Sonho de Valsa*, melodramatic tropes (such as love of family, religion and marriage, finding one's true love, and so on) are treated with surrealist intentions to question myths of love and romance. The film offers up a message that reversing sociopolitical alienation and achieving personal liberation will come from a personal change in perspectives.

The title of the film ("Dream Waltz" in English) conjures up notions of dreams, desires, and romance. The opening credits and first sequence of *Sonho de Valsa* are accompanied by the sounds of violins playing a waltz. Adding to this romantic tone, bright lights and overexposed film create an ethereal, peaceful quality for the image of a Siamese kitten playing on a white rug. The kitten yawns, which is accompanied by the incongruous sound of a lion's roar, suggesting that what is ostensibly cute and sweet may actually have a very sharp bite. Indeed, this initial disjunction of sound and image sets the questioning tone for Ana Carolina's discussion of heteronormative love and romance. There is a cut to a well-lit white room where a man and a woman are being intimate in bed. The woman, who is later identified as Tereza (Xuxa Lopes), rolls over after reaching sexual climax, picks up the kitten to play with and, in voiceover, shares, "Anoite sonhei que me casei com um gatinho" (Last night I dreamt I married a guy). The term "gatinho," which literally translates as "little cat" in Portuguese, colloquially means an attractive young man. This play with metaphors (which occur throughout the film) combines with the nondiegetic woman's voice to make it difficult to determine which parts of the film are "reality" and which are imagined scenarios. The subject of her dream—finding and marrying a man—in this opening sequence speaks to a socially codified, internalized desire to find one's true love and establishes early that the question of love and romance will take center stage.

That the woman refers to a dream she has had combined with the dreamlike mise-en-scéne positions the film within a surrealist mode of representation similar to that found in *Das Tripas Coração*. Sexuality, sexual pleasure, and love were topics frequently addressed by the surrealists. For André Breton, true liberation included the liberation of desire—thus his pronouncement in the Second Manifesto: "Il n'este pas de solution hors de l'amour" (There is no solution outside of love).[58] A fundamental political practice espoused by the surrealists was inserting inner reality into the outer, material world. For Breton, love, as an aspect of surrealist politics, most aptly represented the insertion of the psychological into the political, and vice versa.[59] Whitney Chadwick adds that for the surrealists, eros was seen as having a subversive power and was a consistent leitmotif of Surrealism, but it was a male language of eros that dominated: "The cultivation of *eros* in Surrealism made woman into an active sexual force in the world and in man's creative life, but the language of love, whether expressed in the romantic visions of Breton and Eluard or in the perverse images of Dalí and Bellmer, was a male language. Its subject was woman, its object woman, and even while proclaiming woman's liberty it defined her image in terms of man's desires."[60]

Hence, for the (historical) surrealists, love was a discursive tool used to engage in political debates and for ultimately seeking personal emancipation. Similarly, the melodramatic mode approached the question of love as a way to reflect on (and frequently uphold) social expectations for gender and sexuality. In what may best be understood as a rhetorical conversion, Ana Carolina includes a number of melodramatic tropes in *Sonho de Valsa* and pairs them with a surrealist aesthetic that results in the subversion of myth-like beliefs of romantic love that have been coded, as Chadwick notes, in a male language that has, in the eyes of Ana Carolina, served to repress women's true sexual force and impeded personal, female liberation.

Ana Carolina problematizes the question of love by exploring the different phases in Tereza's psychosexual development, tracing her affective bonds and romantic relationships from childhood to adulthood. The protagonist, Tereza, is seen waking in her bedroom, the same space where the opening sequence had taken place, causing further uncertainty about which segments of the film are intended to represent reality or dreams (or perhaps even within dreams). The brightly lit room with all-white decor and the camera slightly out of focus contribute an ethereal quality to the scene, disconnected from physical reality. She enters a home library where she talks with her father (Arduíno Colassanti) and her brother (Ney Matogrosso) and, although she appears as an adult, she portrays youthful behaviors, playing cat's cradle and obsessing about a zit on her forehead. Tereza sits on her father's lap while he caresses her knee, suggestive of an incestuous or at least unusually close relationship between the two. While the three talk, Tereza—and she alone—sees a Prince Charming in full medieval garb miraculously appear to float on the room's ceiling, waving and winking down at her. Moments later, another "Prince Charming" appears outside the library window with a white horse. Though the sudden appearance of these men catches her attention, she feigns not seeing them and continues talking or listening to the conversation with her brother and father.

The Prince Charming figures reappear later in a party that Tereza and her father and brother attend. Here and in the previous scene, Tereza is portrayed as holding an inordinate devotion for her father and brother and a compulsive need for male approval. It merits noting that the sudden appearances of Prince Charming figures do not go unrecognized by the protagonist. Rather, Tereza's contained confusion at the sight of these men in medieval garb reveals a pulling away from codified beliefs and an initial questioning of romantic myths. What is more, her nervous demeanor in this and subsequent scenes demonstrates a disturbing disjuncture between her desires and society's expectations of her. Her nervousness (and what may even be seen as neurotic behavior at times) embodies a feminist noncompliance with scripted behaviors and roles.

While under the watchful (and possessive) glances of her father and brother, Tereza dances and talks with different men at the party.[61] This party takes place against a dark backdrop with high key lighting, which creates the absence of visual depth and suggests a decontextualized, dreamlike event. She acts very indecisively before eventually meeting a man named Carlos Alberto. Before they leave the party together, Tereza and Carlos come across some people attempting to hit a piñata. Tereza takes a swing at it but hurts herself, prompting her brother to come to her aid. The two sit down, and high backlighting creates a rim of glowing light around the outlines of their bodies, adding a sense of distortion to the scene. Tereza then confides, "Se eu quisesse, ja poderia estar livre" (If I wanted, I could already be free), to which her brother responds, "Se você soubesse" (If you knew how). She further admits great insecurity and that she sees behind every man the shadow of a man who will love her. In this, Tereza acknowledges the central problem of psychophysical freedom, which is tied to her belief that she will (and must) find a man who admires and loves her unconditionally. Although she shows signs here of beginning a process of self-liberation, the party sequence ends when her inordinate devotion to familial male role models overcomes her, and she passionately kisses her brother.

Tereza's search for love, contentment, and a sense of self continues in the next stages of Tereza's development, first with a boyfriend named Marcos

(Daniel Dantas) and then with a husband named Ivan. Exposition of her relationship with Marcos begins in the domestic space of a white bathroom where Tereza bathes and Marcos shaves. Once again making it unclear on what experiential plane the action takes place, Tereza shares with Marcos the details of a dream she has had, envisioning herself walking along a path full of rocks. The self-referential nature of this statement is clear, given that both earlier and then later in the film Tereza is seen walking over rough terrain, which in turn metaphorically refers to the surface of her own life. Tereza brings up issues concerning his possible infidelity. She wants full commitment from Marcos, which he simply cannot offer her. Showing great insecurity with herself and her relationship with Marcos, she pulls and tugs at him. Interrupting their argument, a mermaid suddenly appears and flips around in the bathtub before apparently diving into deep waters to escape. By way of trick cinematography,[62] Marcos appears to dive in after the mermaid, offering a critique that he can be easily drawn to a mythic feminine figure rather than sustain the relationship he has with a real woman, Tereza.

But Tereza does not give up easily. She "dives in" after Marcos and the mermaid. She then crawls through a dark tunnel lamenting the fact that she has lost her love. The tunnel leads to a drainage opening at a road out of which Tereza crawls and she then finds herself immediately in the middle of a military parade. Remarkably, the military forces participated in this parade scene that shows citizens reviewing military forces passing before them. By extension, this scene is highly suggestive of a transition from a military regime to a new democratic era. Going uncannily unnoticed by those around her, she crawls on the ground in front of parade onlookers and weaves in and out of soldiers standing at attention. Tereza catches sight of Marcos, who has himself caught the eye of the mermaid, now a real woman dressed as a marching band flag bearer. Angered, Tereza yells at Marcos, picks up the flag, and waves it threateningly at Marcos before two military police grab the flag from her and ask for her documents. Still dressed in a bathrobe, she whimpers, "Estou sem identidade" (literally: I'm without identity), which in the original Portuguese plays simultaneously on the idea of an "identification card" and "identity." The bartender (Paulo Reis), who later gains the name Ivan as Tereza's husband, then puts his arms around Tereza and tells the police officers that she is a "code 13—dementia" before whisking her away into the backroom of the bar. There, Tereza's neurotic insecurity comes out in full force. Just moments earlier she was angered and trying to whack Marcos with the flagpole. Now she talks hyperactively and shows she is extremely concerned. She asks the bartender (Ivan) if she

Figure 2.9. Tereza, still wearing her bathrobe, crawls from a drainage tunnel and into a parade in *Sonho de Valsa*.

hurt Marcos, if she is what Marcos imagined her to be, and if Marcos is having an affair with the flag bearer.

The scene in the storage room of the bar explores the sentiment expressed at one point by Tereza that "o que os olhos não vem o coração fica louco" (what the eyes don't see, the heart goes crazy). In other words, the scene explores the balance of imagination and reality with identity and desire in heteronormative relationships. The arguments and discussion about relationships, fidelity, and love take place in a back storage room, suggesting that these are debates waged "behind" the scenes of consciousness. Initially, this balance is explored in the scene with imagination taking center stage. An anxious Tereza expresses that her wholeness depends on the opinions of men and their inclinations toward her. The central thesis of *Das Tripas Coração* is recalled when Tereza pathetically cries out at one point in frustration, "Eu não caibo na sua imaginação" (I don't fit into your imagination), asserting that she is a product of an old delirium and that her very existence depends on the mental workings of men. In this, Tereza begins to show an awareness that her lack of a stable identity stems in part from how she has been imagined by men in society and how she has played into the desires and fantasies of others. At a calm point, she admits that everything she has ever done has been to please a man.

The philosophical focus in the storage room scene then shifts toward questions of desire and its impact on one's sense of self. Tereza moves away from Ivan and Marcos and crawls on top of a pile of white sand covered with a layer of silver glitter. This plane of action is interrupted by a montage of erotic images in which the bodies of Tereza, Ivan, and Marcos become entangled and glisten under mobile overhead lighting. Several of the montage stills show the three circled around a black goat, indicating that their sexual acts arise from natural animal instincts.[63] These images correlate with comments made earlier by Tereza that feelings can be the source of knowledge about reality. The surrealist exploration of desire that takes place here— within the original fantasy sequence that led to the bar itself—appears to end when a clothed Ivan stands up in a fully lit storage room and stops a hanging lamp from swaying. Ivan, in non sequitur fashion, encourages the three to talk about what happened—referring either to the preceding erotic scenes or some other incident(s). Underscoring differences of perception, Marcos does not wish to talk and responds, "Não aconteceu nada" (Nothing happened), whereas Tereza corrects him, stating, "Aconteceu sim" (Yes, it did happen). Realizing that she can envision men as she wishes and that she can take charge of her own imagination and identity, she attempts to exorcise Marcos and Ivan from her life (and mind) by yelling "Sai! Sai os dois!" (Out! Both of you, out!).

In the next phase of her personal trajectory, Tereza goes to a party where she meets Ivan, who had appeared as the barman previously. They begin a relationship; soon thereafter, they go for a walk in a park. They stop and sit on a bench, where Ivan casually lays down and places his head in her lap. Tereza then raises the hood of the dress she is wearing and covers her head. With great seamlessness, the two have effectively rehearsed the iconographical image of Michaelangelo's sculpture *La Pietá*. Moments later Ivan crawls into a water fountain and positions himself to look like a Christ figure with lights shining brightly from behind. When Tereza leans down and apparently pays homage to this image, it becomes clear that her ideas about marriage and her relationship as a wife have been greatly influenced by Catholicism. What is more, these images suggest that the notion that women are to be self-sacrificing may emerge unexpectedly in seemingly ordinary activities.

Sonho de Valsa revisits the issue of marriage, which had earlier been addressed in *Mar de Rosas*. After their courtship, Tereza and Ivan appear before a church altar (ostensibly) for their wedding ceremony. There is no diegetic

Figure 2.10. Tereza rehearsing the role of the ideal, protective woman, holds Ivan in her arms in *Sonho de Valsa*.

dialogue in the scene. Rather, an uncomfortable silence reigns over the couple as an enormous beetle swarms around Tereza's bouquet. While she fidgets, the buzzing sound of the insect becomes increasingly louder. Meanwhile, attendants to the wedding appear to leave before the ceremony seems even to start. This line of action is intercut with images of Tereza's brother and father looking in extreme horror toward her as if witnessing a horrible accident, images of Tereza tossing off her veil while extolling how she does not need him, and a shot of Ivan stating that she ruined everything. This montage explores the unexpressed thoughts regarding their marriage and suggests that the seeds of divorce are planted early in a relationship. The tension at the wedding causes Tereza to collapse. Her brother rushes to her aid, but a humanized Christ figure arrives first, lifts her up, and carries her magically to the front door of her father's house, suggesting that a woman's existence falls under the constant protection of a male figure—be it the Holy Father, a husband, or a biological father. Bright lights and overexposed images lend an ethereal quality to Tereza's collapse. The lighting also marks a point of transition where Tereza will begin to move metaphorically toward greater enlightenment. After awakening in her father's house, she decides calmly

Figure 2.11. After crawling out of the hole she had fallen into,
Tereza emerges on new terms in *Sonho de Valsa.*

that she needs a real job, a real life, a real male companion. In a relaxed, confident voice speaking to herself, Tereza states that problems are not solved, but they are sometimes abandoned. The sequence ends as she opens a door and an extremely bright light envelops her.

The last sequences of the film treat Tereza's final steps of giving up illusions and assumed realities. In these final scenes of the film, overt plays on words are brought fully to the surface. The process Tereza goes through shows her walking barefoot over rocky terrain, sitting down at a creek bed, picking up a frog, biting into it and stating purposefully that "é fundamental engolir sapos" (literally: it is necessary to eat frogs), another idiomatic expression similar to "grin and bear it." She talks to herself about finding her own "sonho de valsa" (fantasies) and facing up to the rigors of life while she makes a wooden cross from logs and twine. In an act of gender and religious transgression, Tereza then proceeds to drag the cross with her over rough landscape before she falls into a cavernous pit. The visual images here—eating frogs, bearing a cross—are plays on metaphors reflecting commonly held beliefs and serve to question the value of self-sacrifice.

The final images of the film are particularly powerful. Inside the hole she has fallen into with her cross, Tereza confronts images of marriage, motherhood, and all the men who have passed through her life, including her father, brother, lovers, and the Prince Charming figures. Naked bodies glisten under beams of light that shine from above while Tereza speaks now with a reflective calmness. In her closing words, Tereza is no longer a neurotic, anxious young woman. She is more confident, resolute, and proceeds to climb out of the pit, using her cross as a ladder. Before reaching the opening at the top of the pit, there is an intercut image in slow motion of Tereza thrusting the cross into a mirror, breaking it to pieces; behind the mirror a bright light shines. This act of destruction suggests her liberation from the image of herself that was shown to her and external values she believed she needed to fulfill.

In the final shot, Tereza, with great effort, climbs out of the hole she had fallen into and smiles as she rests herself on the edge of the pit. Tereza has completed her process of psychophysical liberation. She has shed accepted myths and unquestioned beliefs, wakes from numerous layers of dreams, and emerges into open air as if reborn. Unlike the male figure in *Das Tripas Coração*, who remained unchanged after waking from his dream, the female protagonist here emerges transformed. She has left behind useless fantasies. This final scene in *Sonho de Valsa* completes the trajectory of escape from patriarchal oppression that began in the dark night along a highway in *Mar de Rosas*. Here, the female protagonist emerges from the darkness, moves into the light, and reengages with the world on new, unalienated terms.

3

Rescreening the Past

The Politics of Memory
in Brazilian Women's
Filmmaking of the 1980s

Brazilian women's filmmaking during the 1980s emerged at the juncture of several influences. Amid apparent political openings, a pressing desire to reflect on the recent past rubbed up against state-sponsored visions of Brazilian history. A process of developing new senses of cultural and political identity was met with a lingering practice of censorship. As discussed in chapter 1, the grip of authoritarian rule began to loosen during the second half of the 1970s. Students and organized labor once again took to the streets to demand political change. In late 1978, the AI-5, a key authoritarian instrument, was abolished. Shortly thereafter, the passage of the amnesty law in 1979 heralded the beginning of a period of political opening, or *Abertura* (1979–85), and a moment to reassess meanings of *brasilidade* (Brazilian cultural identity). But neither amnesty nor the abolition of the AI-5 translated into immediate relaxation of repression. Right-wing groups attacked high-profile figures, a bomb exploded in a downtown shopping center in Rio de Janeiro, a letter bomb was sent to the headquarters of the Brazilian Press Association, and vigilantes threatened newsstand owners who sold progressive newspapers.[1] The years of political opening before the official end of the military dictatorship can be diagrammed as a zigzagging line where new political freedoms were met with ongoing governmental control and intervention in the culture sector.

Whereas Ana Carolina's films took a psychoanalytical approach to the cultural imagination, other women directors at this time such as Tereza Trautman, Suzana Amaral, Norma Bengell, and Tizuka Yamasaki drew on the melodramatic mode to offer feminist interventions in the reconstruction of Brazilian politics and cultural identity. My discussion here focuses on

Tizuka Yamasaki, another "offspring" of Cinema Novo directors and one of the first women filmmakers, alongside Ana Carolina, to establish a continuous career trajectory in filmmaking. Yamasaki, who claims she inaugurated a "cinema of emotion" in the 1980s, strategically turned to melodrama to comment on Brazil's past in an effort to reclaim overlooked female figures and their experiences in Brazil's history as well as to contribute discursively to a process of redefining citizenship during *Abertura*. At the same time that we can detect an engagement with feminist discourses that were prevalent in the early 1980s, we find that Yamasaki's films strategically mediate Brazilian history and advocate for affective bonds to reformulate civil society on the cusp of a new democratic era.

Although her career spans four decades, Yamasaki's early, highly acclaimed films from the 1980s, including *Gaijin: Os Caminhos da Liberdade* (Gaijin: Paths to Freedom, 1980), *Parahyba, Mulher Macho* (Parahyba, Manly Woman, 1983), and *Patriamada* (Sing, the Beloved Country, 1984) are of particular interest. These films harmonize on a common goal to provide feminist interventions in the reconstruction of Brazilian politics and national identity. Against a backdrop where the military government openly sponsored the production of certain types of historical films that would maintain its hegemony and censored others that criticized contemporary events and authoritarian policies, I explore how Yamasaki's first two works represent iconoclastic, defiant women of the early twentieth century and suture the political milieu of the past to the contemporary push for redemocratization in Brazil. Reflecting greater easing of government control in the mid-1980s, one finds in *Patriamada* a blending of melodrama and documentary modes that engages with feminist discourse of the time and the struggle for a return to democratic elections. Her last film is notable in that it reflects a desire for direct engagement with political life, a spirit that is developed further in women's independent and alternative film and video projects.

History and memory are not synonymous, but they are never fully distinct from one another. While history aims to deal in facts and events, memory is a process of giving meaning to the past. In this process of interpreting the past we find the possibility for the emergence of new understandings of citizenship. Elizabeth Jelin frames the importance of working through the past as a vital process in transition politics. She asserts that interpretations of the past are part of the "difficult road toward forging democratic societies" and key elements "in the process of (re)construction of individual and collective identities in societies emerging from periods of violence and trauma."[2] What is more, reflecting on the past in the present involves rethinking the parameters of politics and justice in the public and private sphere.[3] The (re) interpretation of the past is a vital process in reconstructing individual and collective identities after periods of violence, and memory plays a significant role in strengthening a sense of belonging to groups and communities.[4] At stake for women filmmakers in Brazil as the dictatorship came to an end was offering interpretations of the past that brought excluded political "others" into view and produced new cultural knowledge on which a democratic Brazilian society could be built.

Representing history in Brazil from 1975 to the end of the military regime was a highly contentious enterprise. In the name of national security, the regime began investing more directly in the cultural sector by the mid-1970s. Although development of historic subjects was generally thwarted during the Médici "presidency" (1969–74), the declaration of *distensão* resulted in a pressing need to substitute forceful control of the nation with more subtle methods of maintaining hegemony during a protracted process of political relaxation. At this time, the state was particularly dedicated to solidifying notions of *brasilidade* by way of promoting and protecting traditions and history, evident in numerous programs focusing on national memory and culminating in the creation of the Fundação Nacional Pró-Memória (National Pro-Memory Foundation) in 1979. The story of Brazil that the state promoted was one of homogenized diversity—the contradiction being appropriate. In 1975, the Conselho Federal de Cultura (Federal Council on Culture) published the "Política Nacional de Cultura" (PNC, National Policy on Culture). The PNC, in seemingly benign fashion, defined Brazilian culture as evolving from the "sincretismo de diferentes manifestações que . . . podemos identificar como características brasileiras" (syncretism of different manifestations that . . . we can identify as Brazilian characteristics).[5] Renato Ortiz critiques the conservative ideology of the PNC, which he defines as a Gilberto Freyre–inspired ideology of syncretism where differences (racial, ethnic, regional) and contradictions are elided in favor of a harmonious acculturation.[6]

At the same time that numerous political memoirs were published,[7] the state supported production of historic films first through the National Film Institute (INC, Instituto Nacional de Cinema) and then through Embrafilme.[8] Not only did the government at this time take a new, direct role in film production financing, it also established a special committee to review scripts and select projects it would support. Those representations of history that conformed to the governments need to assert and maintain its hegemonic position were given the green light. Although the military government did not necessarily have a clear idea of what history it wanted told, it is more than likely that directors at the time were aware of what histories could *not* be told. Thus, what we find is a state-sponsored practice of simultaneously codifying those narratives of Brazilian history in Brazilian cinema that were "useful" to the regime while de-memorializing visions of the past that did not help maintain the status quo.

In the 1980s, a number of Brazilian filmmakers developed an aesthetic of naturalism to reflect on contemporary history. However, from the late 1970s to the early 1980s there were a number of limitations to this mode of expression that ultimately made it a compromised aesthetic choice. The political liberalization of *Abertura* combined with a more commercially oriented cinema motivated a tendency toward a certain naturalism, which has been seen as forming part of a "seductive strategy associating cinematic spectacle with authenticity and even audacity in presenting the raw data of everyday life."[9] Although numerous directors sought to treat political experience after years of dictatorship, many of these films were clearly market-oriented works that developed action-filled plots and offered little social commentary.[10]

Two important Brazilian films from this time that draw on a naturalist aesthetic and ostensibly offer a critical vision of Brazilian society are Hector Babenco's *Lúcio Flávio, O pasageiro da Agonia* (1977) and *Pixote* (1980). With specific regard to *Lúcio Flávio*, Randal Johnson notes that director Hector Babenco is reported to have consulted with censors before filming, reflecting a general strategy at the time in which filmmakers and the authoritarian regime struck a tacit agreement that there were political limits that had to be observed.[11] Although director Hector Babenco did develop a plot around the social exclusion of young people in raw fashion in *Pixote*, the film ultimately fails to establish a location for the spectator and consequently leaves little room for social analysis.[12] What is more, Johnson argues that both films develop a documentary tone but are, ultimately, "illusionistic fictions."[13]

Critical, naturalist portrayals of everyday life or direct discussions of the more recent past were met with continued censorship. Actions taken by government censors during the "ambivalent" first years of *Abertura* suggest that filmmakers who wished to treat history, especially recent events, needed to show restraint or opt to develop projects set further away from the contemporary moment. In 1982, former Embrafilme director Roberto Farias released his *Pra Frente Brasil* (Onward Brazil) and, despite its success at the Gramado Film Festival and selection to participate in the Cannes Film Festival, the film clearly tested the degree to which political relaxation had been adopted within the government. Given the green light by two different censorship panels, the film was ultimately blocked ostensibly for its graphic depiction of torture scenes set in 1970.[14] However, the 1982 elections in which citizens voted directly for governors and state senators was the more likely reason to block the film, thereby preventing negative associations with military-backed candidates and maintaining a slower pace of political transition. Another film that touched on the Achilles' heel of the military regime includes Renato Tapajós's *Em Nome da Segurança Nacional* (In the Name of National Security, 1983). The film features violent images of repression, military marches, and interviews with people who suffered under the regime, and it criticizes the guiding philosophy of national security espoused by the military regime as justification for the dictatorship. The film was immediately banned.[15]

Alongside an aesthetic of naturalism, the cinematic melodrama (re) emerges at this time in Brazil with a tendency for developing the historical melodrama. Whether as a potent catalyst for cultural reflection or for its ability to address sociopolitical crises, cinematic melodrama has experienced several "boom" periods in the major film-producing countries of Latin America, taking on particular social functions at critical junctures in the development of national identity. For instance, in her work on Mexican cinematic melodramas of the 1940s and 1950s, Ana López asserts that films from this period, on the heels of the nation-building project of the Mexican Revolution (1910–20), mediated national and gendered identity, staging "dramas of identity" that addressed "pressing contradictions and desires within Mexican society."[16] The melodramatic mode has been highly successful in Brazil, finding an outlet in books, plays, and radio programs before emerging in moving pictures. From the inauguration of sound cinema to the late 1950s, the *chanchada*—musical comedies with a high melodramatic valence—flourished in Brazilian cinema. In his research on this period of Brazilian film history, Cid Vasconcelos suggests that the melodrama was a genre best suited to nationalistic films during the Estado Novo (New State) dictatorship of Getúlio Vargas (1937–45).[17]

Toward the 1950s, however, melodramas began to fall out of favor. Protesting against a Hollywood-style studio system of film production and inspired by the aesthetic proposals and production strategies of post–World War II Italian neorealism, an iconoclastic generation of filmmakers emerged and became known as New Latin American Cinema. Their film practice denounced melodramas for their bourgeois ideology and commercialism while favoring films made in natural settings, using nonprofessional actors and treating popular themes. More interested in substituting emotional responses with rational thought, these filmmakers saw their work as an extension of their political praxis and a way to intervene in debates about cultural dependency and neoliberal development ideology. In the case of Brazil, when the dictatorship turned violent and repressive, these filmmakers found refuge in allegorical representation as a way to discuss the nation while avoiding state-sponsored censorship.[18]

Despite being rejected by Cinema Novo directors, the importance of melodrama in Latin America cannot be overstated. Melodrama has crossed political, cultural, and audiovisual borders throughout the region, perhaps owing to what Hermann Herlinghaus notes as its high degree of intermediality.[19] Others attribute the prevalence of melodrama in Latin America to matters of history and cultural identity. Jesús Martín-Barbero asserts that melodrama in Latin America is an expressive mode par excellence and, regardless of the narrative form in which it appears, "taps into and stirs up a deep vein of collective cultural imagination."[20]

The reemergence of cinematic melodrama at this time can be seen partly as a reaction to state policies and partly as a mode through which history and social relations could be effectively addressed. Shifts in censorship practices created the conditions for women to take up the melodramatic mode. Whereas challenges to the traditional family and gendered social roles had once caught the censors' eyes under the pretext that it was a system to defend morality, by the late 1970s censors were clearly more concerned with preserving the hegemony of the state and its power. However, despite the proliferation of *pornochanchadas* and later emergence of hard-core productions, films with sexually explicit scenes or those that challenged Catholic morality continued to be censored until the redemocratization process went into full swing in 1985.[21] Films that could be socially or politically fractious or, more important, show contempt for the military regime were systematically censored. Thus, a domestic melodrama set in the past (seemingly) did not pose the same threat to a military regime struggling to maintain its hegemony.

Melodrama at this time was a highly effective critical mode. For women filmmakers who were interested in pushing dialogue forward on women's roles in society and changing gender dynamics, the melodramatic form, with its tendency to interrogate gender and interpersonal relationships under the influence of external social factors, was particularly advantageous in the context of early and late *Abertura*. Owing in part to how melodrama has afforded a space for making the personal political, feminist film scholars have taken an interest in the study of the mode for its potential to expose the failings of capitalism and patriarchy.[22] Scholars of Latin American Cinema have noted how melodrama has functioned as a space to subvert or uphold social norms and afforded women more progressive roles.[23] The cinematic melodrama has been seen as providing a sociopolitical compass for societies undergoing dramatic change, when former social narratives no longer offer the guidance they once did.[24] With its stylistic excesses and tendency to elicit emotional responses before the struggle of good versus evil in which virtuous characters prevail, melodramas have allowed for critical reassessment of social roles and the reformulation of political values. The particular joining of emotion and feelings with reflection on the past as found in historical melodramas leads toward new definitions of individual and collective identity. As Elizabeth Jelin observes, when events or moments are associated with emotions, the association triggers a process to search for meaning and departures from learned routines.[25]

Brazilian women filmmakers have demonstrated a consistent concern for intervening in interpretations of history. Acclaimed film pioneer Carmen Santos directed *Inconfidência Mineira* (1948) in which she portrays the revolutionary insurgency of Brazilians seeking independence[26] from Portugal in the eighteenth century and comments indirectly on the illegitimacy of political power during the Vargas Era (1930–45). In turn, Ana Carolina directed the highly acclaimed, feature-length documentary *Getúlio* (1974) in which she examines the dynamics of power and Estado Novo dictator Getúlio Vargas at a time when Brazil was once again in the grips of a military regime.

In the 1980s, a new generation of Brazilian women directors took to the melodramatic mode to discursively intervene in the process of redefining citizenship in Brazil during a key period of sociopolitical transition. Common to these melodramas directed by women in the 1980s is an exploration of the past that not only addresses lacunae in official versions of Brazil's history but also aims to redefine women's roles in a future democratic nation. Portraits of strong female protagonists in the more distant past of the early twentieth century (*Gaijin, Parahyba, Mulher Macho,* and *Eternamente Pagú*) give way to reflections on more recent past and contemporary moment (*Patriamada, Sonhos de Menina Moça, A Hora da Estrela*) as the period of *Abertura* segues into the official end of the dictatorship and beginning of the redemocratization period. In addition to avoiding lingering problems with censorship (as discussed above), these women's films that take up the distant and recent past make the significant gesture of reclaiming Brazilian history while intervening in new understandings of Brazilian cultural identity. Directors such as Suzana Amaral, Tizuka Yamasaki, Norma Bengell, and Tereza Trautman took advantage of the mode's ability to address tensions in the domestic sphere, related to the shifting definitions of Brazilian political and national identity as well as redefinitions of gendered social roles being addressed by the women's movements.

In the heady years of redemocratization (1985–88), Norma Bengell made her directorial debut with *Eternamente Pagú* (1986), a biographical portrait of Patrícia Galvão, affectionately known as Pagú, who collaborated with the modernist Anthropophagic movement and became the partner of the movement's leader, Oswald de Andrade. Her militancy in the Communist Party led to numerous arrests and, during the populist dictatorship of Getúlio Vargas (the Estado Novo), she was jailed for five years and tortured by the military. As a revolutionary who relentlessly fought for liberty, she became an important, symbolic figure in contemporary Brazilian feminism. Although Pagú is studied in relation to the Anthropophagic movement by school children in Brazil, her life had not been portrayed in the cinema. Bengell's film takes up this young, politically defiant woman and portrays her as a figure to respect and admire. That *Eternamente Pagú* opens with the image of Pagú looking out over a modern, late-twentieth-century cityscape makes it clear that the narrative of Pagú's life and political iconoclasm should inform the present and future construction of the Brazilian nation.

Also developing the melodramatic mode, Tereza Trautman's *Sonhos de Menina Moça* (1988), narrates the departure of a family from the Rio de Janeiro mansion where they had lived for forty years, which functions as an extended metaphor for the sociopolitical rupture taking place in a Brazil undergoing a process of redemocratization. The film's characters, whose lives had been molded by the years of the dictatorship, now search for new meanings of existence. Suzana Amaral's *A Hora da Estrela* (1985), an adaptation of the novel by Clarice Lispector, narrates the abject suffering of a young woman from northeast Brazil who finds herself wholly marginalized in the urban, industrialized south. The plight of the film's protagonist, Macabeia, is at once synecdotal and allegorical for the feelings of alienation experienced by a large section of the Brazilian populace and struck an emotional chord with audiences. Amaral's film speaks to social exclusion, inequality, and the debilitating effects of an authoritarian regime. As well, Lúcia Murat's *Que Bom Te Ver Viva* (1989) denounces the dictatorship's use of torture on female political prisoners. Melodramatic soliloquies (by actress Irene Ravache) are juxtaposed with documentary testimonial of victims of torture, creating a synergy of cognitive and affective functions of memory and an intimate work of political protest and recovery from violent trauma.

❏ ❏ ❏

It is during this complicated sociopolitical context in which the government promoted historical films that sexuality and traditional gender roles were discussed more openly, and there was a growing desire for more critical reflection on personal experiences and Brazilian cultural identity that Tizuka Yamasaki, a third-generation Japanese-Brazilian, established herself as one of the most important Brazilian film directors of the 1980s. Of the women filmmakers of her generation, Yamasaki most adeptly employs the melodramatic mode to rearticulate national identity, the tenor of politics, and the practices of citizenship during the years of *Abertura*.

The first three films by Yamasaki evidence some elements learned from working on films by Cinema Novo directors, but she clearly develops her own work in entirely new directions. From Nelson Pereira dos Santos, with whom she worked as an assistant on his *Amuleto de Ogum* (1974) and *Tenda dos Milagres* (1977), she gained an appreciation for Brazil's diversity and a concern for national identity. Working with Glauber Rocha on his film *A Idade da Terra* (1980), in which she assisted in the direction and production, Yamasaki gained a vision of cinema as an arena for political activism and how to transform one reality into something else.[27]

Despite these early experiences with Cinema Novo directors, her work represents significant departures in style and substance. Darlene Sadlier asserts that Cinema Novo was conceptualized "in unconscious ways for a young man's gaze," which rejected supposedly "feminine elements" of capitalist culture and developed a tendency to "substitute pathos, tears, and masochistic suffering for rigorous political analysis and angry calls to social action."[28] However, Cinema Novo never completely distanced itself from what it rejected. After analyzing a short retrospective film, *Cinema de lágrimas* (1995) by Nelson Pereira dos Santos, Sadlier asserts that key traits of melodramatic mode "were never completely absent" from Latin American New Cinema.[29] Nonetheless, Yamasaki's employ of the melodramatic mode in *Gaijin* does differ from her Cinema Novo predecessors in that it openly reclaims a "cinema of emotion" to foreground the "feminine" as part of her political analysis and activism.

Expanding *Brasilidade* in *Gaijin:*
Os Caminhos da Liberdade (1980)

The historical melodrama *Gaijin: Os Caminhos da Liberdade* takes up the history of the first generation of Japanese immigrants to Brazil in the early 1900s.[30] The film received numerous accolades and awards, including one for best picture in the Gramado Film Festival and was nominated to represent Brazil in the Berlin Film Festival. The film also received first prize (El Premio Coral) at the Second International Festival of Latin American Cinema in Havana in 1980. Not only was this the first award given to a Latin American woman, but it also marked the emergence of a new generation of filmmakers.[31] The film's eventual success belies the difficulties Yamasaki had in securing production funds for the film. Despite official cultural policies (discussed herewith) that promoted historical films, Yamasaki began searching for funding for the film in 1976, four years prior to its release. While Japanese and Japanese-Brazilian businessmen largely rejected her proposed project for undisclosed reasons, the Igreja Messiânica (Messianic Church) and the Sociedade Brasileira de Cultura Japonesa (Japanese-Brazilian Society) both contributed production funds. Embrafilme eventually joined in as a co-producer and also distributed the film.

In its representation of exploited workers, recuperation of history, and treatment of gender, the film contributes to a renewing discourse on citizenship in Brazil prior to the end of the military dictatorship. The melodramatic mode allows Yamasaki to address the previously ignored history of Japanese immigration while making political claims on the present. In this and her next two films, Yamasaki employs emotion as a tool to bridge social, ethnic, and political divides and to foster solidarity.

The opening sequence of *Gaijin* pairs a visual montage of contemporary urban São Paulo with an aural montage of samba music, the sounds of traffic, construction noises, and the voices of different people. The visual montage, composed of cars, trucks, subway trains, and people moving across the screen in opposing diagonal vectors, suggests dynamic activity, forward movement, and a celebration of Brazil's economic potential and the intersection of different forces that define and occupy a space. Abundant tropical fruits are piled for export, and there is a cut to a shot of the Liberty (Estação Liberdade) metro station in the heart of the Japanese neighborhood in São Paulo. White-on-black intertitles dedicate the film to all immigrants, declaring, "Este filme é uma homenagem a todos que um dia precisarem deixar sua terra" (This movie is a tribute to those who once had to leave their land). While the film clearly discusses the presence of Japanese in Brazilian culture, the dedication underscores a larger goal of inclusiveness. The Japanese were one of many groups that shaped Brazilian society. Visually, this message of inclusion is punctuated by an image that merges a large sun rising from the horizon (a symbol of Japanese culture) glowing behind modern São Paulo skyscrapers.

There is an abrupt cut to an isolated village in Japan where a notice has been posted on a building. Intertitles inform that the year is 1908, and a group forms around the notice to read the announcement, which states that Brazil wishes to hire immigrant workers. In voiceover, the female protagonist, Titoe (Kyoko Tsukamoto), speaks in Japanese, reminiscing that the year was the Era Meiji 41 and she was only sixteen years old. There is a cut to the young woman dressed in a kimono saying goodbye to her family as three men ride in a wagon, slowly moving away from her. She stands alone in an open field between the family and community she is leaving behind her and the new, makeshift family she has been forced to join taking off without her. As Titoe wipes tears of anguish from her eyes, she explains in voiceover that her brother and cousin had wanted to go to Brazil and, since only families were accepted, she had been married to her brother's friend Yamada Kawada (Jiro Kawarazaki) in a system of arranged marriage called *omiai kekkon*. As Titoe stumbles forward, she recalls in voiceover, "So many years have passed! So many things happened. But now, this past belongs to my memories."

The opening sequences that juxtapose the early-twentieth-century Japan and modern São Paulo serve several key purposes. First, the images of contemporary São Paulo questions notions of Brazilian cultural identity promoted during the authoritarian military regime. During the years of the dictatorship, the military called on positivist ideals of "order and progress" to support its plans for economic restructuring and developed the idea of "O Brasil Grande" (Big Brazil). Brazil was constructed as the country of the future, and an economic powerhouse where *mulata* women danced samba and the national soccer team was the best in the world. This notion of Brazil is one that Yamasaki interrogates in her film, in which she relates current success of the country to the efforts of hundreds of uncelebrated immigrants. Just as the film intervenes in historical representations, it also establishes a temporal and visual bridge between past and present in a gesture that relates past struggles and present resilience in the face of adversity.

Whereas many Brazilian films that have represented history have focused variously on the period of Portuguese colonization or heroic figures of nobility, Yamasaki's debut film focalizes its narrative through the eyes of a humble, impoverished, young Japanese woman to reflect on the history of the Japanese in Brazil. The Japanese had been left out of the ethnic, racial equation—a harmonious blending of Black, Caucasian, and Indian—employed to narrate the foundation of the Brazilian people. During the populist dictatorship of Getúlio Vargas (1930–45) little space was available for Japanese-Brazilians to assert their ethnicity in a political landscape dominated by eugenics and an official policy of ethnic integration.[32] Although Japanese actors did appear in the erotic film industry in the 1970s,[33] prior to Yamsaki's film the Japanese community had been largely left out of the Brazilian cultural imagination.

Here, a spectacular representation of the past, strategically supported by the military regime in its early years, takes a back seat to a personalized, intimate recuperation of previously unacknowledged history.[34] Indeed, the film's narrative largely emerges from Yamasaki's own experiences looking at family albums and listening to the stories of her grandmother, Titoe, who was among the first Japanese immigrants to Brazil. Although her grandmother's name is lent to the female protagonist of the film, Yamasaki has asserted that the film draws from some personal family memories but is very much her own interpretation of her relatives' arrival to Brazil. Thus, the film is at once a narrative of personal (family) memories with added fictional elements that is then moved into the collective sphere.

Although historical films of the 1970s have been criticized for a lack of authenticity and failure to research carefully the historical moments that were being represented cinematographically, Yamasaki bases her film on her own family's experience and her extensive historical research, and she sought to portray the encounter with difference as accurately as possible. Japanese actors were hired to play the primary roles with the belief that they would be more apt to convey the experience of cultural shock and sense of disorientation that the first Japanese immigrants experienced in the early twentieth century. Despite some members of the Japanese-Brazilian community's initial unwillingness to participate, Yamasaki successfully convinced six hundred members of the Japanese-Brazilian population in Atibaia (São Paulo) to participate as extras. In addition, the film was shot on locations in Atibaia—not far from where Tizuka grew up—and in the city of São Paulo.

Just as *Gaijin* recuperates her family's history and the history of Japanese immigration to Brazil, Yamaski's film takes a stand regarding her political and cultural identity. The film afforded Yamasaki a platform from which she advocated for greater awareness of Brazilians of Japanese descent as full members of contemporary Brazilian society. With *Gaijin*, Yamasaki sought to put an end to the discrimination that she had experienced. In an interview granted to the news magazine *Isto É* in 1980, Yamasaki makes it patently clear that her film aimed to fight ongoing discrimination against herself and a limited concept of Brazil's *mestiçagem* (cultural-racial mixing), stating, "Eu tenho uma cara de japonesa, e assim sou vista como estrangeira na minha própria terra. Eu estava a fim de acabar com isso. Todos nós somos filhos de estrangeiros que, direta ou indiretamente, fizemos o Brasil de hoje." (I have a Japanese face, and so I am seen as a foreigner in my own country. I really wanted to end this. We are all sons and daughters of foreigners who, directly or indirectly, made Brazil what it is today.)[35] Indeed, Jeffrey Lesser notes that Yamasaki's film created an important dialogue between cultural and ethnic groups in the early 1980s and helped to explain the presence of Japanese people and products in São Paulo.[36] The film may also be seen as a long trajectory of ethnic militancy on the part of Japanese Brazilians, who interrogated state-sponsored homogenized notions of diversity and aimed to be included in the Brazilian cultural imagination.[37]

The recuperation of the history of Japanese immigration signifies, in turn, a reclaiming of citizenship for all Brazilians. The period of *Abertura* was a transitional political moment for intervening in the shape and direction of a new democratic Brazil. At a time when the state was promoting visions of history that would be amenable to the regime (as discussed above), the histories of the less powerful could have been easily overshadowed. Joan Ramón Resina, who has worked extensively on the politics of memory during the Spanish Transition, asserts that the past can "radicalize the present" and challenge an affect-blind modernity.[38] Similarly, Salvador Cardús i Ros suggests that political transitions from authoritarianism to democracy are moments when complex struggles take place between remembering and intentional forgetting in the process to forge "a *new* political tradition."[39] The juxtaposition of two temporal moments of the two opening sequences connects the past narrative of early-twentieth-century Japanese immigration and Brazil of the early 1980s and constitutes a highly political act. *Gaijin* is, thus, very much engaged with challenging hegemonic notions of Brazilian cultural identity rooted in the past as much as it is directed at inventing a new sociability for the future. As a historical melodrama, the film makes political claims on the present while avoiding direct critiques of the regime. Appropriating the rhetoric of the melodramatic mode, the spectator is positioned to suffer alongside the Japanese immigrants as the plot turns on emotional highs and lows before the young female protagonist eventually triumphs over adversity. The spectator is moved to experience Titoe's anguish in leaving her homeland.

Shortly after leaving the peaceful fields of Japan, a ship named the *Kasatu Maru* docks at the port of Santos. Aboard were the first 781 members of what would become the largest Japanese community living outside Japan.[40] The Japanese immigrants, dressed in Western clothes, disembark with cautious optimism in the strange new land. In a scene that shortly follows the arrival of this first wave of Japanese immigrants, an English capitalist investor and a Brazilian coffee plantation owner discuss their recent labor problems. The Brazilian landowner makes an argument for Japanese workers because, as he believes, they are more disciplined, work harder, and do not complain. The abolition of slavery in 1888 prompted wealthy landowners to replace African slaves with European immigrant laborers, primarily from Spain and Italy, who brought with them anarcho-syndicalist ideas. Their demands for improved working conditions pushed the capitalist elite toward employing Japanese workers, whom they believed were tidy, orderly, and obedient. It becomes clear that the coffee plantation owner desires cheap, easily exploited labor, and he intends to take full advantage of the Japanese laborers. It was not savvy investments or skillful trade negotiations that led to the economic success of São Paulo: the rapid industrialization and economic growth experienced in Brazil during the early 1900s relied on the exploited labor of masses of African slaves and then immigrants from Europe and Asia.

As emotional identification with the Japanese immigrants develops, the narrative explores the irony that the Japanese have been separated from the Brazilian cultural imagination despite their experience that parallels many immigrants to Brazil. Before they arrive at the farms where they will work, the Japanese must travel by train to an immigration center. On the way, a child dies of food poisoning, serving as a harbinger of more suffering to follow. The Japanese émigrés descend from the train and are met with a traditional marching band and great curiosity on the part of the local Brazilian population. Titoe is grabbed by an unknown man standing at the train station, suggesting an erotic, hypersexualized vision held about Japanese women. The spectator is moved to sympathize with Titoe's fear and confusion. At the immigration center, they are separated from the other immigrants, primarily the Italian and Spanish, who are able to communicate among themselves and with the Portuguese-speaking officials sufficiently well. This physical separation is suggestive of the way in which Brazilians of Japanese descent have been isolated from the Brazilian cultural imagination while European immigrants (Spanish, Italian, and German) entered it. Drawing on the work of Maurice Halbwachs, Elizabeth Jelin notes that individual memories are always socially framed and warns that what does not find a place in that framework is subject to being lost or forgotten.[41] Yamasaki intervenes here in conceptions of Brazilian cultural identity by bending the framework of history to include Brazil's Japanese immigrants.

As the émigrés are registered, jokes told by an Italian immigrant, Enrico (Gianfrancesco Guarnieri), bring laughter and smiles, while the fear and confusion expressed in the faces of the Japanese position them as innocent victims with whom the spectator sympathizes deeply. The Japanese immigrants stand quietly as they are immediately informed of their limited rights, being warned by the authorities who arranged for their work in Brazil that they are not allowed to form political associations and will be immediately banished from the country for any labor activism. In effect, the capitalist market in Brazil wanted at the early twentieth century what the military regime demanded of people several decades later—orderly, obedient workers who denied their own rights and did not protest their exploitation. But rather than existing parallel to the development of the Brazilian nation, the history of Japanese immigrants is intertwined with that of other racial and ethnic groups.

At the core of *Gaijin*, one finds a discussion of the politics of labor relations juxtaposed with an investigation of the very concept of foreignness. The narrative establishes a clear dichotomy between the innocent (good) immigrant workers and the greedy, violent (evil) plantation owners and staff. The Japanese workers arrive at the Fazenda Santa Rosa, where they quickly realize they are entering a situation they did not bargain for. Counter to their expectations, they are shown their housing accommodations at the *fazenda*—dilapidated, former slave quarters, thus clearly solidifying they are substitutes for now-freed African slaves. The Japanese are given staples of the Brazilian diet—manioc flour, beans, and dried meat—but, having no idea how to prepare these ingredients, they beg for rice. They struggle to learn the backbreaking work of collecting coffee but manage to keep their spirits high with the motivation of earning a handsome sum at the end of the harvest season. When their earnings are reduced to nill by dubious fines and charges for foodstuffs they did not purchase at the plantation store, they are outraged at such dishonorable behavior. They have unwittingly become indentured servants to the plantation. Tonho (Antônio Fagundes), the plantation's bookkeeper and the one who is forced to take deductions from the worker's earnings, functions as an individual placed in the middle between the immigrants and the plantation owners. He acknowledges what he is doing is unjust and, because he has befriended the immigrants, it pains him to practice such deceit. But he is hesitant to do anything as he, like the

Figure 3.1. Titoe and Yamada learning how to harvest coffee beans in *Gaijin*.

immigrants, fear the plantation overseer Chico Santos (Alvaro Freire), who carries a whip and retains the authoritarian behaviors of a slave master.

Immigrant workers from Spain and Italy are noted for having brought anarcho-syndicalist ideas with them to Brazil, but their protests of low wages and deplorable work conditions were no match for systematic and (frequently) violent repression of would-be labor organizers. Enrico, the Italian who told jokes at the immigration center, embodies the fight for worker's rights. In an early scene, he approaches the coffee plantation owner, Heitor, to request a small bonus to help offset the increasing costs of food sold at the company grocery store where workers are forced to buy their provisions. He later engages in a politicized conversation with a group of immigrant workers about ownership of the fruits of a man's labor. Having identified Enrico as a potential troublemaker, Chico Santos and some of his men break into his house late one night and beat him up. Shortly thereafter, Enrico and his family are seen being evicted from their residence while a legal announcement is read that he is being banished from the country for inciting civil disobedience and disturbing the peace. Given continued labor unrest into the late twentieth century, the film calls attention to the longstanding struggle for workers' rights and indirectly condemns the military coup d'état in 1964, which demanded obedient workers and largely equated demands for work-ers' rights with communist subversion that threatened national security. In short, the authoritarian crackdowns portrayed in the film resonate with labor relations during the military regime in Brazil.

Yamasaki's film brings into frame the excluded "others" of Brazilian so-ciety, past and present, a larger trend that can be detected in films from the *Abertura* period.[42] In numerous sequences, the film explores the notion of outsider and the very meaning of "foreignness." Ceará, the nickname of a migrant worker from the northeastern state of Paraíba, chops down trees one day with Titoe's husband, Yamada. As they work, Ceará talks longingly of his native land and, holding back tears, confesses to Yamada that his dying wish is to be buried in his homeland—a desire shared by the Japanese. En-rico, sharing wine with his fellow workers, points out all the different ethnic groups found at the Fazenda Santa Rosa and jokes about the stereotypes of each group. In another scene, Yamada talks with Titoe and his cousin Ueno about cultivating vegetables and teaching the Brazilians their knowledge of agriculture. When Ueno complains that all they think about is work, Yamada chastises him for only chasing after *gaijin* (foreign) women—meaning here nonethnic Japanese immigrant women. It is Yamada's use of the word *gaijin* when talking with Ueno that more clearly underscores the question of who is the foreigner in this scenario. While the (im)migrant workers do not share a native homeland or language, they share a common experience of being outside, excluded from the inner circle of power with little ability to voice their rights. The film makes the politically significant gesture of equalizing all, including those of Japanese descent, as *gaijin*, or foreigners in Brazil. In terms of resonance with the early years of *Abertura*, Yamasaki draws a com-parison between experiences of being an outsider during the early twentieth century and the long period of political exclusion and social alienation that people had experienced since the coup d'état in 1964.

Driven by a discourse of inclusivity, Yamasaki's film gestures toward the development of affective bonds and the recharging of a communal spirit in the wake of the authoritarian military regime. Numerous scenes in the film portray interethnic camaraderie. Ceará patiently and with great humor teaches the Japanese how to collect coffee. Native speakers of Portuguese offer impromptu classes. Tonho, smitten with Titoe, tries to teach her how to wash her clothes better in a stream. In one of the few moments of leisure, a multicultural group drinks, eats, listens to music, and dances in a circle. Perhaps it was at this party that Ueno, Titoe's cousin, caught the eye of a blonde Italian immigrant with whom he later sneaks off and has a romantic rendezvous. And, albeit never consummated on screen, Tonho's frequent glances at Titoe suggest the possibility of a romance between them.

Although Yamasaki's film blends romance and politics to comment on the inclusion of Japanese immigrants into the Brazilian cultural imagination, some members of the Japanese community in Brazil objected to the representation of interethnic romance, claiming that this would never have taken place at the time.[43] What is key here to understand is that Yamasaki intentionally incorporates in her historical melodrama some strategic acts of fiction. In his work on memory and political transitions, Cardús i Ros asserts that just as memories are narratives that rely on personal and external recollection, they also include "fiction, things forgotten and errors that are *necessary* to make memory coherent and significant."[44] Yamasaki's film *Gaijin* may have lacked authenticity in terms of the prevailing sexual mores of the Japanese community in early-twentieth-century Brazil, but the interethnic romances that she portrays seek to strategically break out of the self-imposed isolation of the Japanese community (which the director herself desired in her own life) while motivating affective bonds with members of the larger Brazilian populace. It would seem as if Yamasaki took a cue from Darlene J. Sadlier, who has noted the sociopolitical potential of the melodramatic mode in Latin American Cinema, stating that it "has the ability to bring women and other groups who have lacked social power into communities of emotional solidarity and strength."[45]

Just as "others" are repositioned historically and politically, the film also aims for new political and gendered consciousness. At first Titoe is portrayed as a fearful and shy young woman who follows familial expectations, but by the end of the film she questions social expectations and becomes a significant agent of social change in her community. She learns to love her husband and eventually gives birth to a girl. But in a scene where Titoe sits alongside a stream with another Japanese woman, the two complain about their additional domestic duties after a full day of hard labor and both reject the unwanted sexual advances of their husbands. In this, Yamsaki's film brings forth tensions located within the domestic sphere, common to the melodramatic mode, to critique traditional gendered social roles. By no coincidence, this critique of women's "double day" was a hot-button topic in the women's movement in Brazil at the time. Titoe is thrust into a new role after the death of her husband Yamada, who had been the de facto leader of the Japanese group. She boldly embraces her unanticipated independence and takes on a leadership role by urging the community to escape their oppression at the fazenda. Titoe's character thus echoes and is emblematic of

Figure 3.2. Titoe reunites with Tonho, fighting for
workers' rights in *Gaijin*.

calls from the women's movement at the time for women to become agents
for social and political change.

As an individual placed between good (immigrant workers) and evil
(greedy landowners), Tonho comes to a new consciousness and demonstrates
his new social awareness. After it is discovered that the Japanese have fled the
fazenda, he is ordered to join the other staff at the *fazenda* to capture them
(as if they were escaped prisoners). Tonho runs into Titoe in the woods but
does not turn her in, urging her to get away. But before she flees, Titoe tells
Tonho, in broken Portuguese, that he also should leave because she knows
that he, too, is miserable at the *fazenda*. Titoe, having gained independence,
become more aware, and shed her fears, ultimately becomes a heroic agent
of action for her own community and pushes Tonho toward a new level of
social consciousness as well.

Years later, Titoe is seen walking to work at a textile mill in São Paulo,
where she has found refuge from the *fazenda*. Dreams of returning to Japan
have been substituted with a focus on being a single mother to her daughter
Shinobu, who speaks Portuguese and shows signs of being very much tied to
Brazil. In the final scene, Titoe walks with her daughter through the streets of
São Paulo, where she sees Tonho, who now stands atop a platform shouting

out demands for workers' rights before raucous street protesters. Matching eyeline shots mark the moment of recognition before a brief flashback montage of moments Titoe and Tonho shared at the *fazenda*. Their mutual affection for one another cannot be denied, and their chance encounter in the streets of São Paulo underscores that they are destined to be reunited. Despite the struggles they have been through and ongoing political strife, the final scene underscores that love can overcome adversity.

History Fueling the Present in *Parahyba, Mulher Macho* (1983)

Whereas Yamasaki's debut film focuses on Japanese immigration to the south of Brazil in 1908, her second film moves north to consider Brazil's political landscape of the late 1920s and early 1930s. In *Parahyba, Mulher Macho*, Yamasaki furthers the discourse of sociopolitical inclusivity that she began in her film *Gaijin*. Against the backdrop of a politically turbulent period before the Vargas Era (1930–45), the film centers on the life of Anayde Beiriz, an intelligent, iconoclastic poet who scandalized her contemporaries in the 1920s and 1930s but had been relatively forgotten before Yamasaki's film was released in 1983. Besides her defiant behavior, Beiriz was perhaps most (in)famous for having engaged in a romantic relationship with João Dantas, a local lawyer and member of a regional landholding elite family who assassinated the much-beloved regional political leader João Pessoa. Blending a narrative of romance and politics, *Parahyba* offers a trenchant critique of patriarchy, clientelistic politics, and vigilante violence while making the contemporary claim that sexual and political freedom are closely linked.

Upon its release, the film raised a number of polemics, including a legal case against Yamasaki by Beiriz's sister for "abalo moral" (moral damages) and widespread criticism that Yamasaki's film disrespected historical reality. Yamasaki defended her artistic license and representation of history stating, "I'm a director. I give reality a poetic interpretation and I tell the stories in the way that I want to. You go out on the street and see that which you want to see. I went out into the history of Brazil and chose a fictional story, but a fictional story that seems to me to be more truthful than many history books."[46] This is not the first time Yamasaki has creatively mediated historical data. As noted above, she received criticism of *Gaijin* for its inaccurate representations of interethnic romance. While certainly concerned with historical facts, Yamasaki's approach to representing history coincides greatly with Hayden White's assertion that history is a mediated assemblage of facts[47] and Elizabeth Jelin's call to consider the tensions between history and memory, where "the most creative, provocative, and productive questions for inquiry and critical reflection emerge."[48]

Parahyba quickly establishes that the narrative unfolding before the spectator aims to intervene in understandings of history, to critique a culture of political corruption, and to bring to light a forgotten story of individual courage and conviction. Opening intertitles explain that in 1930, Brazil lived through a prerevolutionary moment in which political life in the state of Parahyba was divided between João Pessoa (Walmor Chagas) of the Liberal Alliance Party (Aliança Liberal) and the local oligarch "Colonel" Zé Pereira (Oswaldo Loureiro), who supported the Republican Party (Partido Republicano). It is in this scenario, proclaim the intertitles, that "uma anônima cidadã" (an anonymous citizen) by the name of Anayde Beiriz (Tânia Alves) wanted to live a different revolution, wanted to love, explore her thoughts, and have the right to choose the life she wished to live. Beiriz had no idea what was in store for her when she fell in love with João Dantas (Cláudio Marzo), a lawyer and enemy of Pessoa. Yamasaki seems to follow the trajectory of Cinema Novo directors who went northeast to develop critical reflections on Brazilian society. But whereas these films largely focused on male figures, *Parahyba* places female experience on this Brazilian horizon.

The action of the film begins in medias res with men gathered in the streets yelling, cheering for Pessoa, and flocking to get a glimpse of numerous love letters and erotic photographs of Beiriz and Dantas, which were taken from his home under the direction of Pessoa, who had the intention of finding communist materials and publicly shaming Dantas. Beiriz emerges from the chaos in the street, withstanding crude jeers from the crowd as the intimate details of her life are exposed to public ridicule. In voiceover, she calmly asks: "Why are you people doing this to us? What are we guilty of? Is it because I love João Dantas?" An extreme close-up captures her face. A tear runs down her cheek and a sound bridge overlays a dissolve as the narrative then flashes back in time to explain how events have unfolded. This opening sequence leaves no doubt that the film's narrative centers on questions of women's sexuality in the midst of political transition. This scene, in conjunction with the introduction described above, positions the film as an historic melodrama and indicates tragic consequences for an ill-fated romance.

It should be seen as no coincidence that Yamasaki chose to situate her second film in the political climate of the late 1920s. Indeed, in terms of popular uprising, widespread discontent, and popular desire for political reform, a number of parallels can be drawn between the breakdown of "café-com-leite"

Figure 3.3. Anayde walking defiantly through the jeering crowds in *Parahyba, Mulher Macho*.

(milk and coffee) politics of the "Old Republic" (1889–1930) and the erosion of military rule in the early 1980s, when Brazil was on the verge of yet another pivotal political moment. It must also be noted that in the late 1920s, women were breaking through a number of social barriers. Women artists, scientists, and intellectuals were gaining much greater visible presence and exercised increasing influence. Shortly after assuming power, Getúlio Vargas decreed a new electoral law that, among other measures, introduced the secret ballot and granted women the right to vote. Connecting past and present, Yamasaki's film portrays the widespread protests taking place in late 1929 and early 1930 to serve as historic fuel for the resurgence of civil society and the creation of a new democratic society in the early 1980s.

More specifically, Yamasaki's second film takes direct aim at a history of exclusionary politics where few individuals were fully enfranchised members of the community. During the Old Republic, a political system had been established where control of the presidency alternated between elites of the coffee-producing state of São Paulo and of the dairy-producing state of Minas Gerais. Hence, the (unwritten) political system, or "gentlemen's agreement," earned the name "café-com-leite" (milk and coffee) politics. This marginally democratic system was wholly patriarchal, wherein republican elite politicians formed alliances with rural landholding bosses, or *coronéis*. The rural lumpen, middle classes, and growing population of urban residents had little or no say in the political direction of the country. The military-controlled regime that took power in 1964 was arguably as closed as the political manipulations taking place during the republic. In both periods, individuals outside an elite, closed circle were excluded from political participation.

Given the portrayals of the people and culture of the northeastern region of Brazil, one could erroneously be led to believe that Yamasaki follows in the footsteps of Cinema Novo, noted for its focus on the rural cultures of the northeastern *sertão*. While she certainly appreciates the experiences she had working with Glauber Rocha and Nelson Pereira dos Santos, Yamasaki's work differs greatly from films by these and other Cinema Novo directors in terms of style and themes developed. Generally, Cinema Novo films were concerned with the breakdown of traditional patriarchy in the face of modernization and moved spectators to sympathize with debilitated male figures while offering little or no commentary on women's roles in society. In aesthetic terms, Cinema Novo directors tended to move outside urban centers when they wanted to speak allegorically for Brazil as a whole.[49] By contrast, Yamasaki, who demonstrates a keen interest for integration of all members in Brazilian society in the face of longstanding exclusionary practices, eschews totalizing allegories in favor of a melodramatic mode. She directs the camera to pan to the side to allow the previously excluded to enter the political frame. While allegories involve parallels between events, persons, or situations—and, as noted above, cinematic melodramas can certainly possess allegorical qualities—in Yamasaki's film, the political parallels function differently. Consistent with the impulse that drives all historical films in which events or individuals from the past are catalysts for addressing contemporary concerns, Yamasaki's film strategically memorializes the life of Anayde Beiriz, maligned in her own era, in a larger effort to encourage the (re)strengthening of civil society in the present.

A flashback sequence portrays Beiriz as a bright, defiant youth. She challenges Catholic authority and, demonstrating her early sexual liberation, has intimate relations on a beach with a young man (of her choosing). In high school, she is caught daydreaming. When the teacher grabs her papers from her, we see they contain erotic poetry written by Beiriz. When she defends herself by proclaiming a utopic belief that love can conquer all, she earns a hard slap from her teacher. But Beiriz's sharp intelligence garners her the award for the best student at the school upon graduation. Although the best student had historically been asked to return to the school to teach, she is denied the position in favor of a wealthier, lighter-skinned student who will, it may be assumed, not pose challenges to traditional behaviors. Such instances of rigid, conservative thinking and class- and race-based prejudice do not defeat Beiriz who, instead, embodies a spirit of defiance by wearing bright red, flowing dresses and entering a barbershop where she asks to exchange her long flowing locks for a haircut "a la garçon" (like a man). It is in the barbershop where Beiriz catches the eye of João Dantas.

In the sequences that recreate the political period, the film underscores the clientelistic relationships that had prevailed in politics. Protests in the north and northeast broke out in 1929 as a response to the selection of a São Paulo candidate, Júlio Prestes, by President Washington Luiz (also from São Paulo), thus breaking the tacit agreement to alternate the presidency between regions—Minas Gerais, Rio Grande do Sul, and São Paulo—and placing the Partido Republicano in a precarious position. Running under the party Aliança Liberal, Getúlio Vargas (of Minas Gerais) chooses João Pessoa (of Paraíba) as his running mate for the 1930 elections. For his part, Dantas had no interest in changing the bloody clan politics that had prevailed in the north and northeast, as he himself was a member of an elite ruling family and thus supported the "old system" of coronéis and arranged presidencies. In the film, Dantas speaks about the breakdown in established politics with the local oligarch, Zé Pereira, who promises to upset the upcoming elections in his favor. A cut to Pessoa speaking with his advisor reveals they also plan to manipulate the elections to ensure their desired result.

Yamasaki's representation of Anayde Beiriz configures her within Brazilian history as an agent of democratic change and progress against a backdrop of political corruption and recalcitrant conservatism. In terms of its representation of the intersection of gender, female sexuality and politics, her film evidences similarities with melodramatic films from the Estado Novo (1934–45) period. Film scholar Cid Vasconcelos notes that melodrama was employed during the Estado Novo period as a framework (with propagandistic purposes) for representing nationalistic themes and values. Particularly interesting is that during the cultural and political period characterized by the rise of a New Man melodramatic films such as *Argila* (directed by Humberto Mauro, 1940), *Aves sem Ninho* (directed by Raul Roulien, 1939), and *Romance Proibido* (directed by Adhemar Gonzaga, 1944) portrayed the emerging New Woman as a version of the political leader Getúlio Vargas, who in turn symbolically embodied the nation's values at the time.[50] That female characters, rather than male protagonists, were able to play the alter ego of the nation's political leader can be attributed largely to the fact that these films were melodramas.[51] Yamasaki's film *Parahyba* at once reclaims the highly popular melodramatic mode and the cinematic image of the modern civilizing woman who, much like the female characters in melodramas of the Estado Novo period, challenge traditional patriarchal politics and advocate for new roles for women in the realms of politics and interpersonal relationships.

Having been denied a teaching position at the school where she studied and understanding that one's own enlightenment is useless unless others are enlightened with you, Beiriz decides to teach people to read in a rural area. Her actions here comment on longstanding government neglect of education specifically and of the region as a whole. The north and northeast regions of Brazil, historically at an economic disadvantage, have had high rates of illiteracy relative to the south and south-central regions. And, despite its positivist orientation during the late nineteenth and early twentieth centuries, the Brazilian government chose *not* to invest in educating the masses, leaving education largely in private hands. Given that literacy was a requirement to vote until as late as 1988, failure to invest in education has translated historically into the systematic exclusion of the vast majority of Brazilian citizens. Perhaps aware of her own fortune in being able to study at a private institution, Beiriz seeks to enfranchise the poor people of rural Paraiba with the necessary skills to be a citizen.

As the film progresses, Beiriz demonstrates great political awareness in other ways, notably in her relationship with João Dantas. She writes essays to be published in the local newspaper in which she expresses her political viewpoints and she speaks out on women's suffrage. Notably, she disagrees with Dantas about politics. While he, being of an elite family, supports continuation of the traditional rule of the oligarchy, Beiriz asserts that the time has ended for only a few families to rule the region, and she supports the opposing candidates of the Aliança Liberal. In her relationship with Dantas, she sees herself as his lover and political equal. Although he slaps her at one point for disagreeing with him, she refuses to curtsy to her partner's attempt to take a dominant political lead.

Conversations of politics in the film are frequently intertwined with historical reenactments and intimate scenes between Dantas and Beiriz. A parallel is thus established between Beiriz's political awareness and her sexuality. Beiriz does not fear expressing physical affection for Dantas in public and, in scenes of lovemaking, she takes a dominant role. Her sexual freedom is matched by her open political participation, suggesting that in order for women to be able to participate as full citizens in Brazil they should be able to experience their sexual lives to the fullest as well. It becomes clear that there are two revolutions taking place: the struggle for political leadership of Brazil, and Beiriz's fight for greater sexual freedom and individual (female) liberty. In this, the film coincides greatly with second-wave Brazilian feminism. A key debate in the women's movements of the 1970s and 1980s reflected on women's right to sexual pleasure, making women's sexuality a political issue. In literature, collections were published of erotic writings such as Márcia Denser's 1980 anthology *Muito Prazer* (Pleased to Meet You) and a second anthology in 1984 entitled *O Prazer é Todo Meu* (The Pleasure Is Mine). In the case of Yamsaki's *Parahyba*, erotic expression is very much part of Beiriz's personhood, her subjectivity.

Whereas Yamasaki employed images of modern-day São Paulo to frame her historic melodrama on Japanese immigration to Brazil, which served as one way to establish links between the history of Brazil and the current shape of Brazilian cultural identity, the connections between past, present, and future are constructed more overtly in the narrative of *Parahyba*. The traumatic moment of public ridicule Beiriz experienced at the beginning of the film is repeated, bringing the narrative to the present moment of the diegesis. A *corrida*[52] singer, who had previously "dueled" playfully with Beiriz in a bar, steps in to comment on the narrative, singing:

> These are the people
> who are today conquering
> wealth and power
> without ever understanding
> the paths of history
> as they are.
>
> They never learned the lesson
> that who goes up
> swims against the tide
> that always risked a forward step
> without fearing the risk
> and pushed up the hillside of the future
> the heavy wagon of the present.[53]

Visually and thematically, the scene offers metacritical commentary. The corrida singer, who faces the camera and directly addresses an audience, breaks the "fourth wall," creates a reflective distance, and prompts close analysis of the portrayed events. In other words, the corrida singer in the role of narrator reveals the story that has unfolded to be a re-presentation of history with lessons from the past that should be assimilated in the present. The corrida's lyrics position the narrative to overlap past, present, and future and urge a critical assessment of the past in order to encourage the reinvigoration of the disenfranchised to fight illegitimate power and political corruption.

After learning of the public humiliation, Dantas, partly out of revenge and partly to defend Beiriz's honor, arranges to meet Pessoa and then kills him in public. Historically, the assassination of Pessoa by Dantas catalyzed the armed opposition rebellion led by Getúlio Vargas, who, under the pretense of restoring liberty and the purity of the republican regime, ousted the chosen (and elected) candidate Júlio Prestes and installed himself as president of Brazil in 1930. Thus began the populist dictatorship of Vargas and the Estado Novo (1930–45).

As noted earlier, melodramas have historically afforded women a space for more progressive roles in Latin American cinema. However, this has often been counterbalanced with the theme of self-sacrifice. A woman may challenge conventions, but she will have to face consequences for doing so. In writing on this theme in melodrama, film critic Pablo Pérez Rubio has observed that sacrifice in melodramas almost always implies the self-annulment of desire on the part of female characters, which ultimately constitutes an upholding of the patriarchal order.[54] By contrast, the female protagonist in *Parahyba* clearly does not forego her sexual desire and liberation in the pursuit for a more progressive politics, but she does suffer in the end.

In the final sequence, the tragic failure of love points to the condemnation of traditional, patriarchal politics. Dantas is arrested shortly after killing Pessoa amid massive public outrage. Aware that his punishment will be severe, he asks Beiriz to obtain some poison so he can commit suicide before being executed. Unfortunately, Beiriz arrives too late, as Dantas's throat had been brutally slit open in an act of extrajudicial violence. Learning of this, a stunned and despondent Beiriz walks through the street past chaos and fires as the revolutionaries take control of the city. Love has not conquered all, and this moment of great pathos calls attention to the unjustness of Beiriz's suffering and condemns the barbarism of conservative, patriarchal politics. The final scene is accompanied once again by the corrida singer, whose lyrics guide the spectator's interpretation of the narrative and weigh on the images:

> In the aftershocks of the drama
> that rocked the country
> if you see the light
> of Anayde Beiriz
> she offers lessons of the past

remains an example
a face, a name
something that remains
that memory does not forget[55]

The corrida singer urges the audience to remember, celebrate, and emulate Beiriz's resilience and determination. Ending with a dedication to all those who fought for the right to choose their own destiny, the film celebrates individuality, long repressed under the political weight of conformism. Similar to the ending of *Gaijin*, an independent woman who challenges tradition and demands greater political, economic, and sexual freedoms is positioned as an example of historic and political record. The final frozen image of Anayde Beiriz raises the question: How will women's sexual freedom be constituted in the next phase of Brazilian politics?

Engaging the Historical Present in *Patriamada* (1984)

Whereas Tizuka Yamasaki places the narratives of her first two feature-length films in the beginning of the twentieth century, her third film, *Patriamada*, develops its narrative around the fight for direct free elections in the early 1980s (in other words, the *Diretas Já* movement) leading up to the end of the military regime. The three films develop a crescendo toward a more immediate present. Film scholar Julianne Burton brings to light the intricate production process the crew of *Patriamada* undertook, adapting a fictional storyline to daily political developments.[56] Although censorship was lifting during this period, Yamasaki's film picks up where mainstream media had been sorely failing for some time. Brazil's largest, most powerful media outlet, TV Globo, resisted broadcasting images of people protesting in the streets until it became clear that public opinion had swayed.[57] Thus, Yamasaki's film practice serves simultaneously as an important historical register of the time. Indeed, the masses of people who took to the streets in the early 1980s have as much a role in the film as Yamasaki's fictional characters. In *Patriamada*, Yamasaki continues the gesture made in her previous films to unite diverse individuals from different backgrounds. In the case of *Patriamada*, the process of redrawing the boundaries of belonging takes on a decidedly political tone where claims are made on the state to reinstall and redefine democratic institutions and social policy.

The artful weaving of documentary and fictional strategies is initially the most notable characteristic of Yamasaki's *Patriamada*. A melodramatic love story involving a successful businessman (Rocha), an idealistic film-maker (Goiás), and a driven young journalist (Lina) is intercut with clips of testimonials and commentary on contemporary politics and society by anonymous citizens, politicians (including President Figueiredo, Tancredo Neves, and Paulo Maluf), and celebrities (Milton Nascimento, Sonia Braga, and then-union-leader and later-president Luiz Inácio Lula da Silva). The fictional narrative revolves largely around Lina's (Débora Bloch) professional ambitions and romantic liaisons with Rocha (Walmor Chagas) and Goiáis (Buza Ferraz), who is himself making a film entitled *Patriamada*. Segments of television-style reporting cut to images of Lina helping Goiás by conducting interviews with people protesting on the streets of Rio de Janeiro. It is important to note that Yamasaki and her crew shot actual footage of the *Diretas Já* street protests and then wove them into the film structure. In a particularly poignant blending of fictional and realist strategies, Rocha looks out the window of his business office high above the streets of Rio de Janeiro where thousands of people are demonstrating. He decides to join the masses in the streets, where he bumps into Lina before returning to his office. Music by Milton Nascimento plays in the background, and Rocha is visibly touched by the people's enthusiasm.

In *Patriamada*, the fictional melodrama blends effectively with the realist strategies. The absence of marked separation between the two can be explained by scholars whose recent work suggests that melodrama deploys both the rhetoric of realism as well as the rhetoric of fiction to make sense of the everyday. Christine Gledhill argues that melodrama "[takes] its stand in the material world of everyday lived reality and lived experience, and acknowledging the limitations of the conventions of language and representation, it proceeds to force into aesthetic presence, identity, value and plenitude of meaning."[58] Drawing on Peter Brooks's notion of melodramatic imagination, Mariana Baltar explores the existence of the melodramatic in Brazilian documentary. Her findings suggest that Brazilian documentaries have taken up the melodramatic as a way to call attention to urgent contemporary issues and do so by inviting spectators to affectively engage with the private stories of individuals. She further asserts that it is this affective engagement by spectators that "leads the way toward the addressing of public issues."[59] In short, the fictional narrative segments and the documentary-like sequences function synergistically to effect a "melodramatic experience." It is from a more emotion- and thought-provoking position that Yamasaki speaks to the audience and subsequently inspires once-alienated individuals to again love and become engaged in the development of their country.

In writing about this film, Julianne Burton asserts that a combination of realist and fictional strategies found in *Patriamada* creates a "transitional state" that not only references but also speaks to the sociopolitical context of Brazil in the mid-1980s. What is more, the intricate editing process of fictional and documentary footage creates what Burton defines as a meta-meditation on the transitional moment, which in turn engages in a process of historic healing.[60] This healing or reconstructive process in *Patriamada* involves redefining sexual and gendered identities. Regarding individual identity and its relation to society at large, Burton asserts that Yamasaki's film borders on a naive neopopulism in its documentary-style footage while privileging an exploration of an ambitious, urban-middle-class "self" rather than explorations of the "other" in the fictional sequences. To these insightful comments, I wish to add that Yamasaki does, in fact, continue an exploration of "otherness" or different ways of being a member of a redefined Brazilian society. Rather than explore ethnic, political, or class-marginalized "others" in a way that she did in *Gaijin* or *Parahyba*, Yamasaki explores ways of being on *other* gendered and sexual terms, offering alternative feminine and masculine models of behavior.

Belying the progress the military regime boasted it would bring to Brazil, several scenes in *Patriamada* reflect on the country's dire socioeconomic situation. Rocha Queiroz, a wealthy, politically connected businessman and one of the main fictional characters, speaks about the external debt and the need for a government that functions. The concerns of the middle classes and the poor are also addressed. There are scenes of poor people who protest the environmental pollution that threatens the neglected communities where they live, and workers demand better wages and working conditions. The cross-class, poly-vocal representation breaks an imposed silence and speaks to greater solidarity premised on a shared need to fix what is wrong with Brazil. In contrast to the discourses of fragmentation and alienation found in literature and film of the 1970s, here we see an image where individuals from diverse backgrounds are all included to recreate the nation.

As seen in the previous two films by Yamasaki, *Patriamada* focalizes its narrative through a female protagonist and juxtaposes a progressive vision of gender and sexuality with a shifting political landscape. Here, the narrative revolves around Lina, a twentysomething journalist who embraces an androgynous side by wearing masculine clothing (pants and neckties). Lina ambitiously pursues a career in the masculine world of the printed press and balances her affection for two men: Rocha, mentioned above, and Goiás, a filmmaker with whom she collaborates. In terms of promoting nontraditional masculine and feminine roles, *Patriamada* takes a step further than that seen in *Gaijin* or *Parahyba*. Male impotence, single parenthood, divorce, male and female sexual desire, and pleasure are all discussed or represented in a complex, open manner. Lina is shown as the one who initiates sexual encounters, she has more than one sexual partner, and sex scenes focus on her face and the pleasure she experiences. Her friend and partner Goiás cares for the child he fathered with his ex-wife, Elisa, who has left for Paris, where she lives with her lover.

In contrast to the representation of sexuality found in *Parahyba*, neither male nor female characters are the targets of violence or ridicule for leading sexually liberated lives. That said, the film does draw attention to the intersection of women's reproductive health and politics. An unplanned pregnancy functions as a source of narrative tension in the film. Lina is seen leaving a medical clinic where she learns she is pregnant. Rather than cry or become desperate as might be expected in a more traditional script, Lina smiles. She is happy about being pregnant—despite the apparent failure of or lack of access to effective birth control. Her fortunes quickly change. In an allusion to ongoing problems journalists had with censorship at the time, Lina is fired from her job at the newspaper for offending people in power. Later, her relationship with Rocha falls apart after he suffers a heart attack and his family discovers his marital infidelity with her. Following a scene in which she argues with Rocha, Lina is seen lying on a medical table, ostensibly to have an abortion. The dimly lit room in which she waits, clothed in a surgical gown, suggests the clandestine nature of abortion at the time. In the end, Lina yells out "no," jumps off the table, and abruptly leaves the clinic. Given the highly polemical nature of abortion in Brazil (both then and now), Lina's actions can best be interpreted as a sudden realization that, in fact, she did not want to terminate the pregnancy. It is important to recognize more generally how Lina deals with her pregnancy. First, it must be noted that an abortion was an option she considered but which was not legally or safely available to her. Second, for many days, Lina does not tell the two potential fathers, Goiás and Rocha, that she is pregnant, nor does she ultimately pursue finding out which man is the biological father. Her actions, in sum, assert that her body is under her control and that her pregnancy is her choice. At the time of the film's release, this was a highly progressive stance on women's reproductive rights.

Ultimately, this film redefines what patriotism or "love of country" means in the context of the 1980s. Although the film is entitled *Patriamada*—which can be translated more literally into English as "beloved homeland," the film

Figure 3.4. In a crowd demanding direct, free elections,
a pregnant Lina with Rocha and Goiás in *Patriamada*

does not promote a noncritical allegiance to an abstract idea or to traditional institutions. In fact, the film questions the degree to which the state would be the preferred basis for defining a new political community. This is best illustrated by the closing sequence in which Lina, Goiás, and Rocha are at another political demonstration. Both men place their hands on the abdomen of a pregnant Lina, neither knowing if he is the father but both wanting to take responsibility. This last shot suggests a complete reformulation of society. Future generations should not bear unquestioned allegiance to a State or a Father. Rather, nontraditional alliances such as this nontraditional family structure will give birth to a new democratic, civil society that is the responsibility of the collective.

4

Widening the Screen

Independent and Alternative
Film and Video, 1983 to 1988

Just as it is important to bring to light Brazilian women's feature-length filmmaking, it is equally important to address independent and alternative film and video projects that contributed to new definitions of citizenship during the last years of the dictatorship and the transition toward democracy. While the term independent here refers to modes of production wherein media makers work outside commercial media organizations, the term alternative refers to media practices in which the communicative processes arise from or hold close linkages with the socially, politically, and economically excluded. Contemporary feminist film scholars have urged the study of moving image production beyond feature-length films to include audiovisual works by women that have been produced, distributed, and exhibited outside mainstream channels. Thanks in part to the spread of the Internet and the development of digital technologies, there has been a renewed interest in the proliferation of alternative media in recent years. However, alternative media traces its history several decades back. The 1970s and 1980s were witness to a global, alternative media boom. Various modes of alternative media (radio, presses, video, and the like) functioned generally as modes of political resistance and social activism.[1]

With the advent and diffusion of video technology in the early 1980s, Brazilian women's independent and alternative film and video sought to intervene directly in political discourse and, if not at least tangentially affiliated, was directly linked to numerous social movements becoming more prominent, including the women's movements. Concomitant to the goal to define new political and cultural identities, Brazilian women's alternative media at the time sought to reclaim and expand citizenship rights by intervening in understandings of *brasilidade* (Brazilian cultural identity) and shaping debates surrounding issues such as abortion and women's access to healthcare.

With regard to women's filmmaking in an Anglo–North American context of the 1970s and 1980s, Laura Mulvey asserts that a period of consciousness raising and propaganda, where the focus was on registering women's life experiences, preceded a second period in which aesthetic principles of the historic avant-garde were a point of reference.[2] However, the Brazilian context demands a different approach to women's film and video production, owing to the particularities of Brazilian politics and the development of the Brazilian women's movements. The periods Mulvey describes are largely reversed (and then overlapping) in Brazilian women's audiovisual production of the 1970s and 1980s. More avant-garde techniques of representation, such as those found in Ana Carolina's surrealist-informed films, preceded independent and alternative productions that drew on realist representational strategies in film and then video. And then both modes coexisted. In the 1980s, Brazil was home to one of the strongest and most diverse video movements in all of Latin America.[3] Perhaps not surprisingly, to this date, innovative programs aim to democratize access to media making.[4] Some filmmakers took to video technology for economic reasons given that 16 mm and 35 mm film stock was very expensive in Brazil throughout the 1980s. As well, in terms of reception, mainstream exhibition venues were (and generally are) not accessible to Brazil's poor and working classes. Movie theaters have largely relocated to posh shopping centers that strive to keep out "undesirables" with high ticket prices, fences, security guards, and closed-circuit cameras. Alternative media, which are characterized as enacting horizontal, participatory modes of address, was able to reach those who would otherwise be excluded from the community-building ability of alternative media.

Scholars of independent and alternative media have long argued for appreciating audiovisual process over product.[5] Similarly, feminist film scholar Claire Johnston has advocated for an approach to women's audiovisual production that develops an "interventionist conception of textual practice seen within specific historical conjunctures."[6] Scholarly attention to women's film and video has tended to focus on feature-length film. However, it is necessary for scholars to acknowledge a rich history where women have been highly successful in producing moving images and understand more fully how women have made vital contributions to discussions on society and politics. Thus, this chapter proposes "widening the screen" to allow greater appreciation of how Brazilian women's independent and alternative film *and* video were part of a larger social practice that sought to reclaim political rights and expand notions of citizenship in the 1980s.

Aiming to acknowledge the perspectives of different social actors coexisting in parallel struggles for democracy, I chart a historiography of a select group of Brazilian women's independent, alternative film and video production during the 1980s. I explore funding and production practices as well as how women's independent and alternative film and video contributed to the politicization of gender, race, class, and sexuality at a new political and cultural crossroads during the final days of the military regime and during the period of redemocratization from 1985 to 1988. By opening the discussion to other formats of audiovisual production, my discussion moves out of the Rio de Janeiro–São Paulo axis. In the context of metropolitan Rio de Janeiro, I consider works by film and video maker Eunice Gutman, a self-defined feminist whose work has shifted from 35 mm to video over the decades. With regard to metropolitan São Paulo, I address work by the Lilith Video Collective, a group of three women who, like Eunice Gutman, dedicated themselves to bringing greater awareness to women's issues as the Brazilian constitution was being rewritten. In the northeastern state of Pernambuco, the feminist nongovernmental organization SOS-Corpo drew on the communicative possibilities afforded by video to contribute to the developing feminist discourse in the metropolitan region of Recife, the capital of Pernambuco and one of Brazil's largest cities. In the case of SOS-Corpo, my discussion considers women's audiovisual production within an internationally funded women's group and how video became a vital avenue to address the most pressing concerns for feminist activism in the region. This treatment of women's independent and alternative film and video production draws attention to a significant yet understudied area of women's media production that has existed outside the mainstream channels of production, distribution, and exhibition but has greatly contributed to reformulating citizenship in Brazil.

The return to civilian rule in 1985 and the beginning of the period of redemocratization in Brazil involved a dual process of coming to terms with the past and looking forward in order to reconstruct a democratic present and future. On February 1, 1987, the *Assambléia Nacional Constituinte* (National Constitutional Assembly) opened session. The assembly was seen officially as the end of a period of transition which, by way of conciliation, would finish "o ciclo revolucionário" (the revolutionary cycle) in Brazil.[7] What was particularly notable about this process in Brazil was that Brazilians elected representatives to the Assambléia Nacional Constituinte. In other words, the citizens of Brazil would have the unprecedented role of having a say in the drafting of their own constitution.[8] Given that a constitution regulates the organization of the state and the branches of government as well as oversees areas of social, economic, familial, educational, cultural, and political interaction, the stakes were high for women (as individuals and working together in groups) to have their concerns incorporated into the new constitution. Some of the areas where women sought reform included family life and structure, labor rights, access to healthcare, educational and cultural opportunities, and combating violence against women.[9]

A key success during the period of redemocratization occurred in the area of healthcare reform. With great effort and perseverance, the popular movement to reform healthcare in Brazil succeeded in incorporating their demands into the 1988 constitution. As defined in this document, the Sistema Único de Saúde (SUS, Universal Healthcare System) was proposed to oversee the state's constitutionally defined commitment to providing Brazil's population with complete, quality medical care, which would be managed by municipal, regional, state, and national councils on healthcare. Prior to this, uneven economic development—particularly acute in northern and northeastern regions of the country—had made access to healthcare difficult.

The SUS measure followed a highly progressive program launched by the Ministry of Health in 1983: the Programa de Assistência Integral à Saúde da Mulher (PAISM, the Program for Integrated Women's Health Care). Started before the return to civilian rule, the PAISM was a watershed program for women in Brazil and became a point of reference for international agencies.[10] The program was the first in which the Brazilian state proposed a (partial) program for fertility and the first to propose an integrated view of women's healthcare as opposed to offering isolated family planning measures.[11] The PAISM revealed a new body politics in Brazil; indeed, the concept of women's integrated healthcare revealed a break from the logic that had previously guided the state's control of women's bodies (when state-run programs were limited to pregnancy and childbirth), expressed a social change in the position of women, and gave new dimensions to the female body in the social context.[12]

Central to the efforts of many women's organizations was a new understanding of gender and making gender-specific (healthcare, decriminalizing/ legalizing abortion) and gender-related (labor rights, childcare) demands part of the new Brazilian democracy. Alongside other methods of communication, video was a key tool in educating and advocating for their demands. Alvarez observes that the multifaceted communication efforts in the Brazilian women's movement (including feminist video collectives, alternative publications, and conferences), "all attest to the vitality of autonomous society-centered feminist thought and action in postauthoritarian Brazil."[13] What should be noted is that nongovernmental organizations not only made possible women's independent, alternative media but these media went on to function as key tools in creating and sustaining a productive tension between civil society and the state.

Eunice Gutman, Independent Film and Video Director

As an independent film and video maker, Eunice Gutman has been firmly committed to fighting for greater civil, social, and political rights for women and the underprivileged. Gutman studied at the Federal University of Rio de Janeiro before moving in 1965 to Belgium to escape the military regime and to attend the INSAS (Institut National Supérieur des Arts du Spectacle), where she learned the techniques of filmmaking and television production.[14] When she returned to Brazil in the early 1970s, she found that questions that had been raised in Europe at the time regarding the structure of the family and sexuality were at an incipient stage in Brazil. The country had manifestly fewer freedoms and was more conservative.[15]

After returning to Brazil, Gutman edited films, produced photonovelas for magazines, and taught screenwriting and directing at an experimental school in Niterói. She also worked in television, including at the public station TV Educativa and for a brief time at TV Globo. Early in her career Gutman established her own production company, Cine Qua Non, and has since continued working as an independent producer and director, benefitting from programs in place in Embrafilme in the early 1980s and receiving substantial production funding from nongovernmental sources, such as the Ford Foundation, UNICEF, UNESCO, Frauen-Anstiftung, the Pathfinder Fund, ISER (Instituto de Estudos da Religião, Institute for Religious Studies), MOBRAL (Movimento de Alfabetização de Adultos, Movement for Adult Literacy), Espíritu da Coisa, and Negritude Brasileira, among others.[16] Gutman's first documentary film, *E o Mundo Era Muito Maior Que a Minha Casa* (1976), in conjunction with MOBRAL, treated a literacy program located in rural Rio de Janeiro.[17] The rising costs of production in 16 mm and 35 mm film combined with the absence of or insufficient state support for independent filmmaking and advances in video technology prompted Gutman to start working in Betacam video in the early 1990s. Most recently, the National Council of Catholic Bishops of Brazil awarded her the *Prêmio Margarida da Prata* for her documentary film *Nos Caminhos do Lixo* (In the Paths of Garbage, 2009), which treats the creation of a recycling cooperative founded by poor women in Nova Iguaçu (Rio de Janeiro). The documentary registers their efforts and reclaims the citizenship of these women, who are often abandoned by their husbands. Throughout her career, Gutman has focused on the disenfranchised, popular cultural practices, and the roles of women in society, while at the same time being dedicated to the belief that moving images can be a way of transforming the world and yourself along with it.

Exploring Gender in Só no Carnaval? and Vida de Mãe é Assim Mesmo?

In *Só no Carnaval?* (Only During Carnaval? 1982), Gutman combines an investigation of popular cultural practice with a challenge to traditional notions of gender. This short film registers the thoughts of several men who for generations have dressed as women to form the *bloco das piranhas* ("whore brigade") in Carnaval parades. The film opens with a traditional *choro* tune playing in the background while close-up shots capture women helping their husbands put on false eyelashes, lipstick, wigs, and dresses. Unlike the more artistic practices of transvestite performers, there is no attempt in this case to approximate a more "authentic" representation of women. Their makeup is exaggerated, and they don large prosthetic breasts and use pads in their borrowed undergarments to give the impression of well-endowed derrières. While they dress, the *choro* song lyrics comment on this tradition of men dressing as women during Carnaval and cavorting with their male buddies all night.

Although this celebration is all in good jest, humor transforms into skepticism. Situated in the context of Carnaval—a time when quotidian hierarchies are reversed, social norms are challenged, and the disenfranchised rise to the top for a few hot, sweaty days before Lent—this short documentary film reveals the underlying misogyny of the normal gendered social order and, in doing so, ultimately questions the degree to which there will be a reversal of this gendered order in the reconceptualization of the nation-state undergoing redemocratization.

The men seem truly to enjoy themselves. Gutman directs the camera toward a man sporting a bushy moustache, wearing a black dress and a black wig. As he bounces joyfully from side to side, a hand-held camera shot closes in on him. Several elements in this scene make clear that a film recording is being made, including the microphone (momentarily visible within the frame), questions asked off screen (to which he responds), and his being positioned squarely facing the camera while directly addressing it. As such, the film comments on its own production and eschews filmic practices that seek to make seamless the modes of representation. More to the point, the "un-seamlessness" of the representation contrasts with the "seamlessness" of the men's reproduction of femininity. The man adds that the dress belonged to his great-grandmother, then his grandmother, and then his mother. But he claims proudly, "Now I wear the dress!" before he lifts the hem and asks that the camera get a shot of his (sexy?) leg. What is curious here are the generations of women who have worn this dress that he now wears and the joy he experiences in being objectified while wanting to maintain a degree of subjective control over his own representation.

A second man, wearing a red dress, large wig, and sunglasses, pauses as he leaves his house to join his comrades. Addressing the camera, he explains that he is a police officer and professor during the year but all this gets turned upside down during Carnaval. His recorded comments continue as a voiceover to images of other men getting dressed, riding on the tops of cars down the street, shaking their fake pregnant bellies, and grabbing their prosthetic bosoms. He explains that it is easy to make yourself a woman, referring simultaneously to the construction of femininity both for him as well as women. All one needs is some courage, a dress, some makeup, and a wig. His voiceover fades out as the camera focuses on the *bloco* of men singing a song "Olé, Olá. Long live the whores." But dressing as a woman is not all fun and games. The man's voice fades in again to confess that he greatly dislikes wearing makeup and a wig. He never uses high heels. Then he admits, "It must be horrible to be a woman, this stuff of wearing false eyelashes. If I return in another incarnation, I want to be a dog but not a woman!"

The nondiegetic space of the man's voiceover contrasts sharply with the men jumping around and having fun. The disjunction between the man's voice and images of playful practice reveals marked inconsistencies in social expectations for gendered roles and behavior. The man's comments are certainly misogynist, but his words also reveal displeasure with an idea of womanhood that he himself has absorbed and portrayed. The hyperbole of their performance here takes a 180-degree turn toward denouncing the very representation in which they participate.

A group of women standing along the parade route make it clear that what is at stake are socially sanctioned definitions of what it means to be a woman. The camera turns to the women, and they give voice to their displeasure. These women look directly at the camera to critique and challenge the values upon which this time-honored practice is based. They make clear how this cultural practice makes them feel and, thus, hold the men accountable for their actions. As one of the few moments where sound and image are synchronized, the scene makes a subtle audiovisual demand for existential coherence.

The history of this cultural practice is made clearer at the closing of the documentary, when there is a cut to still shots of aged, sepia-colored photographs of men dressed as women during past celebrations of Carnaval. The photographs regress backward from a still photograph taken in approximately the 1960s, then the 1940s, before the camera focuses on the last still shot, from 1913. In the nondiegetic sound space, a contemporary samba rhythm can be heard. This sound bridge connects the past with the present and illustrates the historical trajectory of this humorous but demeaning tradition. The contrast of image and sound here underscores that cultural practices of this type, which reveal underlying misogynist beliefs that do not likely exist "only during Carnaval," belong to the past and are out of place in present society.

Whereas *Só No Carnaval?* engaged in a broader questioning of femininity, Gutman's next short documentary film, *Vida de Mãe É Assim Mesmo?* (Can This Really Be Motherhood? 1983), directly politicizes the intersection of sex, class, and gendered social roles as it takes on the question of abortion, a woman's control of her own reproductive cycle, and the responsibilities of the state to provide adequate healthcare. Gutman's film situates itself in the larger debates surrounding the struggle to decriminalize abortion in the 1980s. Women's groups argued for the decriminalization of the practice of abortion in light of several public opinion polls taken in Rio de Janeiro in 1980. These surveys revealed that the majority of Brazilians opposed abortion on moral, ethical, or religious grounds but did not believe that the state should penalize those who seek or perform an abortion.[18] From 1983 to 1987, abortion was hotly debated in the mainstream press, medical journals, government press bulletins, and publications by the women's movements. Several key events relevant to the struggle to decriminalize abortion took place in the early 1980s. In March of 1983, a national meeting was held in Rio de Janeiro, at which Gutman's film *Vida de Mãe É Assim Mesmo?* was screened and discussed.[19] Thus, Gutman's film participated alongside other channels of communication to shape the debate on access to and decriminalization of abortion.

The beginning of *Abertura* politics allowed the feminist movement to formulate more openly its approach to the abortion debate. Access to safe, legal abortions was seen as part of a larger demand for the right to healthcare for women. In 1986, in conjunction with the INAMPS (National Institute of Medical Assistance of the Social Security Administration), the Ministry of

Health, the National Council for the Rights of Women, numerous feminist groups, and the PAISM, a policy was outlined and had the stated objectives to avoid the need for abortions through education about and access to contraceptive methods.[20] Nongovernmental organizations such as SOS-Corpo oversaw some of these educational campaigns where the state failed to fulfill its social responsibilities. By the end of the decade, however, the debate shifted away from the practice of abortion toward the widespread practice of female sterilizations.[21]

In *Vida de Mãe*, Gutman employs direct-address testimonial and voiceover commentary by women of different classes and ages in order to build consensus and raise consciousness about abortion. The film opens with images that undermine romantic notions of motherhood divorced from lived reality. The opening shots show round, carved stone statues of smiling female figures in public parks and plazas. These frozen images of women caught in maternal bliss are the only references in the entire film to a culture that holds idealistic views of women as mothers. Distancing itself from abstract ideals, moral lectures, and religious hierarchies, the pragmatic, secular approach to the film becomes clear with a quick cut from the stone figures to a shot of a woman in labor lying on a gurney in a hospital delivery room.

Three women representing different ages, classes, ethnic/racial background, and marital status figure centrally in the documentary: a teenager living in the Zona Norte, a sociologist in her thirties residing in an upper-class neighborhood in Rio, and an older woman who works as a maid and lives in a favela. Husbands and father figures are mostly absent, save the brief mention of husbands from whom the women are separated or with regard to the sociologist, who states that she is married. In this way, bearing and rearing children are represented as the responsibility of women. With each woman speaking about her own experiences with pregnancy and motherhood, the documentary provides cross-class viewpoints that support the proposal for safe, legal access to abortions. Although wealthier women can pay for abortion procedures in private clinics, poor women are forced to bear a double burden of female poverty in a patriarchal system. In each of the interviews, tightly framed close-up shots in which the women directly address the camera are juxtaposed with their commentaries overlaying images of them going about daily activities. The result is in an effective blending of the personal and political.

In the film there is a cut to a woman standing outside a concrete-block home washing dishes. A very young woman of slight build passes by with a bucket in her hand as she heads toward a well. There is another cut, and the camera, repositioned in front of the young woman, captures her squarely in a tightly framed close-up shot. She then tells her story of having to drop out of school, avoiding public humiliation for being pregnant so young, and giving up her freedom to take care of her child. After the direct address, her spoken words overlay images of her working at a textile factory, and we learn that an unwanted pregnancy has directly affected her autonomy, her lifestyle, her current and future economic status, and her educational goals. But there is more to the history of this teenage girl. In the next scene, shot inside her family's home, the mother reveals that her daughter was the victim of rape at the age of twelve. Indeed, the young girl's story was at the center of a legal case covered extensively in the Rio de Janeiro press in 1980.[22] Despite her efforts to obtain an abortion as legally allowed in cases of rape, no doctor would do so for fear of being labeled an abortionist. The mother speaks of the channels through which they sought recourse but, by the time the legal system had resolved the issue, her daughter was too far along in the pregnancy. Notwithstanding her legally sanctioned rights, the state's negligence and delays effectively took those rights away.

The next two interviewees elaborate on the socioeconomic issues involved in access to abortion. The film cuts to a new location in Rio de Janeiro, and the camera tilts down from a high-angle shot of abundant trees surrounding a well-kept house. The woman in the scene states that she is age thirty-two, a sociologist by profession, married with two daughters, and does not wish to have any more children. Panning shots of her house and the surrounding area are accompanied by a voiceover of the woman as she further explains that she has always used birth control but that she would seek an abortion if her chosen contraceptive method failed. Having accompanied two friends who had abortions, she states that she finds the practice of clandestine abortions to be humiliating to women and dangerous, as the conditions in these clinics are not always ideal. What is key in the interview with this woman is that it shows that access to contraception and legal (safe) abortions crosses class lines. Yet, as an educated, economically advantaged woman, she has been able to make choices that have allowed her the freedoms that the previous young woman will likely never have.

The third interview focuses on a fifty-two-year-old woman who works as a maid and lives in a favela. The camera pans over the horizon and captures a high angle shot of the Zona Sul below. We see the woman in her kitchen stirring a pot. She then raises her head and speaks directly to the camera to tell her story. She has always worked as a maid. When she was married, she got pregnant seventeen times; she had six children and had eleven abortions.

She further explains that her last abortion was fifteen years ago and that she has been separated from her husband for the past eleven years. As the woman provides additional information about her marriage and the worsening financial situation in which she found herself, her words overlay images of her cooking, cleaning, and washing clothes. Her husband, who would not allow her to take the Pill and did not want her to have an abortion, provided no economic assistance. She states that her last abortion was botched and she ended up in the hospital. This woman's life has been clearly affected by lack of access to effective birth-control methods. What is more, her life has been put in danger because of a patriarchal state that does not allow a woman to take birth control without her husband's permission and that has refused to provide safe abortions that would avoid risks to women's health.

The personal segues into the political in the final scenes. Women in positions of power call for the legalization of abortion and state-funded access to safe abortions. A medical doctor and head of an infertility clinic in Rio de Janeiro, Elza Puretz Hersjenhut explains that improperly performed clandestine abortions scar women's reproductive organs. To protect women's reproductive health, she calls for access to abortion procedures in safe, government-run hospitals. A long-time advocate for women's rights, Romy Medeiros da Fonseca argues that the Brazilian penal code is out of date. She calls for the decriminalization of abortion and for access to abortion procedures to be part of the national social security program. In both cases, these women define access to abortion and reproductive healthcare as issues of political import that affect all women of Brazil.

Redefining People and Places in A Rocinha Tem Histórias and Duas Vezes Mulher

Rio de Janeiro is perhaps as famous for its breathtaking natural landscape as it is for the favelas that cling to the hillsides bordering middle- and upper-middle class neighborhoods. In the 1960s, favela communities began organizing to seek improved urban infrastructure and greater distribution of municipal resources. During the transition to democracy in the 1980s, these neighborhood associations took on vital roles in the redefinitions of civil society.[23]

Faced with the neglect of the poor by local, state, and federal governments, increasing numbers of women got involved in their communities to provide needed services such as schools and health clinics, and to lobby for basic services like post offices and running water. In 1985, Gutman directed *A Rocinha Tem Histórias* and *Duas Vezes Mulher*. Both films focus on residents of two Rio favelas and provide a space for members of these communities to reflect on their lived realities. As they speak, the relationship between personal development and community development becomes clear. Ultimately, these documentaries reveal the forging of new sociopolitical identities during the transition to democracy and the community solidarity needed to bring about social change. The dictatorship may have exacerbated social inequalities, but these films reveal in the end that grossly underprivileged sectors of society have survived and persevered in the face of numerous obstacles.

In *A Rocinha Tem Histórias* Gutman returns to a concern for education and literacy that she developed in her first film, *E o Mundo Era*.[24] In collaboration with a project funded by FUNARTE (National Foundation of the Arts) that aimed to create an anthology of stories by school-aged children living in the favela Rocinha, Gutman combines a concern for education with an interest in the mobilization of this community. The two works—book and video—imply a joint line of action between the state and community efforts in Rocinha to bring about change.[25] The film registers the transformation of Rocinha where individuals work together to improve their physical and social environment and, in turn, serves as a model for the rest of Brazil faced with the larger transition to a democratic culture.

The film develops a testimonial style of documentary techniques, including interviews with educators and child authors, from whom we learn about their daily chores and their dreams for the future. Each child is positioned in a schoolroom setting, in the home where she or he lives, or in the streets and areas where they play. As they read their stories aloud and talk about going to school, their words overlay images of individuals carrying water in buckets up the hill, a hillside area where people dump their garbage, and raw sewage running down channels in the walkways of the favela. These images add stark visual effect to the stories the children tell and make their expressions of hope and determination extraordinary. They will not be victims of their environment.

Handheld camera work reveals the vital, complex relationships among people. Alongside images of women and children fetching water and washing clothes, there are shots of a newly constructed community center and men working to build additional community schools. Over these images, the women discuss how the community desperately needed formal schools in order to educate their children, which were not offered to them by the government.[26] The film visually rejects Brazil's history of structured inequality. Those outside the favela are called on to effect social change as well. High-angle shots from within the favela capture images of the nearby beach and adjacent high-rise apartment buildings where the upper middle class resides in luxury. The proximity of the beach and these buildings serve to locate the favela as a part of the metropolitan area. The community, like the work that goes on within the favela, should not remain invisible.

What is more, those living near the favela should be aware of the role they play in the life of its community members. In this, the film does not shy away from issues of class and unspoken racial discrimination. The women educators reveal that children from their community were not welcome in the public schools below (in other words, in mainstream Rio de Janeiro). They were treated unfairly because they were poor migrants from the northeast living in a favela, and no attention was paid to the economic factors that prevented these children from succeeding. Dilma, the director and teaching coordinator of one of the community schools in Rocinha, underscores the need for an educational system that recognizes the different life experiences of these children. Reflecting on the discrimination she experienced when she left Rocinha to go to high school, Dilma further explains, "The objective is not to raise children to live in a ghetto but to make them full members of society. Education is a right for all people." The comments made by Dilma bring to light an important facet in the redemocratization process. Different groups will define their most pressing needs, which will in turn define the social and political rights to which they are entitled.[27] Thus, the push for democratic reform and expanded citizenship is not a homogeneous struggle. The needs of the community in Rocinha are not likely those of the wealthy that live below them; nonetheless, the two communities are juxtaposed to indicate that their lives are connected in a larger democratic, public sphere.

On one level the documentary *A Rocinha Tem Histórias* focuses on children and their educational needs. On another level it is a documentary of women's self-empowerment. As the women in *A Rocinha Tem Histórias* share their experiences of living and working in the community, they also reflect on how their efforts have empowered them to see themselves as political actors. Both this film and Gutman's next documentary, *Duas Vezes Mulher*, offer visual evidence of what James Holston has referred to as a new urban citizenship or "insurgent citizenship." In his work, Holston describes how members of lower economic classes became citizens through a process of *autoconstrução* ("autoconstruction"), in which people built their own houses and neighborhoods and, in the process, constructed new modes of political participation and rights. Moreover, the insurgence of the local transformed national democratization.[28]

The empowerment of women to engage in political participation as an outgrowth of their efforts to build and improve their communities is developed further in *Duas Vezes Mulher*. The film's narrative portrays two women: Jovina, a woman in her seventies, and Marlene, a younger, middle-aged woman. Both are originally from the northeast, moved to Rio de Janeiro, and found jobs as domestic workers. What is more, both live as single women in the favela Vidigal, where they have built their own homes and raised their children and, in the case of Jovina, built the homes of her children and the street on which they live.

Issues surrounding the production and exhibition of this film tie into a significant juncture in the women's movement in Brazil. First, the closing titles indicate that the film was based on a research project entitled "O impacto da urbanização sobre a participação da mulher de baixa renda" (The impact of urbanization on the participation of poor women) by the Núcleo de Estudos sobre a Mulher (Women's Studies Department) of the Pontífica Universidade Católica (Pontifical Catholic University) in Rio de Janeiro (known generally as NEM-PUC-RJ). This film does not develop out of direct interaction with a grassroots community but instead emerges from an institutional base within the women's movement. Notably, the women's movement was becoming more institutionalized and professionalized by the mid-1980s, owing to political openings in the Brazilian government as well as funding from international organizations. Financial support to make the film came from UNESCO-Paris, UNICEF, and NEM-PUC-RJ. Also, the film was shown outside Brazil at the World Conference on Women held in Nairobi in 1985, a year marking the beginning of the redemocratization in Brazil and the end of the U.N.-declared "Decade of the Woman" (1975–85).

Gutman's film is reminiscent of the cinema vérité documentary form and, as such, brings forth three key questions regarding the ability of realist codes to change consciousness, the construction of the profilmic event, and the notion of a unified self.[29] The film opens with shots of Arpoador and the favela, Vidigal, situated at the end of the upper-class neighborhoods of Leblon and Gávea. The camera pans over the landscape and, again, the geographically marked class structure of Rio de Janeiro is revealed. The poor live in shelters clinging to the hillsides, and the middle and upper classes live in well-built homes on stable ground. As was not the case with her other films, Gutman includes herself in the audiovisual text. There is a cut to the interior of Vidigal and her words overlay handheld camera shots of the humble dwellings and narrow streets of the favela. She congratulates the people on the improvements the community has made with their courage, their own toil, and perseverance. As the handheld camera continues to focus on images of the tidy, narrow streets and concrete-block houses built closely together, Eunice introduces the two women she will speak with, Jovina and Marlene. This opening sequence sets the stage for the interviews to follow.

There is a cut to an older woman sitting in front of a sewing machine. The camera is positioned directly in front of her and captures her in a medium one-shot. Jovina begins to tell her life story. Married at age thirteen, mother to ten children, separated form her alcoholic husband, she migrated from the state of Bahia to Rio de Janeiro, where she found work as a maid. The interview with Jovina celebrates the resourcefulness of this matriarch and, as was the case in the previous documentary, respects her having taken control of her destiny and defined the space in which she lives. This becomes most apparent when she relates her experience defending her home from foreign investors who wanted to evict her. While she speaks, images are shown of her surrounding neighborhood.

Toward the end of the interview with Jovina, there is a break between the space and time represented visually and the asynchronous aural space of Jovina talking. Images of Jovina looking out a window of her home and images of her with her family have been shot at a time different from the moment of speaking. The spatiotemporal break gives visual force to her assertion that "[s]ocial roles should change . . . women must have a sense of their own value." The sense of self-worth that women have for themselves and the roles they undertake should be defined by themselves as individuals engaged in autonomous interaction with their social environment. If one of the key structuralist, semiological critiques of realism was this filmic mode's inability to draw attention to its representation as a representation,[30] then the aural and visual breaks in the representation of Jovina draw attention to the film as a film. Thus, Jovina is positioned within the social and economic context, but she is not constructed by the social institutions that surround her. Rather, her life is a practice that signifies the possibility for some other institution, some other way of constructing the world around her.

In many respects, Marlene's experience parallels that of Jovina. With the camera positioned at the end of a hallway and slightly overexposed, the first image of Marlene is a profile shot while she sits on a sofa in her living room. While Marlene continues to speak, there is a cut and the camera is repositioned in front of her, filming her in a medium one-shot. Marlene shares a great deal with Jovina—she is from northeast Brazil, separated from her husband of eighteen years, mother to four children. She, too, fought to prevent the destruction of her home from land developers and observes positive changes in women's roles. Marlene explains that her increased participation in her community, stemming from the fight to save her home from developers, precipitated the separation from her husband, who thought community activism was no place for a woman, who should just work and stay at home. Her activism was a bittersweet success. While it led to the dissolution of her marriage, it also led to an increased sense of self-worth and self-empowerment. This change has made her more aware and critical of society. Marlene's final words reveal an awareness of discrimination against women and especially black women like herself. What is important, she affirms, is to continue fighting to contest poor treatment until she is recognized as an equal member of society.

With the exception of the use of a close-up shot of Marlene when she was greatly saddened while talking about the death of her mother, tight framing is avoided in this documentary. By avoiding a tightly framed "talking head," Gutman ensures that Jovina's and Marlene's words are not isolated from the contexts in which they speak. Rather, a regular pattern of intercutting between a medium one-shot of the women speaking and handheld camera shots of the favela and their homes serves to combine subjective and "objective" perspectives. In this way, the film contributes to the forging of embodied, sociopolitical identities as it combines the subjective knowledge of personal testimony with "objective" information from handheld shots of the communities in which the people live.

Both *A Rocinha Tem Histórias* and *Duas Vezes Mulher* focus on collective action and the development of women's sociopolitical identities as an outgrowth of their efforts to improve their communities. This process is one that Alberto Melucci has observed in his work on social movements and the development of collective and individual identity. Specifically, he asserts that "[t]he social construction of collective action and identity . . . involves complex interactions along three axes: ends, means, and relationships with the environment."[31] If one of the goals of feminist film is to resist populist cultural history that avoids unreflective representations of the social collective,[32] then both films discussed here suggest that political and cultural subjectivity are not established realities but are, rather, discursive practices between individuals and larger social collectives.

The Lilith Video Collective: Encountering Race and Gender in *Mulheres Negras*

Rare are the cases of women like Eunice Gutman who have developed the skills to work in both film and video production. More common during the 1980s were women's independent media groups in which members contributed specific skills. One such group is the Lilith Video Collective, founded in 1983 in São Paulo by Jacira de Melo, Marcia Meireles, and Silvana Afram. By 1985, Lilith Video had established an intense work schedule.[33] As one of the first two women's video groups founded in Brazil,[34] Lilith Video joined the ranks of many women's media collectives in Latin America, including Cine Mujer–Colombia, Cine Mujer–Mexico, and Grupo Miércoles (Venezuela).[35] Dedicated to offering alternative visions of women,[36] Lilith Video coincided in goals and practice with other women's video collectives in Latin America. For instance, Goldman notes that Cine Mujer (Colombia) sought to create counter-hegemonic representations of women, re-envision women in the national imagination, and establish direct mediation between community groups, the state, and NGOs.[37] However, the Lilith Video differed from these other groups in terms of technology. While organizations such as Cine Mujer–Colombia and Cine Mujer–México were able to secure funding from government sources and work with 16 mm and 35 mm film, Lilith had limited access to funding and worked with less expensive video format. Although Lilith Video received no funds from Embrafilme, they did produce federally commissioned videos.[38]

Indeed, government institutions in the state of São Paulo played a key role in the development of women's independent video production in the region. After 1985, the Conselho Estadual da Condição Feminina (State Council on Women's Condition, CECF) and the group Sáude da Mulher do Instituto de São Paulo (Women's Health Group of the São Paulo Health Institute) developed projects for the production of audiovisual programs.[39] In 1987, Lilith Video received funds from the CECF to produce a five-hour television series called "Feminino Plural" (Feminine Plural). The work of the Lilith Video Collective and this project specifically illustrate a unique collaboration between the local state, broadcast television, and independent women media producers. Fully funded by the state of São Paulo, the program "Feminino Plural" is noted for being the first feminist series broadcast on television in Brazil.[40]

State funding was essential to the success of women's independent video production. In 1986, approximately 50 percent of women's video production in the state of São Paulo was made possible by the support of the CECF and the Saúde da Mulher section.[41] In 1987, these two institutions supported 70 percent of video production treating women's issues.[42] The year marks a high point for women's video production in São Paulo, which can be attributed to three key factors. First, there was general enthusiasm surrounding the democratizing potential attributed to the new video technology, combined with financial support from the indicated state agencies in São Paulo to facilitate production. In addition, increased interest in showing video programs motivated increased production. These new venues included an increase in the use of video in women's movements for didactic purposes as well as the organization of video festivals dedicated exclusively to videos produced by or about women. Notable is the I Vídeo Mulher (Video Woman Festival) organized by Maria Angélica Lemos in 1987.[43] However, 1987 was also the beginning of a decline. From 1988 to 1991, there was a significant decrease in video production, due largely to eliminated or decreased support from the CECF and the Grupo de Saúde section,[44] but this did not mark the end of women's alternative video production. In 1992, the Associação Brasileira do Vídeo Popular (ABVP, The Brazilian Association of Popular Video) with support from the Ford Foundation, sponsored a national contest for popular video.[45]

After nearly a decade of working together, the original members of the Lilith Video Collective decided to go in different directions to pursue individual goals.[46] Silvana Afram enrolled at the University of São Paulo.[47] Jacira de Melo completed additional university studies and more recently has directed the Instituto Patrícia Galvão—Comunicação e Mídia (Patricia Galvão Institute—Communication and Media).[48] Marcia Meireles and Maria Angélica Lemos founded a new organization to house the Lilith Video archive and to continue working in audiovisual production. This new organization, Co-Mulher (Comunicação Mulher, Women's Communication) has gone on to produce videos treating issues such as women and HIV/AIDS, violence against women, and environmental feminism.[49]

A multitude of women's groups organized in the mid-1970s under a generic umbrella to fight for women's rights (such as making divorce legal, punishing crimes of domestic violence, and the like) and gender-related issues (such as daycare centers, price increases). What had taken on a unified front vis-á-vis the military regime began to diversify after 1979.[50] Conflicts arose within and among women's groups to define the most appropriate strategies to effect social and political change as well as what issues should be placed at the forefront. Alvarez observes that, at this time, "generic" activities "gave way to more 'genderic,' issue-focused ones."[51] Part of this greater specificity involved addressing race. In the early 1980s, black feminist organizations emerged to articulate the specific needs and concerns of black Brazilian women.[52]

In the 1980s, few audiovisual works in Brazil confronted race or racial discrimination. More common in Brazilian cinema are representations of black Brazilians as archetypes and/or caricatures: the slave, the sambista, the sultry mulata, and so on.[53] From the introduction of cinema to the late 1980s, very few black Brazilians had directed feature-length films.[54] Inspired by the film movement Dogme, young black Brazilian director Jefferson De formulated a Brazilian version in 1999, calling it Dogma Feijoada. In this, De called for an authentically black Brazilian cinema that, among other traits, should privilege the life of the average black Brazilian. Notably, De recently directed *Bróder* (2010) which went on to win the award for best film at the Gramado Film Festival in 2010 and has played internationally. De and numerous others have helped bring attention to the problems of racism and racial representation in Brazil. But whereas a few Afro-Brazilian men have been successful directors and producers, we have yet to see an Afro-Brazilian woman break through in the profession.[55]

In keeping with the goal to offer alternative views of women, Lilith Video produced a short video, *Mulheres Negras* (Black Women of Brazil, 1986), particularly notable for directly defining racism as a problem in Brazil and for disaggregating questions of race, which had been obfuscated and subsumed in discussions of economic class. The work also shows a transition in the discourse of citizenship that moves from the conquest of rights to an expansion of the concept of citizenship—what it means to be a full member of Brazilian society. This video was one of the first videos produced by Lilith Video under the sponsorship of the CECF and is one of the first (and few) videos that directly address the intersection of race and gender in Brazil.[56] Equal parts celebration of Afro-Brazilian culture and open denunciation of racial discrimination, the video documentary includes personal statements from a broad cross-section of Brazilian women to encourage the development of new sociopolitical identities.

Similar to the works of Eunice Gutman, this documentary includes testimonial direct address for building consensus and raising consciousness. Early in the documentary, a young woman states frankly, "There is racism in Brazil." This is followed by interviews with a broad cross-section of Afro-Brazilian women who add contour to the debate and outline a number of ways in which racism has affected their lives. In terms of the labor force, one woman states that black women always earn less. Another woman describes being suspiciously rejected for a position she applied for after the potential employer saw that she was black. A hairdresser perceives that there is less confidence in her because she is black. And a schoolteacher reveals she has had problems in the classroom because formal, dominant education does not accept authority from black people. Some of the interviews take place on the street with women who have been stopped randomly. Their unrehearsed, affirmative responses to the existence of racism makes patent that the issue is one of sincere and common concern. What is more, these women effectively address the practice of racism in their everyday experiences in the public sphere. These are women who position themselves as able to contribute to society, but they are not allowed to fully participate *in* society.

The documentary clarifies how racism permeates Brazilian culture, specifically in terms of how black women are (not) represented. The camera slowly pans by images of a very fair-skinned, blonde woman and white man in an outdoor advertisement while a woman's voice overlays these images, critiquing the fact that whiteness is the model for beauty. A black woman who works as a model asserts that the only time images of black women circulate in Brazil is during Carnaval and other events of that type. This, she firmly states, is racism. Her words contradict the widely held notion that the black or mulata woman dancing in scintillating garb is a celebration of Afro-Brazilian identity. In effect, the woman critiques a form of racism in which black women are not represented within a full range of human activity. Rather, they are acknowledged as members of society in a very limited fashion—as sexualized dancers during celebrations such as Carnaval. In other words, black women are portrayed as objects within but not subjects that shape Brazilian society.

A television actress relates a similar experience playing the part of a maid in a *telenovela*, a centerpiece of Brazilian popular culture. One of her lines was to tell a white character that she knew her place in this world. She chose to ignore the line during shooting, was confronted by the director, and he fired her the next day. Apparently, her place in this world was not to fight for the dignity of women and those of African descent. As well, a middle-aged woman confesses that she grew up thinking she was ugly because she was never asked out on dates. But she came to an important revelation: "Eu comecei a perceber que o que era considerado a minha feiura eram os traços de negritude que eu carregava no meu corpo" (Then I began to realize that what had been considered my ugliness were the marks of blackness that I carried on my body). Rather than be crushed by false images and prejudices, these women have decided to come to new terms with their blackness. They demand recognition of their blackness and of their exclusion. And this must change. These women instrumentalize their experiences to denounce racism. Zezé Mota appears briefly, encouraging black women to be proud of their heritage and persist in calling for change.

The documentary could very well have ended by making a claim against racism and supporting its argument. However, the video moves beyond denunciation and provides a parallel space to illustrate how these women will not be oppressed by the color of their skin, the shape of their noses, or the texture of their hair. These women reference African traditions—clothing, music, religion—that have been suppressed in mainstream Brazilian culture.[57] This is done in part to counteract what one interviewee poetically describes as "blackhood, in exile, without any reference points in its own country." This is a central problem posed by the documentary: the lack of attention paid to how race intersects with other facets of everyday life in Brazil. What are the larger consequences of this? The last interviewee explains: "Until people accept blacks and other people that coexist in Brazil, nobody can talk about national identity." This final statement, and the documentary as a whole, position race as a key factor in redefining the people of Brazil and national identity. The politics of whitening will no longer be accepted. The new Brazilian democracy must be racially aware and inclusive.

Video and Feminist Activism in SOS-Corpo: Making Sex a Public Concern

Shortly after the declaration of amnesty in 1979, social organizations no longer had to rely on protections from established institutions such as the Catholic Church. For women's groups, this meant no longer having to sideline feminist discourse in the name of general, social welfare. While NGOs had played a decisive role in the process leading up to the end of the military regime, during the period of redemocratization (1985–88) these organizations served as increasingly important channels of dialogue between civil society and the state.[58]

For SOS-Corpo, a feminist NGO in the northeastern state of Pernambuco, one way to shift the relationships of power was to develop videos to provide information on women's health and reproduction to the citizens of the greater metropolitan area of Recife. Although this area of women's audiovisual production has been largely overlooked in media studies, it represents a significant component in the struggles waged by social movements in Brazil prior to and during the period of redemocratization. Contributing to the empowerment of women (and civil society in general), video made sex an issue of public concern and made it possible to extend feminist-based discourse to segments of the population that otherwise would not have been educated about vital healthcare issues.

SOS-Corpo is a middle-class, urban, feminist organization situated in Recife, one of the largest cities of Brazil. Originally structured as a feminist entity supported by the work of voluntary activists, the organization came into being in 1980 and officially formed as an NGO in early 1982. To help further its work related to women's reproductive health and sexuality, SOS-Corpo began receiving funding from international institutions such as the Ford Foundation, SACTES (Serviço Alemão de Cooperação Técnica e Social), Novib (Netherlands), Oxfam, and the MacArthur Foundation. Originally known as SOS-Corpo—Grupo de Saúde da Mulher (SOS-Corpo—Women's Health Group), the organization changed its name to SOS-Corpo—Gênero e Cidadania (SOS-Corpo—Gender and Citizenship) in 1991[59] to reflect a revised perspective on gender and women's healthcare as it relates to larger questions of social inclusion and individual autonomy.

SOS-Corpo has since become a point of reference for women's organizations nationally and internationally. At the international level, SOS-Corpo has developed contacts with institutions aligned with women's movements throughout Latin America, Europe, and North America.[60] Representatives from SOS-Corpo have attended numerous national and international conferences and symposia on women's health. During the 1980s, SOS-Corpo sought to intervene in the drafting of the PAISM and the new Brazilian constitution. In the state of Pernambuco, SOS-Corpo has developed and maintained strong alliances and working relationships with a number of local NGOs and neighborhood women's associations.

SOS-Corpo has consistently developed and maintained educational and political practices grounded in feminism. Notable among their projects are educational outreach programs working with middle-class women, women residing in impoverished areas of the urban periphery, and male and female youth. Their programs have also targeted the specific needs of women, such as pregnant women and domestic workers. Women educators have conducted classes on female anatomy, physiology, sexuality, and contraception, and they have held open conversations on the feminine condition. These classes have been conducted at SOS-Corpo's institutional space, at community centers in the greater metropolitan area of Recife, and in the rural areas of Pernambuco. Lacking adequate educational materials, the organization has dedicated itself to extensive research, publications, and mass informational campaigns. SOS-Corpo has produced numerous resources, including print (brochures, pamphlets, posters, reports) and audiovisual materials (slides, videos) for use in their own organization as well as to lend or sell to other women's groups in Brazil and elsewhere in Latin America.[61]

Communication has been a key component of SOS-Corpo's activities since its founding. In the early 1980s, the group developed radio programs to reach women in rural, isolated areas of the state. By the middle of 1984, the organization realized its work had been greatly reinforced by the use of radio, which they saw as not only a way to spread information about women's health but also as a method of pedagogical outreach to a wider audience they would not otherwise be able to reach.[62] A second key communicative method employed by the organization was the development of community-based theater, which allowed for fruitful exchange between activists and the women of the respective communities in which they were working. Theater served as an outlet for women to express their reflections on issues affecting them in their communities. For feminist activists, the knowledge gained from community theater helped shape the language, work methods, and concepts later used by the organization.[63] Specifically, their approach shifted toward a more integrative approach to the female body, which brought about new understandings of sexuality and a greater awareness of the heterogeneity between and among different women despite their apparently similar life conditions.[64]

Working with women in the urban periphery led SOS-Corpo to realize it needed to improve their teaching instruments. Against a backdrop of general optimism about the democratizing potential of new video technology and an increasing demand from new and established women's groups for presentations on women's health and sexuality, SOS-Corpo developed an alliance with TV VIVA in 1985[65] to produce a series of thirteen short documentary segments called "Transas do Corpo"[66] to discuss issues related to women's health and human sexuality. The series was included in TV VIVA's Community TV—a program in which large screens and video projectors were set up in open areas (such as parks, plazas, and other gathering spots) of metropolitan Recife. Internal documents indicate that the work methods of SOS-Corpo—the definition of topics, the development of scripts, for example—was a highly collective process.[67]

SOS-Corpo's production, use, distribution, and exhibition of video documentaries were highly successful. During redemocratization (1985–88), SOS-Corpo produced nineteen videos of which 490 copies were sold to various resource centers and other nongovernmental organizations and entities working with women in the movement for healthcare reform.[68] It is important to note that SOS-Corpo, in conjunction with TV VIVA, established an alternative model of production and distribution, producing and selling copies of their own videos to groups and individuals who requested their works. In 1986 alone, SOS-Corpo's videos were sold to 104 different associations and institutions. From January 1986 to December 1988, these videos were shown at 211 separate events in urban and rural areas of Pernambuco. This figure does not include the number of showings these videos had in TV VIVA's Community TV program. While the actual number of people attending these exhibitions in public plazas is impossible to determine, internal documents estimate that videos by SOS-Corpo were seen an additional seventy-five times in these free, open-air, public venues.[69] In sum, these works by SOS-Corpo secured a considerable degree of distribution and exhibition within an alternative framework.

The growth in video production during the 1980s led to the creation of festivals dedicated to alternative and women's video as well as spaces for video within mainstream film festivals. SOS-Corpo's videos were shown in national and international festivals, including Fest-Rio, the Festival de Vídeo Sobre a Mulher promoted by the CNDM in Brasília, special screenings organized by the ABVP, the Latin American Women's Video Festival in Peru, Videofest/Medien Operative in Berlin, and the Festival of New Latin American Cinema in Havana.[70]

The information transmitted in SOS-Corpo's programs was vital in the northeast. Like other activists in the women's movement, SOS-Corpo remained vigilant that the state would not largely disregard the PAISM and simply promote a program of birth control. Their suspicions were well founded. The military regime shifted its population policy from a pronatalist position during the economic boom years of the late 1960s and early 1970s to propose a national family-planning program in the early 1980s under pressure from the International Monetary Fund. A privately funded branch of International Planned Parenthood, BEMFAM (Sociedade Civil Bem Estar Familiar no Brasil), distributed birth control pills in clinics, primarily concentrated in the impoverished northeast, where population control was promoted in lieu of industrial or agricultural development.[71] In neo-Malthusian fashion, controlling poor women's fertility was seen as one solution to widespread poverty. Unfortunately, the distribution of birth control pills from these clinics went largely unregulated. Women would receive free packets of pills without proper medical attention and advice regarding the side effects of the daily doses of hormones. Meanwhile, the state indirectly promoted "voluntary" female sterilization as a birth control method by not questioning the abnormally high number of Cesarean sections being performed and paid for by the National Healthcare System (INAMPS). During these unnecessary C-sections, women paid out-of-pocket (and under the table) to have doctors perform tubal ligations.

Although access to contraception was, in fact, one of the goals of the women's movement, the measures taken by the state did not coincide with the feminist goal of teaching women that their bodies belong to them and that they should have control over their reproductive cycle. Rather, the state failed to fulfill its social obligations. In the mid-1980s, there were 614 health-care posts in the state of Pernambuco. Of these, only 144 had gynecologists and at only twenty-five of these clinics could women be screened for cervical cancer.[72] In this northeastern Brazilian state with the highest rates of cervical cancer in the world, this is evidence of gross negligence on the part of the local, state, and federal government.[73] Throughout the 1980s, the women's movement dedicated a significant amount of energy and resources to address women's healthcare—making sure legally ratified programs were implemented, protecting hard-won reforms from retrograde politics and educating women (and men) about reproductive healthcare.

Having secured key (progressive) legal measures in the 1988 constitution, the goal starting in the 1990s for SOS-Corpo was to protect acquired rights, hold local, regional, and national government accountable to their own agreements, and continue their efforts to increase women's reproductive and healthcare rights. Notwithstanding new economic crises brought about by the Plano Collor, SOS-Corpo continued producing audiovisual materials that responded to the key issues arising from tensions between the women's movement and the state.

At this juncture, the organization began to produce fewer but longer videos. This reflects a shift in how the videos became a part of their outreach work and can be attributed to a shift in focus of international funding agencies such as the MacArthur Foundation. Once democracy was ostensibly reintroduced to Brazil, the focus of attention shifted to other areas of the world, such as regions affected by the then-recent fall of Communism.

The general professionalization of the women's movements in Brazil saw SOS-Corpo become less active in grassroots mobilizing. But despite increased professionalization and the need to respond to international funding agencies, SOS-Corpo continued to address women's specific health concerns in their own region, such as abnormally high rates of cervical cancer, maternal morbidity and preeclampsia. What is more, their culturally sensitive printed materials and audiovisual work filled in where there were gross acts of negligence and incompetence on the part of the federal government.[74] Videos formed part of specific campaigns, including the legalization of abortion (*Aborto: Desafio da Legalidade*, 1995); the realities of rural women living and working in the Brazilian outback (*Sertanejas*, 1995), prevention of cervical cancer (*Quem Faz Sexo, Faz Prevenção*, 1995/96), continued calls for access to healthcare (*Em busca da saúde*, 1993), and a retrospective work on pioneering women activists in the northeast (*Almerinda*, 1991).

The 1995 documentary on abortion illustrates how SOS-Corpo and its work were shaped in the post-Collor, democratic era. The video speaks to growing concerns in the Brazilian women's movement regarding retrocessions in political process. While politicians have voted to guarantee access to voluntary sterilization in the public health system, they voted to suppress text in proposed laws that would guarantee medical assistance in cases of legally permitted abortions.[75] The documentary on abortion reflects a dedication to the central tenets of SOS-Corpo's work that reproductive rights and women's access to healthcare were legal and human rights.

SOS-Corpo Presents "Transas do Corpo"

The first series of videos produced by SOS-Corpo took the body politics of the time into the street and questioned the relationship between society and the politics of gender. What is more, the videos produced by SOS-Corpo served as a mechanism for political development that did not rely on traditional mechanisms of political action such as clientelistic controls and political cooptation.

With technical assistance from TV VIVA and financial support from Novib, SOS-Corpo was able to produce its first four videos in 1985: *O Quê Faço Com Essa T*[76] (What Do I Do With This T), *Tá Ligada Nessa?* (Are You Clued In on This?), *Atendimento Médico* (Medical Care), and *Atreve-te a Saber* (Dare to Know).[77] Ranging in length from seven to fifteen minutes, each video was included in TV VIVA's Street TV program. Thus, they were seen by an untold number of individuals in the greater metropolitan areas of Recife and Olinda. Internal documents state that these four videos greatly expanded the organization's outreach efforts.[78]

As part of an outdoor television project, the videos produced by SOS-Corpo included strategies of representation common to television. Intended to be viewed by diverse groups in the urban periphery, these segments employ a highly accessible language and style. Each video includes a woman who introduces the topic to be discussed.[79] Using clear, down-to-earth vocabulary, she speaks into a handheld microphone, similar to in-the-field news reporters of the period. At the end of every video, the woman encourages further deliberation about a given issue and announces the phone number at which SOS-Corpo could be reached if viewers had questions.

Issues regarding women's social roles and their health receive balanced treatment whereby the complexity of an issue is explored and presented for further consideration. Thus, the videos promote the idea of communication as a process rather than presentation of facts. In an effort to address the nuances of a presented topic, the SOS-Corpo representative asks questions of men and women on the streets and other locations of Recife. The faces of people interviewed are generally done in close-up format, which personalizes their statements and facilitates viewing on outdoor screens or on a collectively viewed TV sets indoors.

The segments *Tá Ligada Nessa?* and *Atendimento Médico* highlight the inadequate healthcare system in Pernambuco, while the segment *Atreve-te a Saber* encourages women to get involved in local women's groups to learn more about ways to protect their health. *Tá Ligada Nessa?* opens with a medium shot of Ângela Freitas asking people on the streets of Recife: "Qual é a melhor maneira de evitar filhos" (What is the best way to avoid having children?). Presenting the issue of contraception as a question opens the issue up to a number of people with different points of view. It also allows for sharing what people feel is scientific or factual information with personal experience and belief. Thus, different views (objective and subjective) are allowed to coexist for comparison.

A second critique is launched at the under-the-table practice of tubal ligations. By the mid-1980s, tubal ligations had become the most popular form of birth control, with more women in Pernambuco having their fallopian tubes severed than numbers of women taking birth control pills. The interviewer asks several men on the street if they would be sterilized. They answer no, reasoning that this would reduce their masculinity and that birth control is women's responsibility. Additional interviews with women who have had tubal ligations ask them to reflect on their feelings about having done so. Their reactions are mixed—some are satisfied, others regret the operation. The interviewer remarks that opting for a tubal ligation is opting to modify your body for survival and then asks: What happens to a woman who has been raised to be a mother and then can no longer be one? Asking men and women on the street about the best contraceptive methods reveals the cultural beliefs regarding gender and sexuality as well as touches on the politics behind determining the best birth control method. The video presents information and asks more questions than it answers. The power to make final decisions is in the hands of the people.

The next two videos by SOS-Corpo develop a similar goal to inform a wide audience about healthcare problems and motivate them to take action. The principal goal of the video *Atendimento Médico* (Medical Care) is to bring awareness to the problems with the healthcare system in the state and makes healthcare a question of citizenship. The SOS-Corpo interviewer speaks with several women waiting outside a hospital and a group of women sitting on benches just outside their homes. This image of people chatting is a familiar scene and suggests the SOS-Corpo interviewer has casually joined in on an outdoor conversation. The scene also suggests that the issues being discussed in the video are of shared concern and interest. The participants complain about how long they have waited at health clinics, the poor treatment they have received, or the lack of treatment after waiting for long periods.

The video then shifts into political gear. The SOS-Corpo interviewer speaks with a woman who encourages other women to be empowered to demand their rights. The women bring up the question of class differences and access to healthcare. Rich people can afford to pay for efficient, accurate, private care, whereas poor people must rely on an under-funded system. The women themselves assert that access to good healthcare is a right. The SOS-Corpo interviewer then provides statistical information of the inadequate health-care system for women in the state of Pernambuco over images of local clinics. The significant gesture this video makes is in how it effectively shares audiovisual space: the local women speak on-camera and define what they see as problems with the healthcare system; SOS-Corpo, as an institution and represented by the interviewer, provides more precise data on the extent and shape of the problem that these women define. The content and shape of the video is then a collaborative effort between the people and the nongovernmental organization.

In 1986, SOS-Corpo continued to produce short videos on contraception and healthcare to be shown in open, public spaces where the objective was to catch the attention of onlookers, motivate discussion, and inform viewers of the existence of the organization. It also produced a few slightly longer videos to be part of workshops sponsored by SOS-Corpo as well as other women's groups. These videos were also used for didactic purposes but in closed environments with fewer distractions.

One of the videos from 1986, the documentary *Por Quê Não?* (Why Not?) took on the highly sensitive issue of abortion and sought to change public opinion while influencing state policy. The abortion debate in Brazil has certainly not ended. In 1995, SOS-Corpo produced a second twenty-six-minute documentary on the subject, entitled *Aborto: Desafio da Legalidade* (Abortion:

Challenge of Legalization). Legal access to abortion is still today only permitted in cases of rape and when a pregnancy presents a grave risk to a woman.

The documentary *Por Quê Não?* asks people to reflect on this issue that affects all of society. Similar to the shorter videos from 1985, this video features several people who are stopped on the street to offer their thoughts regarding abortion. Their comments blend traditional concepts of morality with patriarchal, classist, often illogical statements regarding women's sexuality and abortion. With these stereotypes and potential for legal backlash, it is not surprising that the women who speak about abortion on camera do so timidly or with their identities disguised, reflecting a more conservative sociopolitical context. Notably, the statements made by these women are not like the tight-framed close-ups in which women directly faced the camera when speaking in Eunice Gutman's 1983 documentary (filmed in Rio de Janeiro). The SOS-Corpo interviewer quietly asks a woman if she thinks abortion is a sin. The woman, shot in profile, in the dark, circumspectly states that she does not know. Another woman is filmed in her kitchen preparing an herbal infusion that she hopes will provoke an abortion. This small-framed woman explains that she already has four children and can't have any more. The representative from SOS-Corpo asks her what else she will try if the infusion does not work. The woman mentions having heard of some drops that she might try. With her head tilted downward, glancing away from the camera, the woman defends herself, explaining, "Não é que eu não quero, é que não posso. Não posso" (It isn't that I don't want to [have a baby], it's that I cannot. I cannot).

The statements by the men and women on the street are intercalated with facts offered by the SOS-Corpo interviewer and the opinions of doctors and lawyers well versed in the public-health and legal concerns surrounding the practice of abortion. The SOS-Corpo interviewer states that women use a variety of household objects to provoke an abortion, underscoring the unsafe practice of at-home abortions and the desperation women must feel to use such crude instruments. Against images of women in hospital gowns and in obvious physical distress, the SOS-Corpo interviewer states that the actual number of abortions performed each day is unknown, but it is estimated that there are approximately eight per hour in Brazil.

There is a cut to an interior space where a woman sits facing the SOS-Corpo interviewer. The woman, sitting in profile and whose face is not fully visible, is asked by the SOS-Corpo interviewer to explain what women do to themselves to provoke abortions. As a gynecologist, she explains that she performs curettage on many women who provoke abortions at home. She adds that she sees a great deal of tissue damage from what she believes to be acid-based drops. Thus, the practice of clandestine abortions gains a different tone. It is not about religious belief, personal integrity, or hormone spikes. The practice of clandestine abortions is redefined as a widespread, dangerous practice and represents a significant healthcare crisis. She sits sideways, not allowing the viewer to fully see her face, and she insists repeatedly that she does not perform abortions.

The SOS-Corpo interviewer next speaks with a lawyer. Positioned facing the camera with book shelves behind her, the woman refers to article 124 of the Brazilian penal code, which defines severe penalties for a woman who has an abortion. She further explains that in Brazil's history, penalties were much less severe and adds that many European countries have already legalized abortion. In the end, the woman argues that laws can be changed according to the political forces and social groups in the country. For a population exiting twenty years of military rule during which time the government dictated policy, suggesting that laws can be redefined by civil society is a very radical move.

This documentary by SOS-Corpo is significant in three ways. First, it takes an important step toward making abortion an issue of public concern. Second, it reveals the differences of feminism in Brazil in terms of cultural, regional, and class differences. Third, as with other videos by SOS-Corpo, it shows the society to itself. In this, the video bridges individual thoughts and opinions with social beliefs and public policy.

Shifts in SOS-Corpo Video Production: Denise (1988) and Dupla Jornada (1989)

Later in the 1980s, SOS-Corpo made changes in its approach to video production. With continued financial support from international funding agencies and experience amassed from working on the "Transas do Corpo" series, SOS-Corpo chose to produce fewer but longer videos. Two important video projects from the late 1980s by SOS-Corpo took inspiration from social projects initiated or supported by the organization. Consequently, each involved increased research and collaborative input and resulted in rich discussions that addressed cultural beliefs, social practices, and state policy. In 1989, one year later, SOS-Corpo completed a short documentary entitled *Dupla Jornada* (Double Day) that focused on women agricultural workers in different regions of Pernambuco.

In 1988, SOS-Corpo produced a medium-length drama entitled *Denise* that marks a notable shift to fiction to impart information about women's reproductive health. In contrast to the documentary strategies found in other videos, a short drama is developed in this work to discuss the use of a diaphragm as a method of contraception. In effect, the diaphragm and learning about women's reproductive health is at the center of a discussion of women's paid labor, access to healthcare information, and interpersonal conflicts that arise when women become more aware of their bodies.

This video also illustrates an innovative and collaborative work process. The video emerges out of a research project conducted by SOS-Corpo and local health authorities in the state of Pernambuco. A total of fifty women from Recife tested the use of the diaphragm as a form of birth control and then reported their experiences, from which a script for the video *Denise* was drafted. Nonprofessional actors and actresses from Recife played the roles in the video.

The title of the video, *Denise*, refers to the protagonist of the drama, a young married woman and mother. The narrative follows Denise over the course of several days and develops a relatively conventional plot with an introduction, the development of conflicts, a peak moment of interpersonal tension, and a quick resolution. Throughout the video, there are images of locations, people, activities, and the speech typical of northeastern culture, and Pernambuco specifically. These elements make the plot accessible and indicate that the narrative is intended for a specific audience and spectators in or near the state of Pernambuco.

Denise revolves around self-empowerment and the difficulties one encounters when trying to make changes in one's life. The drama reveals that something as ostensibly benign as a diaphragm can bring great liberation and intense frustration. The protagonist confronts suspicious disapproval from neighbors for attending women's group meetings, must negotiate with her husband regarding use of the diaphragm, deals with neighborhood gossip, and confronts authority figures who try to pressure her into taking the Pill or being sterilized.

The video relates birth control to opening professional opportunities to women and the improvement of economic situations for families. In one scene, Denise walks in downtown Recife where there are many shops and where she sees a job announcement in a window. Denise grabs the sign, enters, and then exits with a smile on her face. While she shows great excitement in this scene, in the next there is a cut to Denise who lies down and dreams about her recent decisions. Her restless movement indicates that there are fears and doubts involved in taking big personal steps such as accepting a job outside the home. Change is not represented, then, as a seamless process. There are highs, lows, and moments of fear and personal doubt.

In her work on feminist audiovisual production, Julia Lesage considers of paramount importance the relationship between production processes, political goals, and the formal construction (for example, the use of music or narrative structure) of a work.[80] In terms of the relationship between those who produce an audiovisual work and those who are represented, Lesage argues that the ultimate goal is to allow the community to express itself *to itself*.[81] With this in mind, the fictional representation of learning to use a diaphragm and the experiences that are associated with developing greater awareness of one's body—which is based on the profilmic research project—are quite effective. First, the drama reveals that finding an appropriate, adequate birth control method takes time. It is also a process of working with a woman's (heteronormative) sexual partner. Second, greater sexual liberation may lead to unforeseen opportunities that can result in unexpected tensions within a community. The fictional representation in *Denise* highlights the process that one individual woman may go through. Third, for sensitive topics, the fictionalized representation—again, based on profilmic research—may be a particularly effective mode in smaller, tight-knit communities. For example, video viewers in a workshop can talk about what a character did and the choices she or he made without having to bring up aspects of their own private lives. In other words, a fictional piece allows for an open critique of the social, political, and economic circumstances involved in a particular issue without making a direct critique of personal practices.

During the 1980s, women's participation in the paid labor force rose dramatically. This occurred in part due to rises in unemployment and financial crises, which resulted in the loss of real wages and necessitated additional income per household. In the labor market, Brazilian women were generally paid less than their male co-workers and occupied jobs in the tertiary or informal sector. Their work outside the home did not mean they abandoned domestic duties. After the quitting bell, women frequently headed home to complete the numerous domestic chores that awaited them. Thus was born the expression "the double day."

Discussion of this phenomenon must take into account socialized gender identities, family structures, and larger economic and political processes. The double day is a phenomenon where the private and the public spheres collide, requiring structural changes in both arenas to make women's sociopolitical roles more egalitarian. While some women were unaware of their labor rights or resisted giving up their roles in the domestic sphere, mass media outlets continued to promote women as mothers and housewives, and the state paid little attention to the influx of women as members of the economically active population.

Internal documents at SOS-Corpo reveal that during the IX Encontro Nacional Feminista (Ninth National Feminist Meeting) held in early September 1987, appeals were made to address the needs of black and rural women. Subsequently, in September 1988, SOS-Corpo drew on its history of working with women residing in rural areas and women working in the agricultural sector in Pernambuco to hold a conference on women and work, entitled *A Dupla Jornada de Trabalho* (The Double Work Day) in Jaboatão, PE—a city outside Recife. With financial support from Oxfam, the Ford Foundation, and UNICEF, the conference was sponsored by the Centro de Estudo e Ação Social (CEAS, Center for Study and Social Action) and SOS-Corpo. The video *Dupla Jornada* (Double Day, 1989) emerged out of this conference.

The video itself incorporates two documentary functions. In one sense, it is a historical record of the proceedings at the conference, with images of women participating in group reflection sessions, listening to presentations, and role playing in skits. In another sense, the video serves as a platform for women agricultural workers to encourage other women agricultural workers to demand labor rights, and it lobbies for a more egalitarian distribution of domestic chores. The documentary itself is part of a larger campaign. SOS-Corpo produced a thirty-eight-page brochure on the double day to be shared with other women's groups in the region. SOS-Corpo's objective was to encourage women to construct new social identities and offer an alternative approach to discussing the double day, taking into account the pedagogical practices of feminist groups.[82]

But the video reveals that there is much more to the matter of having to complete a full shift at home after working a full day in the fields. The images and interviews in this video seek to valorize women as an autonomous labor force and encourage women to separate femininity and the domestic sphere. Images of women working in the countryside segue into shots of women doing a number of domestic chores (sewing, cleaning, preparing food, and so on) while their children eat and their husbands sit. Additional images show women working in sugarcane fields, women washing clothes, and men putting loads on the backs of horses. The effect of these images is to draw similarities between men's and women's labor. While cutting and stacking sugar cane is similar to stacking wood on the back of a horse, the men do not assume additional domestic work.

These images are overlaid with an aural quilt of women's voices. Different women, in a heterodiegetic, asynchronous parallel visual and aural space, critique the way they have been educated and call for socializing their children differently in order to break this cycle. But there is some doubt that social roles will change any time soon. Individual women's voices are heard, but there are relatively few tightly framed close-up interviews. This underscores the fact that women's labor is not an individual issue. Rather, women are an important collective force in society whose social identities should not be limited by a common obligation to the domestic sphere.

There are important questions not addressed directly by the video: Why should the general public care about women and the double day? What do private disputes between family members over washing dishes or taking out the trash have to do with the public sphere? Simply stated, a larger sociopolitical crisis (women entering the paid labor force) results in pressures placed on the private sphere (completion of domestic chores), which leads back to women's ability to participate in the public sphere. If a woman has some time each day to engage in activities that are for herself—relaxing, sleeping, watching TV, or reading a book—this has an effect on how and to what degree she can participate in public life. In sum, the double day translates into larger questions about social and political subjectivity.

❏ ❏ ❏

In his 1983 text *Technologies of Freedom*, Ithiel de Sola Pool poetically asserted that freedom was fostered when the means of communication were easily available but warned that the effects of negotiations between technology and institutions were not immediate. It is impossible to know for certain who viewed the audiovisual works by Eunice Gutman, the Lilith Video Collective, and SOS-Corpo, but their independent and alternative films and videos bridged class, race, and regional differences to bring about greater awareness to issues affecting the lives of all women. We can be certain that, as they helped shape debates about reproductive and labor rights and configured women as agents of sociopolitical change, these works contributed to the reshaping of citizenship in a redemocratizing Brazil.

5

Developments under Democracy

Brazilian Women's Filmmaking in a New Era

The years encompassing the transition from an autocratic regime to democracy in Brazil did not progress without challenges. Director Lúcia Murat's 1996 film *Doces Poderes* highlights the importance of the moving image to intervene in democratic reconstruction of the nation and speaks to a key turning point in Brazil's recent political history. The film's protagonist, a television journalist, Bia (Marisa Orth), travels to Brasília to cover the political campaigns for upcoming gubernatorial elections where a white, conservative man linked to an established, inner network of political power, and a black, progressive male candidate run for office. Bia's democratic ideals regarding the role of the media in the new democratic electoral politics come up against corruption inside political parties and the manipulation of the media to shape party politics. Discursively engaging with a growing popular sense of political empowerment, Bia asserts her right as a citizen of Brazil by holding firm to ethical principles guiding her role as a journalist and denounces the manipulation of the media. At one point in the narrative, a politician named Chico (Antônio Fagundes) is interviewed on television about the state of politics in Brazil. The interviewer asks Chico about perceived unusual alliances between parties of the Left with a party that had been affiliated with the military regime. Chico normalizes the situation, espousing the need to move beyond the past and concerns with political purity and arguing that political pragmatism is the reality of "um país de terceiro mundo em transição" (a third-world country in transition). More than a decade later, few would still unhesitatingly refer to Brazil as a third world country, but many would agree that Brazil continues to transition toward an increasingly stronger democracy.

Painting a New (Socio)political Portrait

Just as Murat's film reflects on concerns about political instability, the fragility of political parties, and governability that characterized the first period of transition to democracy, the film simultaneously points toward ongoing concerns with solidifying democratic practices and consolidating citizenship rights. The first period of Brazil's democratic transition ended roughly in 1994 with the election of Fernando Henrique Cardoso and when then-president Itamar Franco decreed (during the last six months of his administration) the Plano Real. According to political scientist Timothy Power, the economic reforms of the Plano Real and Cardoso's effective management of power sharing effectively "rebooted" the democratic regime in the mid-1990s, diminishing authoritarian cleavages lingering in the late 1980s.[1]

Indeed, the second phase of Brazil's democratic transition has been notable for a number of political and social accomplishments. When former union organizer and cofounder of the Worker's Party, Luiz Inácio Lula da Silva, was sworn in on January 1, 2007, it marked the first time in Brazil's history that a democratically elected president—Fernando Henrique Cardoso—turned over power to a democratically elected president who was then able to serve out a complete term in office.[2] During his tenure in office, Lula implemented and expanded a number of widely recognized social and economic programs (such as Bolsa Escola, Bolsa Família) to improve the quality of life of the poorest segments of society and to begin to reverse years of social exclusion. In conjunction with an increasing awareness of individuals' rights and their ability to put pressure on government officials, Brazil's urban poor have challenged a regime of differentiated citizenship and radically redefined the meanings of *cidadão* (citizen) and *cidadania* (citizenship).[3]

The increasing strength of Brazil's political systems should not overshadow numerous problems that continue to limit the reach of democracy. While individual Brazilians may have a redefined concept of citizenship, at the same time corruption, violence, and concerns with security hamper the full exercise of citizenship rights. Alongside a new awareness there are increasing frustrations. Despite greater stability in the political process and positive economic growth, there is an ever-decreasing tolerance for ongoing social exclusion. Historian and anthropologist Janice Perlman reports a marked disenchantment with and lack of faith in Brazil's political system.[4] Years after the end of military rule in Brazil, the nation's citizenry still demands transparency and accountability in politics. The promises of democracy have not brought immediate improvements or fully enfranchised citizenship for all.

The elections of November 2010 in Brazil mark yet another important phase in the recent history of Brazil's (relatively young) democracy. The election of Dilma Roussef, the first woman to be elected president and a former Marxist guerrilla activist who was imprisoned and tortured during the military dictatorship, indicates not only great political stability but also continued hopes for a nation that will successfully address its marked social inequalities. Meanwhile, the country gains an ever-increasing presence as an important player in the world political and economic scene. On the eve of her election, Roussef dedicated her victory to Brazil's women and declared the eradication of abject poverty a priority. While some in Brazil enjoy a quality of life similar to that found in highly developed nations, others lack equal opportunities and struggle in extreme economic disadvantage.

Whereas a more closed relationship between individuals and the state may have once been a useful (and appropriate) approach to think about citizenship, what is crucial in the current context is to focus on what Margaret Somers calls "relational practices." In this, one may examine relationships among public spheres, community associational life, and patterns of political culture.[5] It remains worthwhile to consider how gender, class, race, ethnicity, age, and sexuality are related to a persistent unevenness of citizenship in Brazil. Regarding this, Nick Stevenson argues for an analysis of cultural dimensions that will allow for considering how citizenship is experienced.[6] This transition has been reflected in women's filmmaking. Where there was once great focus on a struggle for the acquisition and consolidation of rights in the 1970s and 1980s, one finds from the mid-1990s to the present an increased exploration of differentiated experiences of belonging in Brazilian society and an examination of the quality of democracy that has emerged.

New understandings of citizenship undoubtedly owe a great deal to the current health of civil society organizations[7] as well as social movements that began demanding change decades earlier. Of these, the Brazilian women's movement was key in remodeling the social, cultural, and political patterns for women, children, and the disenfranchised. Discussions surrounding femininity, masculinity, gendered social roles, and sexual identity have evolved. Gone are the heady days of the 1970s and 1980s when the Brazilian women's movement concomitantly focused on ending the military dictatorship and sought changes to women's sociopolitical status. A new generation of women who were born during or after the dictatorship has come to consciousness in a context where life and work opportunities have opened up for them and they have (ostensibly) secured their rights as full citizens. Similar to situations found in Europe and the United States in the 1980s and early 1990s, when fighting over redefinitions of gender seemed suddenly passé, continued advocacy for women's rights seemed out of place in a newly redemocratized Brazil in the early 1990s, which was triply marked by a severe economic crisis, concerns about governability, and the impeachment of president Fernando Collor de Mello, whose policies contributed to the weakening of the women's movement in the early 1990s.[8]

While it is certainly true that second-wave feminisms in Europe and (Anglo) North America helped bring about the establishment of greater equality of opportunities and the freedom of sexual expression for women—which has subsequently raised concerns regarding the degree to which the current nature of female sexual liberation can be an adequate measure of women's freedom and progress, the same conditions cannot be said to have generally taken root in Brazil. Like many other countries in Latin America, Brazil demonstrates great regional and class differences and an uneven process of modernity, which translates into divergent life conditions and unequal advances for women. But it would be a mistake to believe that feminist activity has disappeared when, in fact, feminist discourses on gender, femininity, femaleness, women's rights, and women's positions in society have circulated and become integrated into institutional political practices and individual attitudes. What we find in the current context is a realignment of feminist discourses among numerous (mostly nongovernmental) organizations in Brazil with a focus on human rights and ongoing problems of social exclusion.

The Shape of Women's Filmmaking in a New Era

Just as political practices and the activities of social movements have changed, so has the shape of filmmaking in Brazil altered since redemocratization. Murat's film *Doces Poderes* was one of eighteen films released in Brazil in 1996 and was one of five films directed by women that same year. What is more, Murat's film appears during the critical first years of the Retomada, which prompts a series of questions regarding women's filmmaking in the new era. What distinguishes women's filmmaking in the current context? To what degree do feminist discourses exist in women's filmmaking today, and how are these discourses framed? How do more recent women's films address questions of feminine agency? This chapter aims first to examine how women's filmmaking has negotiated the current context of production and then sketch out notable tendencies with regard to the evolution of feminist discourses in contemporary women's filmmaking. Of these tendencies, what are particularly interesting are the representations of youth in recent Brazilian cinema, which, as I contend, has allowed women's filmmaking to further the process of gendered redefinitions of citizenship through representations of female youth. Recent films by directors Sandra Werneck, Lúcia Murat, and Tata Amaral featuring youth characters push understanding of citizenship beyond a question of legal or political status to engage with cultural and sexual facets of full membership in Brazilian society.

The cancellation of the Sarney Law (No. 7,505) and the closure of Embrafilme and Concine in 1990 during the Fernando Collor de Mello presidency dealt a significant blow to Brazilian cinema. A series of alternative measures were set in place to resuscitate film production, including the passage of fiscal incentive laws—the 1991 Rouanet Law (No. 8,313) and the 1993 Audio-Visual Law (No. 8,586), and the creation of a Brazilian Cinema Rescue Award (1993–94). Government involvement eventually led to the creation of ANCINE in 2001, charged with expanding and enforcing legislation for the film industry.[9] On the heels of the box-office success of Carla Camurati's film *Carlota Joaquina: Princesa do Brasil* (1995), the state became more inclined to support filmmaking, yielding a marked increase in film production. While only nine films were released in 1992, the total number of Brazilian films reached an average of twenty-five by the end of the decade.[10] Hence, the period starting in the mid-1990s has been termed the Retomada or "rebirth" of filmmaking. However, not everyone has boldly celebrated this increased film output, and some have commented that filmmakers are now more tied to the state than ever before. A number of critics have noted that there has been no (import) protection for an *industry* to flourish.[11] Indeed, the vast majority of feature-length films released from 1995 to the mid-2000s relied on monies collected from fiscal incentive laws, creating what has been referred to as a system of "incentivized patronage."[12]

Lacking readily identifiable aesthetic trends or ideological cohesiveness, films of the Retomada have been noted for their great diversity and the number of newcomers brought to the art form. Some critics, however, have critiqued the rhetoric of diversity as a specious, misleading observation.[13] Perhaps owing to the entrée in the mid-1990s of several new women directors, including Carla Camurati, Tata Amaral, Monique Gardenberg, Daniela Thomas, and Jussara Queiroz, along with a general increase in the number of films directed by women, film critic and journalist Susana Schild asserted that women were at the forefront of the Retomada.[14] During the first half of the 1990s, women's film production hovered around 5 percent, but by the second half of the decade, Brazilian films with women at the helm represented approximately 17 percent of all production.[15] From 1990 to 2010, no fewer than forty-five women directed feature-length films, for which they have received numerous awards. Yet, while women's participation in the film industry has greatly improved over time, female directors have hardly dominated the field. Cacilda Rêgo observes that relatively few women have produced with Globo Filmes, an "independent" producer of films eligible for tax-deferred monies but one that also has access to talent and distribution networks.[16] And, although women have successfully positioned themselves as feature-length film directors, they face a general film production context in which it is increasingly difficult to realize aesthetically and ideologically challenging works, let alone count on continued access to production funds.

The razing of state support for filmmaking in the early 1990s created a paradoxical situation. Although new talent could direct their first films, the resultant level field on which all were forced to play prompted complaints that veteran directors had to compete unfairly for funding alongside novice filmmakers.[17] A number of women directors who debuted with feature-length films in the 1990s did not direct again in the first decade of the new century. Similarly, some have experienced very long delays between films. Critic Fernando Veríssimo attributes the general phenomenon of the "one film syndrome" to an "autistic" (rather than artistic) style that lacks auteurist proposals that would allow films to engage in larger debates.[18] However, women's careers as directors are more likely tripped up by an incentive system that focuses on production to the detriment of adequate distribution and exhibition. Such has been the case of Betse de Paula and her film *O Casamento de Louise* (2001), which had limited exhibition in art-house circuits, where its popular aims and origins received a poor reception and the film earned low box-office receipts.[19] Government measures taken in the early 1990s have resulted in a cinema where influence, known names, megabudgets, and glamour have earned primacy. While Sandra Werneck has successfully managed directing the smaller-budget documentary *Meninas* (Teen Mothers, 2005) and played the "big budget game" in her feature-length films such as *Cazuza—o Tempo Não Pára* (Cazuza—Time Doesn't Stop, 2004), filmmaker Lúcia Murat has ventured outside the national funding scenario and sought out transnational coproduction funds for her more recent projects. Other women directors of the new generation include Sandra Kogut who has relocated to New York City to pursue opportunities in the United States. In the Belgian-French-Brazilian coproduction *Un Passeport Hongrois* (A Hungarian Passport, 2001), Kogut, whose grandfather is Hungarian, speaks with a representative of the Hungarian consulate about whether she may apply for a Hungarian passport. As the film's narrative takes shape around official application procedures, the documentary offers a highly personal examination of transnational identity where one finds a sustained tension between personal and familial constructions of history and identity and larger national narratives. The multitalented Anna Muylaert has successfully combined work with television (TV Cultura, SBT, HBO) and her work in cinema. Both of her feature-length films *Durval Discos* (2002) and *É Proibido Fumar* (2009) have received praise from critics and numerous accolades at film festivals.

From one angle, the era of big budgets during the Retomada has muted opposition to expensive, large-scale productions, while alternative visions of the nation and Brazilian culture rub up against increasing globalization and the absence of a broad viewing public—now composed mostly of middle-class patrons in shopping centers. And while Veríssimo may observe an "autistic" quality of "one-film" filmmakers, this should be put into perspective. For women directors, an auteur approach to filmmaking has been and continues to be a vital mode for offering sociopolitical insights. First, proposing and following through with an auteurist approach can be easily rejected under the current system of film financing in favor of more consumable, accessible works. It is important to note briefly that use of the term "auteur" for our purposes should be understood as not only an indication of a style or film practice that is distinctive but also as a director's acknowledgement of a unique responsibility in the creation of moving images that represent others. Second, initial success in short or medium-length films (in either 16 mm or 35 mm gauge) does not guarantee future funding opportunities for those who do, in fact, have clear, auteurist proposals.

The Future of Auteur Cinema: The Case of Betse de Paula's *Celeste & Estrela* (2005)

If Lúcia Murat's film *Doces Poderes* offers a reflective critique of the first phase of the new democracy while critiquing the role of the media in political process and pointing toward new understandings of citizenship rights, then Betse de Paula's 2005 film *Celeste & Estrela* takes the pulse of contemporary (women's) independent filmmaking by reflecting on, with great humor, the difficulties experienced by a young woman director with auteurist goals trying to work in the production context of the Retomada period.

The opening sequences introduce Estrela, a young man who waits at the airport in Brasília for Celeste to return from a trip abroad. While he waits for her flight to arrive, he chats with a quirky female airline employee about his relationship with Celeste, thus providing the structure for the film as remembrances in a series of flashbacks that in turn lead to the present moment of the diegesis. As an employee of the Ministry of Culture where he reviews submitted film scripts, Estrela explains he first met Celeste at the Brasília Film Festival, where he handed her one of numerous awards she received for her short, 16 mm film "Brasília: Anatomia de uma Cidade." Given her numerous accolades, it would be a safely assumed that Celeste would go on to produce and direct an equally laudable feature-length film. But, as the film's narrative reveals, great promise and talent can be exhausted and crushed in the current context.

After winning more prizes than she can carry, Celeste is encouraged to produce her feature-length film, "Amores Impossíveis" (Impossible Loves)—an homage to director Sandra Werneck's *Amores possíveis* (Possible Loves, 2001), which she has been thinking about for some time and in which she aims to discuss (with her fellow Brazilians) an alternative history of Brazil writ large. Thus the drama begins, and what seems to become increasingly impossible is for Celeste to work in the film industry. Indeed, the difficulty the film's protagonist has in obtaining production financing for her film is a veritable encyclopedia of the highs and lows of filmmaking in the Retomada. Celeste's endeavor to make her film launches a critique of auteurist goals that conflict with international expectations and influences alongside local systems of film financing, production, and distribution. She first takes an iconoclastic course on filmmaking with an older, famous scriptwriter named Jean Jacques. Despite his French name, Jean Jacques speaks in Portuguese with an accent thickly inflected by Southern Cone Spanish, thus embodying a transnational spirit that seeks to inform (or inspire?) Brazilian directors about how to make good films. Celeste later takes a course with a British instructor who, also in thickly accented Portuguese, instructs his students on the classical Hollywood-style structure of a filmic narrative with appropriately timed plot points and development of narrative tensions. The foreign expert on film scripts is presented in close-ups with a blackboard full of chalk diagrams of plot structures. Reminiscent of a coach giving instructions to his athletes on how to win the game, the scene suggests that filmmaking is a game for which you need a strategy to win.

These two scenarios can be understood as making multiple commentaries on the current difficulties of producing films with auteurist proposals in Brazil. On the one hand, Celeste takes these courses in an apparent effort to improve the "quality" of her film by improving her film script, but her own ideas about filmmaking come up against outside influences such as those portrayed as absurd, schematic rules of Hollywood-style filmmaking. On the other hand, the Spanish-speaking instructor metonymically references the success of directors in the New Argentine Cinema that has appeared in recent years, suggesting that Brazil should take a cue from its neighboring country's successful new model of cinema where there has been a renewed interest in and institutionalized financial support for first-time filmmakers.[20] And still, that Celeste takes these courses with international instructors could be seen as a critique of efforts to reach a broader, international viewing public. Nonetheless, Celeste stands firm in her goal to speak to Brazilians about Brazil.

Celeste abandons the professional lectures and ventures out to secure funding for her film, and she encounters a byzantine network of film-financing operations. Having filed the requisite government forms required under current audiovisual legislation, Celeste commences her efforts to persuade companies to invest in her film. On the hunt, she meets two female professional lobbyists hired by big-name directors to obtain huge amounts for their pending film projects. When a famous television soap opera actor named Rodrigo leaves the office of a potential investor, the film offers a double critique of the film industry's cult of personality. The female lobbyists express frustration, informing Celeste that Rodrigo is making a film that takes all the money available for film production. They kindly and indirectly inform her that getting film financing is about having connections and looking the part, encouraging her to dress better in order to compete in this professional landscape. The quest for financing is filled with great irony, and it becomes difficult to determine what is more so: that Celeste's modest-budget film cannot get the smallest investment while megabudget productions secure multimillion-dollar contributions, or that Celeste keeps running into Rodrigo at every turn.

Whether part capitulation or part pragmatism, Celeste opts to fight glamour with glamour by sprucing herself up, dressing better to please potential investors in her film, and even appears (by accident?) in the same outfit as a woman she lobbies—offering a critical wink at the degree to which directors have to please others to secure funding under the current system. It is not so surprising, then, when the woman executive she speaks with indicates that her company would be interested in investing in her film provided they could slip in some product merchandising at opportune moments. The absurdity (and ethics?) of the executive's proposal is underscored by a cutaway shot that shows the company's modern-day farm tractor anachronistically positioned in the proposed nineteenth century setting of Celeste's film.

Later, during a meeting with a bank executive, Celeste's financing odyssey points to unfortunate loopholes in the film-funding system. After Celeste pitches her project to a bank representative, he kindly informs her that she cannot have any money from them because the bank sends all its tax-deferred funds to its own foundation through which they produce their own films. In other words, there is no actual incentive for this company to invest in her independent film project. In this, Betse de Paula's film points out a major flaw in the system of tax-deferred investments in cultural production, which are funds owed to the state and, as such, should be managed by a public entity, not diverted back into institutions whose potential conflicts of interest exclude them from balancing private and public commitments.

Securing financing is not the last major obstacle Celeste faces. Having finally managed to produce her film, she encounters the problems of adequate film distribution in the current context. In what could be a clear autobiographical reference to Betse de Paula's own experience with her film *O Casamento de Louise*, Celeste and Estrela inquire about how many tickets have been sold to see her film. After she is informed of the pitiful number, she is crestfallen. But her spirits lift when she eventually receives a call from German TV, which is interested in buying her film. This fortunate news offers the ironic commentary that there is, in fact, an audience interested in her work, but, by and large, it will not be composed of her fellow Brazilians for whom the film was originally intended.

While never making direct calls for change in the current system of film production, what *Celeste & Estrela* conveys by way of its female protagonist is a simultaneous celebration and questioning of past successful models of auteurist cinema such as that of the French New Wave. A number of elements of *Celeste & Estrela* are clearly reminiscent of the *nouvelle vague*. Indeed, the playful, casually connected narrative trajectory of Betse de Paula's film is reminiscent of the films of François Truffaut, Jean-Luc Godard, Jacques Rivette, and Eric Rohmer. In addition to a critique of standardized concepts of filmmaking and narrative construction, the youthful vigor and spur-of-the-moment actions by Celeste resemble the seemingly aimless protagonists of New Wave films such as Michel Poiccard in *À Bout de Souffle* (Jean-Luc Godard, 1960) or Antoine Doinel in *Les Quatre Cente Coups* (François Truffaut, 1959), or even the young Zazie in *Zazie dans le Métro* (Louis Malle, 1960). But what perhaps most clearly ties de Paula's film is Celeste's overtly professed love of cinema and her earnest desire to produce a film about Brazil, its people, and its history. According to David Bordwell and Kristin Thompson, the French New Wave produced original and valuable films, but it also showed that "renewal in the film industry could come from talented, aggressive young people inspired in large part by the sheer love of cinema."[21] If it was a group of determined young people with great moxie and an ardent love of cinema that renovated French cinema in the 1950s and 1960s, then, by extension, Betse de Paula's film proposes that a more genuine renewal (or Retomada) of the Brazilian film industry necessitates infrastructural support of dedicated directors with auteurist objectives, and, no matter how business-like filmmaking may become, it must not be forgotten that film is an outlet for artistic and cultural expression.

The protagonist of *Celeste & Estrela* demonstrated great perseverance and a dedication to auteurist proposals for her film despite the obstacles she faced while launching a humorous critique against a crass, commercial mode of cinema. Undoubtedly, women who were beginning their careers in the 1970s and 1980s faced challenges similar to those experienced by Celeste, but many of them have been able to continue to use film as a platform for expressing alternative visions of Brazilian cultural identity.

Celeste & Estrela ultimately raises concerns about the (im)possibilities of auteur practice within the current financing structures. While it is not my intention to survey the decades-long debates surrounding auteur theory, the notion of the author in film, which originally emerged as a way to lend credibility to film as an art form on par with literature and painting, has never fit perfectly with the collective nature of film production. That auteurism was originally associated with celebration of individual male virtuosity and tacit ownership of stylistic elements brought forth feminist objections. A key feminist critique concerned the focus on a lone male genius in cinema, which often ended up relegating women to the obscure annals of film history. More recent approaches to film authorship have moved beyond notions of origin, unique aesthetic signature, and "thematic motifs"[22] toward discursive practices.[23] Janet Staiger observes that revised theories of agency come from either speech-act theory or poststructuralism with the objective to "rescue the expression of the self as a viable, if contingent, act—a potent one with real effects."[24]

Feminist film critics have upheld the vital importance of authorship in cinema.[25] Despite concerns about essentialism or the repetition of dominant models, those concerned with minority expression continue discussions of film authorship in favor of a conscious subjectivity. While approaches to film authorship continue to be refined, Janet Staiger reminds us of the importance of revisiting the concept of the auteur in its relation to a history of political activism, warning that "forgetting authorship and individuals takes away a history necessary for social activism and utopic imaginings."[26] The issue of agency in women's films needs to be theorized further to take into consideration changing production paradigms and film practices. A director's work may evolve due to technological innovations, to increasing mastery of the craft, or to shifts in production funding structures. Of irrefutable importance for the study of contemporary Brazilian women's filmmaking is to pay attention to issues women filmmakers take up in their films, the degree to which cultural policies support women directors, and institutional practices that women negotiate in order to be able to direct.

Notable Trends

As several directors have indicated in personal interviews, cinema has served as their outlet for taking a stand on issues they found to be of pressing sociopolitical importance. For directors Ana Carolina and Lúcia Murat, their films reveal a consistent meditation on the encounter with ideological and cultural differences. As discussed in greater detail in chapter 2, Ana Carolina's groundbreaking trilogy (*Mar de Rosas* [1978], *Das Tripas Coração* [1982], and *Sonho de Valsa* [1986]) presents the emerging feminist subjectivity of a young, middle-class, urban woman who rebels against a repressive patriarchal culture. In her first film released during the Retomada, the narrative of Ana Carolina's *Amélia* (2000), distributed by RioFilme, centers on the famed visit of French actress Sarah Bernhardt to Brazil in the early twentieth century. This film shares a number of similarities with the director's earlier works. Actresses Xuxa Lopes (*Sonho de Valsa*), Miriam Muniz (*Mar de Rosas, Das Tripas Coração*), and Cristina Pereira (*Mar de Rosas, Das Tripas Coração*) also appear in *Amélia*, where once again one finds an improvisational style of acting that stretches toward the outer edges of expected social decorum and ironic juxtapositions that destabilize the locus and exercise of authority. Although the metaphoric plays on image and sound found in *Sonho de Valsa* are generally absent, at the core of *Amélia* we find a synecdotal structure wherein the visit by Sarah Bernhardt is an embodiment of (presumably superior) European ideology and culture that is embraced by the Brazilian elite but clashes with the realities of the local context in what translates into a feminist meditation on Roberto Schwartz's notion of "misplaced ideas." Given the director's distrust of authority figures and a fondness for baroque aesthetics as a way to transcend mundane abuse of power, it should come as no surprise that the director's *Gregório de Mattos* (2003) delves into the life of seventeenth-century Brazilian poet Gregório de Mattos e Guerra, famous for his lyrical wit and biting satire of the bastions of authority of his time.

Whereas Ana Carolina's work has tended to concentrate on the clash of wills between authority figures and individuals, a meditation on the tensions between different sociopolitical groups while maintaining hope for negotiation underpins the collective works of Lúcia Murat. What is more, Murat's films consistently reflect on Brazil's history, cultural identity, and (sometimes) violent reactions to ideological disagreements and cultural diversity. While Murat's debut feature-length documentary, *Que Bom Te Ver Viva* (1989), visualizes the memories and experiences of survivors of torture under the military dictatorship, and her *Doces Poderes* (1996) investigates political corruption in the media, Murat's films in recent years delve further into the factors that have shaped Brazilian cultural identity as she establishes a historical trajectory that exposes the clash of cultures and ideologies rooted in the colonial past (*Brava Gente Brasileira*, 2000) and the confrontations of race, class, and political orientations during the years of the dictatorship but which extend to the contemporary period (*Quase Dois Irmãos*, 2004). As one of the few filmmakers in Brazil to break the code of silence surrounding Brazil's assumed racial democracy, her successful foray into the musical genre in *Maré—Nossa História de Amor* (2007) bridges differences between black/white and rich/poor segments of contemporary urban Brazilian society (which she took up previously in *Quase Dois Irmãos*) and offers a vital counterpoint to recurrent, misleading representations of poor youth as criminals. It should be noted that in both *Maré* and *Quase Dois Irmãos* Murat collaborated with author and screenwriter Paulo Lins, whose novel *Cidade de Deus* and subsequent screen adaptation contributed significantly to contemporary debates on Brazil's favelas and social inequalities. As well, in the nonfiction format, Murat's *Olhar Estrangeiro* (Foreign Gaze, 2006) extends the concern over misleading representations—the pivot point in *Doces poderes*—where the director addresses stereotypical visions of Brazil as found in international media portrayals of Brazil and its people.

For other women filmmakers, a recuperation of the position of women in Brazilian history and reflection on their relation to the Brazilian cultural imaginary motivates their work. While Cinema Novo actress Ana Maria Magalhães sought to position women in the history of Brazilian cinema with her early exposé of women's work in front of and behind the cameras in the nonfiction film *Mulheres do Cinema* (1978), her more recent biographical drama *Lara* (2002) treats the life of Odete Lara, muse of the Cinema Novo film movement who abandoned her acting career at its height. Similarly, Helena Solberg provides an intimate reflection on the transnational reception and cross-cultural positioning of the 1940s screen icon Carmen Miranda in

Carmen Miranda: Bananas is My Business (1995). It merits noting that former Cinema Novo actress Helena Ignez claims a role as director, releasing her first feature-length fiction film *Canção de Baal* (Baal's Song) in late 2008.

Other women directors have chosen to locate female agency in Brazilian history more generally. Tizuka Yamasaki, whose *Gaijin: Os Caminhos da Liberdade* (1980) focuses the experience of Japanese migration to Brazil through the eyes of a young female protagonist, revisits her protagonist and the historical melodrama in *Gaijin: Ame-me como sou* (Gaijin: Love Me As I Am, 2005), where she treats the contemporary history of the "reverse migration" of Brazilians, regardless of ethnic or racial ancestry, to Japan as *dekassegui*, or immigrant workers. Both films, which won awards for best film in 1980 and 2005 at the prestigious Gramado Film Festival, have contributed significantly to expanding the Brazilian cultural imagination to include Asian immigrants.

These more serious reflections on Brazilian history find comic relief in Carla Camurati's *Carlota Joaquina, Princesa do Brazil* (1995). While frequently labeled as the film that inaugurated the Retomada period, Regina Félix asserts that the film's surprising success with the public can be attributed to the fact that the film captured the zeitgeist of the post-Collor years of political debacle in which the Brazilian populace, disenchanted with failed democratic promises, got cathartic, humorous revenge by laughing at its history of incompetent and unethical political leaders.[27] In terms of the Brazilian film industry, the film's box-office success offered the first optimistic (financial) sparks of the Retomada, convincing agencies to once again invest in Brazilian cinema as a viable arena of cultural production.

A number of films released during the Retomada by both "veterans" (whose careers began in the 1980s) as well as debut directors evidence a feminist use of documentary film and video to denounce systemic social inequalities and the abuses of power. In noncinematic formats, Eunice Gutman, whose works from the 1980s in 16 mm or 35 mm film and video formats were closely linked to organized social movements, has continued independently to produce and direct documentaries to expand discussion on prostitution (*Amores de Rua*/Street Loves, 1994), focus on women's presence in religious practices in Brazil (*Feminino Sagrado*/Sacred Feminine, 1995), address gay rights and lesbianism (*Segredos de Amor*/Secrets of Love, 1998), and reveal the impact of the AIDS epidemic on Brazilian women (*O Outro Lado do Amor*/The Other Side of Love, 2000). In 2009 she was awarded the prestigious Margarida da Prata by the CNBB (Conferência Nacional dos Bispos do Brasil) for her documentary *Nos Caminhos do Lixo* (2008) that brings to light the efforts of a women's collective to generate income by recycling garbage outside Rio de Janeiro. Sharing in Gutman's efforts to promote dialogue on social equality, Ana Luiza Azevedo links reproductive and human rights in *Ventre Livre* (1994), a nonfiction film taking as its subjects the high percentage of Brazilian women who are sterilized, lack access to effective contraception, and seek out (illegal and unsafe) abortions. Thereza Jessouroun revisits the topic of abortion and the ramifications of its clandestine practice in *Fim do Silêncio* (End of Silence, 2009). Meanwhile, in *O Aborto dos Outros* (The Abortion of Others, 2008), Carla Gallo questions why abortion continues to be illegal in Brazil.

Not all who engage in denouncing abuses of power have so clearly foregrounded issues of public health, gender, or female sexuality. Veteran journalist and former exile during the military regime, Tetê Moraes has directed several documentary films that have explored struggles against political repression. The documentary *Terra para Rose* (Land for Rose, 1987), cited as inspiring the creation of the Landless Movement (Movimento dos Sem-Terra), focuses on the female protagonist/activist, Rose, who, alongside hundreds of other families, invades an abandoned farm in an effort to obtain a tract of land to farm to become self-sufficient. The film offers a critical exploration of economic exclusion and a denunciation of lingering authoritarian violence when the film's protagonist is found dead at the side of a road. Moraes revisits the people she met in the late 1980s in *O Sonho de Rose—Dez Anos Depois* (Rose's Dream—Ten Years Later, 1997) and reveals the progress and setbacks they have faced. In 2006, Moraes directed the documentary *O Sol: Caminhando contra o Vento*, which treats *O Sol*—a short-lived alternative press that was established in 1968 and included the participation of key countercultural voices.

Echoing concerns raised by filmmakers in the 1970s and 1980s, a new generation of women filmmakers has also explored institutional violence and the (ab)use of official authority in the legal system as part of a larger social structure that is designed to work against those lacking education and financial resources with works such as the documentaries *Justiça* (2003) and *Juízo* (2008) by Netherlands-based Maria Augusta Ramos, and a shocking exposé of police and drug violence in Brazilian-American Kátia Lund's *Notícias de uma Guerra Particular* (1999), which alongside Paulo Lins's (eponymous) novel became the audiovisual precursor to the widely screened *Cidade de Deus* (directed by Fernando Meirelles and Kátia Lund, 2002). Claudia Priscilla offers further reflections on the Brazilian penal system in the feature-length documentary *Leite e Ferro* (Milk and Iron, 2009), a film that explores the constitutionally protected right for women to nurse their newborns but who are also eventually separated from their children—sometimes permanently—while they serve out their prison sentences. Daughter of director Jorge Bodanzky, Laís Bodanzky is equally notable for her dedication to explorations of social inequity, violence, and abuse of official authority. In her debut feature-length film, *O Bicho de Sete Cabeças* (Brainstorm, 2001), she explores the mistreatment of mental health patients at the hands of medical authorities. Her second film, *Chega de Saudade* (The Ballroom, 2007), an endearing romantic comedy, focuses on a group of middle-aged and older friends who gather at a decaying ballroom in São Paulo—reminiscent of Mexican director María Novaro's *Danzón* (1991)—and was nominated for numerous awards at film festivals. In her third film, *As Melhores Coisas do Mundo* (2010), she explores contemporary society through the lens of youth, developing a narrative around a young boy whose family fragments after the departure of his father. In this, Bodanzky's film coincides with numerous contemporary films from Latin America that focus on youth at the intersection of social, political, and economic change. Bodanzky has also been at the helm of one of the most successful, contemporary forms of cine-activism in Brazil. Her documentary film *Cine Mambembe—O Cinema Descobre o Brasil* showcases the efforts to screen short Brazilian films in public spaces throughout Brazil, sometimes to people who had never seen a movie before. The documentary developed from an itinerant cinema project launched in 1996 by Laís and her husband, Luiz Bolognesi, in which they screened Brazilian short films in public plazas and schools of São Paulo. With better equipment and support from the Ministry of Culture, the project moved to all regions of Brazil and earned the name Cine Mambembe. The project, now known as Cine Tela Brasil, has secured economic partnerships to guarantee its continuation. In recent years, Cine Tela Brasil added workshops led by cinema-educators and launched a website, Portal Tela Brasil, to further their outreach efforts.[28]

In her discussion of auteurism in women's filmmaking, Geetha Ramanathan encourages scholars to explore the representation of feminist discourses and the imprint of feminist authority in women's filmmaking.[29] Advocating for new definitions of gender and female sexuality were hot-button topics at the forefront of political discussions in the 1970s or 1980s. Femininity certainly remains a topic explored by today's women directors, but the nature of the discussion has changed. Regardless of geosocial location, it remains clear that feminism today has arrived at a new point in its trajectory. While disparate ideas may be launched regarding how to define the current state of feminism, Ann Braithwaite argues for a postfeminist perspective, which she asserts takes into account that the "breadth of feminist issues is now much broader than before," crossing "a range of political, social and cultural issues, and intersecting with a variety of theories about gender, race and ethnicity, sexuality, class and even corporeality."[30] At the beginnings of the twenty-first century, a number of conceptual and discursive shifts have clearly taken place such that a feminist imprint subsequently leaves audiovisual traces in women's filmmaking that differ from decades prior. Indeed, a number of films (but certainly not all) by women directors in Brazil engage in postfeminist discussions of femininity and female sexuality not generally found in masculinist, mainstream cinema.

For debut and veteran women directors in Brazil, the romantic comedy has proven to be fertile ground for explorations of feminine/feminist subject positions. Mara Mourão's *Avassaladoras* (2002), which subsequently turned into a twenty-two-episode series on TV Record from February to June 2006, develops the trope of the professionally successful but romantically deficient singleton in which Laura (Giovanna Antonelli) ultimately leaves Brazil to test her fortune in New York City. The final scenes of the film, which show Mourão's protagonist standing in front of the World Trade Center Towers—still standing at the time of filming—leaves a tripartite feeling of unease. That the film was released to audiences in Brazil in early 2002, only months after the terrorists' destruction of the skyscrapers in New York City, merges with Laura's apparent inability to embody a fulfilling gendered identity and sexual subjectivity in Brazil and her aim to find a new subjectivity abroad within an ostensibly beneficial yet occasionally detrimental neoliberal economic order. In addition to Mourão, other women directors have drawn on the genre of the romantic comedy and family melodrama to explore postfeminist femininities. For instance, directors Betse de Paula (*O Casamento de Louise*, 2001), Sandra Werneck (*Pequeno Diccionário Amoroso*, 1997; *Amores Possíveis*, 2001), and Rosane Svartman (*Como Ser Solteiro*, 1998; *Mais uma vez Amor*, 2005) debate where women (and men) stand in the contemporary context with regard to balancing professional opportunities, newfound sexual freedoms, and the contemporary dynamics of romantic relationships. By measure of its English-translated title, Eliana Fonseca's *Coisa de Mulher* (Chick Thing, 2005) could be easily dismissed as a pink-hued, superficial treatment of the lives of urban, upper-middle-class women's romantic problems and sexual dissatisfactions were it not for the (humorous) juxtaposition of different feminist/feminine subject positions: the (un)happy housewife and mother, the overloaded superwoman, and the independent single professional woman. If at first Fonseca's film engages in a renegotiation of femininity in the contemporary social and cultural context, it settles for a formulaic dénouement. With the exception of one lesbian character, the narrative of Fonseca's film succumbs to what is ultimately a traditional, (hetero)normative resolution whereby the sexually frustrated women find solace and redemption in their domestic (male) partners. Lastly, Anna Muylaert follows the successful *Durval Discos* (2002) with equally lauded *É Proibido Fumar* (2009). In this second film, Muylaert redeploys the subtle, ironic (and sometimes dark) sense of humor she developed in *Durval Discos* to reflect on the quirky experiences of a middle-aged, unmarried protagonist, Baby (Glória Pires), who falls somewhere between two models of contemporary femininity, being neither a hard-hitting career woman nor mother to a demanding family like her two sisters.

Engagements with Youth

Of those films (directed by women) that take up the feminine condition, the majority focus on the experiences of adult women. However, the most critical explorations of gendered relations and sexuality are found in contemporary cinematic representations of youth. Indeed, it is in representations of youth where scholars can find the most marked differences between mainstream, masculinist cinema and women's cinematic contributions to debates surrounding femininity, citizenship, and Brazilian cultural identity.

It should be noted that as part of political shifts that took place in the early 1990s, the citizenship status of minors in Brazil underwent significant reconstitution and redefinition. As the women's movements and feminism in Brazil were becoming more diffuse and facing new challenges in the political landscape of the late 1980s and early 1990s, concern was increasing for children and youth. Paradoxically, during the administration of Fernando Collor de Mello, when numerous social programs were defunded and institutions were dismantled, children and adolescents were identified as a political priority. The Estatuo da Criança e do Adolescente (Statute on Children and Adolescents, Law No. 8,069), signed on July 13, 1993, not only endorsed the 1959 United Nation's Universal Declaration of the Rights of Children but also formally recognized children and youth as citizens with fundamental rights (for example, with regard to access to education, healthcare, respect for life, liberty, and so on).

The representation of youth is certainly not new in the history of Latin American cinema generally or Brazilian cinema specifically. During the dictatorship in Brazil, some of the most scathing critiques of the military regime, its policies, and its repressive effects on society came from portrayals of youth figures. Film movements such as Udigrudi and Marginal Cinema are populated with young, rebellious, disillusioned characters. Jorge Bodanzky and Orlando Senna's film *Iracema—Uma Transa Amazônica* (Iracema: An Amazon Odyssey, 1976) portrays the life of a young native Brazilian woman who becomes corrupted and turns to prostitution. Unfortunately, the young girl's subjectivity gets lost behind the film's prevailing goal to critique the construction of the trans-Amazon highway and the government's economic development plans. The growing concern for urban *meninos da rua* (street children) in the 1980s received treatment in Hector Babenco's *Pixote* (1980) and the opening scenes of Tizuka Yamasaki's film *Patriamada* (1984).

Recent cinematic representations of youth afford similar explorations of citizenship in that they comparatively bring class, generational, racial/ethnic, and gender differences to the foreground and motivate reflection on differentiated life opportunities and trajectories. While the representation of youth in recent Latin American cinema has sparked numerous debates on violence, social equality, and democracy, the focus has been almost exclusively on young males, the troubles they face as they enter adulthood, and a general crisis in patriarchy.[31] Meanwhile, few directors or academics have paid attention to the experiences of young females and how poverty and violence intersect their lives differently.

Besides a limited focus in terms of gender, the aesthetic tendencies of recent male-centered youth films have tended to impede understanding of favela communities and their residents. Feeding into widespread fears of violence, internationally successful Brazilian films such as *Cidade de Deus*, its cinematic sequel *Cidade dos Homens* (directed by Paulo Morelli, 2007), *Última Parada: 174* (directed by Bruno Barreto, 2008), and *Tropa de Élite* (directed by José Padilha, 2007) have brought great attention to social inequalities while also contributing to the stigmatization of young, poor (mostly black) males as delinquents who engage in theft and drug trafficking.[32] The cinematic representation of youth living in favelas has become a significant trope in recent films, but, as Beatriz Jaguaribe observes, contemporary representations tend to code the favela within an aesthetics of realism as a violent space filled with young, dangerous, individualistic, and immoral thugs. What is more, these recent representations of the favela have established "an interpretive code of realism" relying on the "shock of the real" that have subsequently shaped discussion of Brazilian urban realities.[33]

While young, poor males have been constituted as a criminal threat to civil society, young, poor females have been positioned within a cloud of moral panic regarding their sexual behavior, specifically as young female sexuality is linked to rates of teen pregnancy and prostitution. Sandra Werneck, whose work has shown a consistent concern for youth and the feminine condition since she began directing in the 1980s, explores the experiences of teen motherhood in the documentary film *Meninas* (Teen Mothers, 2005). In the feature-length fiction film *Sonhos Roubados* (Stolen Dreams, 2010), Werneck mobilizes images of young female prostitution to illustrate how female youth inherit social exclusion, poverty, and abandonment, and how they are subjected to gender-based abuses of power and corruption. These films simultaneously examine girls and young women's intracommunity relations and reveal gender- and class- and race-based configurations of social exclusion.

With funding from Petrobras and screened at the 56th Berlin International Film Festival as part of the Panorama section, Sandra Werneck directed and coproduced the documentary film *Meninas* with Giros Filmes and her own company Cineluz Produções. *Meninas* follows the pregnancies of four teenage girls living in favelas in and around the metropolitan area of Rio de Janeiro. It should be noted that this is not the first nonfiction work in which the director focuses on youth or marginalized subjects: prior to her breakthrough as a successful feature-length film director, Werneck independently produced and directed documentaries on child prostitution (*Damas da Noite*, 1979), Rio de Janeiro transvestites (*Ritos de Passagem*, 1979), and women prisoners (*Pena Prisão*, 1983). Although her work reveals a consistent feminist discourse, her audiovisual practice has evolved markedly. In the 1980s, Werneck, like numerous independent women directors at the time, was able to coproduce her works with financial assistance from the state and in varying degrees of collaboration with social movements and nonprofit organizations. The case of *Meninas* shows that women directors are still able to produce discursively feminist audiovisual works even though the state has largely substituted a direct stake in such independent films via tax incentives offered to large companies.

The issue of teen pregnancy was widely discussed in Brazil in the 1980s and 1990s but emerged as a hot-button issue at the turn of the century. In 1999, prominent politician (and future presidential candidate) José Serra published the newspaper article "Child-mothers," which helped fuel debates surrounding the moral decay of Brazilian society and the social risk of young female sexuality. Major Brazilian newspapers fed concerns regarding an ostensible scourge of young female promiscuity in recent decades. And during a two-month period in 2005, the widely circulated *O Globo* made teen pregnancy the topic of front-page news and editorials.[34] Ill-informed discussions have frequently aligned criminality with unwanted births. In response, researchers in the area of public health have tried to douse fears and downgrade exaggerations by warning against neo-Malthusian interpretations and asserting that current patterns of sexual culture among young people are consonant with long-standing social norms.[35] But this continuation of established norms combined with an absence of sex education aimed at youth and high levels of poverty are particularly problematic.

In an interview, Werneck explains she was interested in exploring how pregnancy fit into the lives of these young women.[36] Her work opposes scandalous tones used in mainstream media and offers up a complex portrayal of these teens' lives as they visit doctor's offices, deal with a variety of life issues, and idle away the days while not attending school. Although the original context for the film was limited to the last trimester and birth, the closing sequence updates the viewer on Evelín, one of the four pregnant teens portrayed in the film, and her life since planned filming ceased. As she carries a wreath of flowers in a cemetery, white intertitles announce that the father of her child (whom she had since married) had been killed in a drug-related incident. Now, at age thirteen, Evelín has become a widow and single mother to a four-month-old infant.

Absent in the discussion are the voices of authorities who offer commentary on the need to change sexual behavior or rates of teen pregnancy and unwed mothers. Rather, Werneck opts to observe how these girls' lives unfold, record their experiences, and register their thoughts about being young and pregnant. Her film, however, is not a repackaged version of direct cinema, noted for a seemingly strict observational approach to documentary filmmaking. The (relatively) "noninterventionist" approach used by Werneck affords an opportunity for young women to speak about their own experiences, otherwise lacking in mainstream debates surrounding teen pregnancy, and, despite the absence of "expert opinion," manages to successfully blend the descriptive and the explanatory. However, what is even more conspicuously absent in the documentary is the practice of official government policies intended to fully enfranchise all Brazilians. Notwithstanding scenes in the documentary showing the teens receiving healthcare at public clinics, the documentary brings to light the government's failure to fulfill its pledged obligations to protect minor's fundamental rights (detailed in the 1993 Estatuo da Criança e do Adolescente) as well as other democratic rights provided for in the 1988 constitution, wherein the state outlined its role in providing education and access to family planning. In this regard, Werneck's documentary not only describes the "unevenness of citizenship" but also points toward explanations for the impeded potential and cyclical exclusion of young, poor females from full membership in Brazilian society.

Reportedly, while working on the film *Meninas*, Sandra Werneck discovered the testimonial novel *As Meninas da Esquina: Diários dos Sonhos, Dores e Aventuras de Seis Adolescentes do Brasil* (2005) by journalist Eliane Trindade, who transformed her book into the screenplay for the feature-length film *Sonhos Roubados* (2009). Owing to Werneck's previous work addressing child prostitution, Trindade was willing to sell the rights to her book, which includes investigative work by the author and the personal reflections of six young women living in urban peripheries who prostitute themselves to cover basic costs of living or to acquire desired objects (clothes, mp3 players, and the like). The film condenses the stories of the six girls in Trindade's work to three protagonists in Werneck's film, Daiane (Amanda Diniz), Jessica (Nanda Costa), and Sabrina (Kika Farias). The film explores their experiences with emotional and physical abuse but refrains from offering a full resolution. While Daiane and Jessica apparently manage to find more stable lives, the final scene shows Sabrina back on the streets joined by new young faces and thereby points to the cyclical, ongoing problem of child prostitution. Both *Meninas* and *Sonhos Roubados* join an unfortunately short list of Brazilian films that focus on the experiences of girls and young women in poor communities. Indeed, in an interview Werneck expresses her dismay and concern regarding the lack of representation of girls, noting that Brazilian cinema has always talked about boys but that the universe of girls is never addressed.[37]

In effect, *Sonhos Roubados* is a feminist counterpoint to the widely successful films such as *Cidade de Deus*, *Cidade dos Homens*, *Tropa de Élite*, and *Última Parada: 174*, whose narratives are almost entirely from the point of view of male characters. Indeed, in her discussion of *Cidade de Deus* by Paulo Lins, Marta Peixoto observes that the novel's perspective is "relentlessly male" and wholly uninterested in female trajectories or subjectivities[38]— the adaptation does little to modify the novel's perspective. Werneck's film clearly differs from these male-focused films in that female points of view predominate. Nonetheless, *Sonhos Roubados* evidences a similar productive process to these male dramas in that her screenplay is based on the personal accounts of young girls compiled by and included in Eliane Trindade's work. In this, it is important to recall that the screenplay of *Cidade de Deus* was based on the personal reflections of one of its former residents, Paulo Lins, while *Élite da Tropa*, the collective memoir by former Rio de Janeiro police officers André Batista, Rodrigo Pimentel, and Luiz Eduardo Soares, served as the departure point for the internationally successful film *Tropa de Élite*.

In her study of representations of Brazil's favelas, Flora Süssekind notes a trend in literary representations which she defines as "an intense neo-documentalism," characterized by the combination of factual and fictional resources.[39] A film such as *Cidade de Deus* draws on the spirit of this multi-layered textuality (for example, the first-person point of view through the protagonist Buscapé who takes photographs for a local newspaper) and is one of the ways that a film such as *Cidade de Deus* makes claims to authenticity. While *Sonhos Roubados* does an equally good job of blurring the lines between fact and fiction, it is far more successful in drawing on the diary accounts of the text *As Meninas da Esquina* to develop the interiority of its young female protagonists. Unlike the "shock value" realism put forth by its male-centered cinematic precursors, *Sonhos Roubados* lacks special effects and dramatic nondiegetic music and progresses at a much slower pace, which grants a creative space in which the female characters' world of fear, loss, love, and friendship develops.

In her work on adolescent males and females living in poverty, Duque-Arrazola notes the direct relationship between levels of poverty and difficulty to change preestablished gender models. The more severe and pressing the condition of poverty, the greater difficulties women have to confront and transgress the demands of gender placed on them by their social environment.[40] Whereas the pregnant teens in *Meninas* may seek to become more significant members of their communities by becoming mothers, and whereas not all of the young women in *Sonhos Roubados* are able to successfully escape from prostitution, two recent films by Brazilian women directors take up women's presence in popular Brazilian music and challenge established notions of femininity. While Tata Amaral's fiction film *Antônia* (2006) considers the São Paulo hip-hop scene, Denise Garcia's nonfiction film *Sou Feia Mas Tô Na Moda* (I'm Ugly but I'm Trendy, 2005) focalizes its discussion of the Rio de Janeiro funk scene through the eyes of its female participants. Despite their formal differences, the female figures in both films radically resist traditional gender norms. What is more, in the process of taking up women's presence in musical subcultures, both films underscore the cultural facets of contemporary citizenship and offer reinterpretations of impoverished communities.

If one of the challenges of contemporary feminism is to wrest associations of victimhood from femininity, then Tata Amaral's film *Antônia* (2006) builds on the director's interest in popular music as both an outlet for Brazilian culture and mode of resistance.[41] Amaral's female protagonists defy the odds set against them and embrace a contemporary womanhood where social expectations do not supersede personal goals. That young women's participation in Brazilian popular music and its subcultures has been egregiously overlooked in academic studies would come as no surprise to scholars Angela McRobbie and Jenny Garber, who have noted that girls and young women are frequently overlooked or misrepresented in studies of youth subculture.[42] Intervening in this oversight, Amaral's film features real-life hip-hop and R&B singers Leilah Moreno (Barbarah), Negra Li (Preta), Jacqueline Simão (Mayah as Quelynah), and Cindy Mendes (Lena) in the lead roles of a narrative about four young women from the outskirts of São Paulo who face down violence, racism, and sexism in the pursuit of their dream of succeeding as a hip-hop band called Antônia.

In terms of Amaral's career trajectory, Antônia is located at the conflu- ence of some apparent contradictions and continuities. That Amaral was a former media activist who advocated for community television stations and questioned the government's role in authorizing radio and television station concessions[43] in the 1980s may seem to conflict with her engagement with media monopoly TV Globo in the transmedia production of the series Antônia and the eponymous film backed by Globo Filmes. However, the link to TV Globo should be seen as a practical move by the director to secure produc- tion funds and an encouraging gesture on the part of the Globo organization to support the positive representation of Brazilians living in marginalized communities. Antônia also reveals a continuation of the director's interest in the experiences of modern, urban life as noted in her short films on the affective malaise of postdictatorial, urban Brazil in Poema Cidade (1986) and the challenges faced by a young office boy in Viver a Vida (1991). That said, her more recent works reveal a shift from focusing on male experiences (in her short films) to primarily focusing on the experiences of female characters and their affective relationships as seen in her first and second feature-length films Um Céu de Estrelas (1997) and Através da Janela (2000). Notwithstand- ing the assertion that these two films alongside Antônia form a trilogy that explores feminine archetypes, there are notable differences among them. The tight framing and narrative focus on women in domestic isolation favored in Um Céu de Estrelas and Através da Janela as well as the representation of the female body in a state of danger get revised in Antônia, where strong-willed, self-reliant female characters fully engage in activities that cross public and private spheres.

While Amaral's film shares the same producers of Cidade de Deus, the film distances itself from this cinematic precursor in that it develops an uplift- ing, positive image of young people who are committed to "looking forward"

(*olhar pra frente*) while emphasizing community solidarity. The female protagonists certainly face numerous obstacles, but in the end one finds a progressive woman/motherhood wherein women are not dependent on men or
repressed by traditional gender roles. Notably, Preta (Negra Li) balances being
a single mother while seeking professional success. And Lena (Cindy Mendes)
refuses to be sidelined by an unexpected pregnancy and a domineering male
partner. Unlike other highly successful Brazilian films of late that represent
poor communities, Amaral sought to humanize her subjects and rejected the
assertion that only a mix of poverty, violence, and action-adventure would
sell.[44] And, while the gesture to humanize poor subjects has been frequently
translated into a bildungsroman format (*Central do Brasil, Cidade de Deus,*
and *Cidade dos Homens* are three examples), Amaral avoided the tendency
to cultivate pathos via a coming-of-age story focused on one individual. In
contrast, Amaral's can be seen as a collective-development story that brings
into view the alliances between members of the same community and a celebration of connections with transnational Afro-diasporic communities as
evidenced in the adoption of hip-hop musical rhythms and aesthetic styles
(Bob Marley t-shirts, braided hair, sideways-worn visors, and so on).

Although *Antônia* was able to take advantage of all the technical polish
afforded a TV Globo–backed production, Denise Garcia's independently produced documentary *Sou Feia Mas Tô Na Moda* offers an interesting point of
comparison in that it seems to embrace its (relatively) poor technical quality and unpolished structure. Focusing on the participation of women in
Rio de Janeiro's funk scene, a style of music still largely seen as a marginal
musical mode due in part to its sexually explicit and sometimes demeaning
lyrics, it seems wholly appropriate to embrace this technical "ugliness" as a
celebration of an excluded but make-do spirit that prevails in Rio de Janeiro's
poor neighborhoods. Not only does the film offer a class-differentiated view
of progressive femininity, it also illustrates how funk music has become a
feminist outlet for these women.

Similar to Murat's *Maré*, representations of the favela space in *Antônia* and
Sou Feia reject the "cosmetics of hunger" employed elsewhere in Retomada-
era Brazilian cinema[45] in favor of an aesthetics of the quotidian in which the
favela space is shot (primarily) in daylight; greater focus is paid to the daily
life of community residents whose activities are not overlaid with special
effects (such as nondiegetic music or rigged explosive devices intended to
mimic gunfire). Notably, in *Sou Feia, funkeira* star Denise da Injeção redefines
her favela community Cidade de Deus as a tranquil and creative space as she
leads a group of (mostly male) friends and neighbors through (relatively) tidy

streets, narrating the history of male-dominated carioca funk and taking intermittent breaks wherein local residents show off their rhythmic talent and verbal wit. She is as much an owner of the history of funk as any of her male colleagues. Notwithstanding the marked aesthetic differences between *Antônia* and *Sou Feia*, both can be equally praised for acknowledging the presence of young women in Brazil's musical subcultures.

The films discussed here make an overt gesture to demarginalize their young female subjects within the spaces of their poor urban communities. Be it by way of a slow-pan tilt shot down into favela where we see Jessica riding her bike through favela streets in *Sonhos Roubados*, the stretching salutations of Mayah on the rooftop of her home against the sprawling backdrop of São Paulo in *Antônia*, the tightly-framed conversations with *funkeira* women in *Sou Feia* who comment on gender stereotypes, or even shots of a pregnant Edilene shopping for baby clothes in *Meninas*, each film cinematographically establishes young female figures as vital members of their communities while offering unique explorations of the world(s) of girls and young women in Brazil.

Conclusion

In addition to recent efforts by President Rousseff to bring attention to Brazilian women artists, the year 2004 marked a watershed moment in contemporary Brazilian women's filmmaking. Coinciding with the declaration of 2004 as the Year of the Brazilian Woman and Rio de Janeiro's holding a special summit on women of the Mercosul/Mercosur, the first edition of the Femina International Festival of Women's Cinema (Festival Internacional de Cinema Feminino) took place. By its eighth edition (in 2011), the Femina Festival has become a premier mobilizer for women's filmmaking, establishing connections between Brazilian women's filmmaking and the rest of Latin America while also positioning Latin American women's filmmaking within a larger framework of world cinema. With recent financial support from the United Nations, the Brazilian Ministry of Culture, and major corporations, it is highly likely that the festival will continue to be one of the most important venues for showcasing and promoting Latin American women's filmmaking. As venues for wide public exhibition, film festivals help solidify the presence of women filmmakers and serve as opportunities to interact with other film professionals, develop liasions for funding opportunities, and allow a point of contact for distribution firms to potentially "pick up" women's films for national and international distribution. What is more, such film festivals are vitally important for drawing attention to women's works that may otherwise be overlooked or works that may markedly diverge from mainstream, commercial cinema. In addition to the efflorescence of women's filmmaking in Brazil—such that it is difficult to keep an accurate "census" of directors—the fact that the Femina Festival has not only confirmed its presence but also diversified and formed links with other international women's film festivals (such as the Films des Femmes festival in France) shows that women's film-making in Brazil (and Latin America more generally) is a dynamic, established category within world cinema.

To summarize, in broad strokes, where Brazilian women's film practice stands today, one would quickly come to the conclusion that current women's film practice in Brazil continues and furthers past practices. As noted in chapter 5, contemporary Brazilian women's films regularly return to issues of gender and female sexuality but now from a postrevolution, postdictatorial perspective. As discussed in chapters 2 and 3, the groundbreaking filmmak-ers Ana Carolina and Tizuka Yamasaki developed feminist discourses around women's civil rights and female sexuality, proposed new visions of belonging in Brazilian society, and, despite their marked aesthetic differences, shared a goal in the late 1970s and early 1980s to counter a patriarchal authoritar-ian state. Similarities aside, Yamasaki notably expands the discussion of *brasilidade* by including Brazil's ethnic and racial "others." During the slow retraction of the military state during the 1970s and 1980s, Brazilian women filmmakers were at the helm of works that increasingly challenged practices of exclusion. As discussed in chapter 4, they produced films and videos that expanded perceptions of Brazilian womanhood, focused on the emerging political consciousness of disenfranchised women, and intervened in class-based demands for improved healthcare.

With regard to the issues raised by contemporary Brazilian women's film practice, one notes parallels to the overall trajectory of feminist ideology in recent decades. Throughout the 1990s and in recent years, one finds an increasingly intersectional approach whereby gender and female sexuality have been studied in conjunction with age, class, race, ethnicity, and other markers of power and social exclusion. The sociopolitical issues raised by women directors from the past find echo in current debates surrounding Bra-zilian women's filmmaking. Concerns raised in the 1970s regarding women's representation in the media continue to be hotly debated in the current con-text. One finds also a dedication to social, political, and cultural issues that affect women's lives (in other words, the feminization of poverty, abortion rights, domestic violence, the legal system, and so on). In this, we find that Brazilian women's film practice retains an impulse to use moving images as a way to denounce social inequality and fight for justice. Whereas Eunice Gutman (discussed in chapter 4) once stood virtually alone with her film on lesbianism in Brazil (*Segredos de Amor*, 1998/99), she is now joined by more directors (Verônia Guedes, Eloísa Fusca, Maria Angélica Lemos) who also address lesbian experience. In sum, discussion of "as múltiplas mulheres" (multiple women) in Brazil becomes richer daily.

As the area of Brazilian women's filmmaking receives increasing attention from academics, analysis of women's filmmaking in Brazil needs to further examine funding strategies women employ to make their films while also expanding its focus to include other arenas in film production, distribution, and exhibition in which women have been involved. In recent years, women have increased their presence behind the cameras in roles other than as directors. For instance, Elena Soarez wrote the screenplays for *Eu, Tu, Eles* (Andrucha Waddington, 2000), *Cidade dos Homens* (Paulo Morelli, 2004), *Redentor* (Cláudio Torres, 2004), and *Vida de Menina* (Helena Solberg, 2004). Similarly, Melanie Diamantas has penned numerous scripts for film and television, including those for films directed by José Joffily (*Olhos Azúis*, 2009), Marcos Bernstein (*O Outro Lado da Rua*, 2004), Mara Mourão (*Avassaladoras*, 2002), and Carla Camurati (*Carlota Joaquina, Princesa do Brasil*, 1995). It is also important to address the presence (or absence) of women who work at distribution firms. To what degree are they able to contribute to decisions made regarding the films that are picked up at festivals and then screened nationally and internationally?

Returning to the questions posed at the outset of this work regarding how Brazilian women's independent and alternative film and video reformulated sexual, cultural, and political citizenship in Brazil: it seems that the contemporary period in which Brazil has begun shedding its status as an economically "at-risk," underdeveloped country and has begun repositioning itself among other nations on the ascendant—namely the "BRIC" nations (Brazil, Russia, India, and China)—suggests that there is an opening for as well as a pressing need for a full range of voices to intervene in the development of new concepts of Brazilian cultural identity at home and abroad. Economic prosperity and international recognition will be joined by new challenges to full citizenship. It seems ever more imperative to consider those audiovisual works in Brazil that continue to reformulate gender, sexuality, race, ethnicity, and other markers of social inclusion/exclusion. In the 1970s and 1980s, a renewed concept of citizenship was a central concept around which social movements organized to bring about an end to the military dictatorship and establish a democratic government. Until significant sectors of Brazilian society are fully enfranchised (culturally, economically, and politically), the concept of citizenship will continue to be a central concept in multifaceted efforts to improve the quality of democracy and bring about a more inclusive Brazilian society.

Notes

Introduction

1. Rosalind Gill, *Gender and the Media* (Malden, Mass.: Polity, 2007), 40.

2. See for example, Randal Johnson and Robert Stam, eds., *Brazilian Cinema* (New York: Columbia University Press, 1995); Ismail Xavier, *Allegories of Underdevelopment: Aesthetics and Politics in Modern Brazilian Cinema* (Minneapolis: University of Minnesota Press, 1997); and Randal Johnson, *The Film Industry in Brazil: Culture and the State* (Pittsburgh: University of Pittsburgh Press, 1987).

3. Elice Munerato and Maria Helena Darcy de Oliveira, "When Women Film," in *Brazilian Cinema*, eds. Randal Johnson and Robert Stam (New York: Columbia University Press, 1995), 340–50.

4. Shortly after this date, the studio was renamed Brasil Vita Filmes. Ana Pessoa, *Carmen Santos: O cinema dos anos 20* (Rio de Janeiro: Aeroplano, 2002), 163, 173.

5. Indeed, this is an area of inquiry in Brazilian Film Studies that merits a study of its own.

6. Heloisa Buarque de Hollanda, ed., *Quase catálogo: Realizadoras de cinema no Brasil (1930/1988)* (Rio de Janeiro: CIEC, 1987), 8.

7. Ibid., 9.

8. Amélia Cohn, "A questão social no Brasil: A difícil construção da cidadania," in *Viagem incompleta: A experiência brasileira: 1500–2000*, ed. Carlos Guilherme Mota (São Paulo: SENAC, 2000), 389–92.

9. Evelina Dagnino, "Culture, Citizenship and Democracy: Changing Discourses and Practices of the Latin American Left," in *Culture of Politics, Politics of Culture: Re-visioning Latin American Social Movements*, eds. Sonia Alvarez, Evelina Dagnino, and Arturo Escobar (Boulder: Westview, 1998), 48.

10. For a thorough historical account of the women's movements in Brazil, see

Sonia M. Alvarez, *Engendering Democracy in Brazil: Women's Movements in Transition Politics* (Princeton, N.J.: Princeton University Press, 1990).

11. See T. H. Marshall, *Citizenship and Social Class, and Other Essays* (Cambridge: Cambridge University Press, 1950), 1–24.

12. See Margaret Somers, "Citizenship and the Place of the Public Sphere: Law, Community, and Political Culture in the Transition to Democracy," *American Sociological Review* 58, no. 5 (1993): 587–620.

13. Nira Yuval-Davis, "Women, Citizenship and Difference," *Feminist Review* 57 (1997): 6.

14. Paul Thompson, *The Voice of the Past: Oral History* (New York: Oxford University Press, 2000), 1–24.

15. The director's full name is Ana Carolina Teixeira Soares, but she has signed her film works as "Ana Carolina," dropping her surnames.

Chapter 1. Brazilian Women's Filmmaking and the State during the 1970s and 1980s

1. Randal Johnson and Robert Stam, *Brazilian Cinema*, 340.

2. Paul Thompson, *The Voice of the Past: Oral History* (New York: Oxford University Press, 2000), 1–24.

3. GEICINE stands for Grupo Executivo da Indústria Cinematográfica, or the Executive Group for the Cinema Industry.

4. José Mário Ortiz Ramos, *Cinema, estado, e lutas culturais* (Rio de Janeiro: Paz e Terra, 1983), 19–23.

5. Helena Solberg, interview by author, tape recording, Rio de Janeiro, Brazil, November 27, 2001.

6. Randal Johnson, *Film Industry*, 132.

7. Ibid., 114–19, 121–23.

8. Numbers drawn from Hollanda, ed., *Quase catálogo*.

9. Suzana Amaral, interview by author, tape recording, São Paulo, Brazil, November 14, 2001, and Helena Solberg, interview by author, tape recording, Rio de Janeiro, Brazil, November 27, 2001.

10. Tereza Trautman, interview by author, tape recording, Rio de Janeiro, Brazil, November 29, 2001.

11. Tata Amaral, interview by author, tape recording, São Paulo, Brazil, November 13, 2001.

12. For example, at this time, the news segment Globo Repórter was filmed on 35 mm film stock and then edited to show on television.

13. Sandra Werneck, interview by author, tape recording, Rio de Janeiro, Brazil, July 16, 2002.

14. Julia Lesage, "Women Make Media: Three Modes of Production," in *The Social Documentary in Latin America*, ed. Julianne Burton (Pittsburgh: University of Pittsburgh Press, 1990), 315–47.

15. Werneck, interview, November 13, 2001.

16. Ana Maria Magalhães, interview by author, tape recording, Rio de Janeiro, Brazil, November 28, 2001.

17. Ana Carolina recalls that there were approximately four female students in a group of about thirty when she studied at the Escola de São Luiz in São Paulo starting in 1966. Note that she is unclear during the interview when the school closed and when she stopped studying there. In contrast, Tizuka Yamasaki recalls one other female student when she studied in Brasília and then in Rio de Janeiro. Ana Carolina Teixeira Soares, interview by author, tape recording, Rio de Janeiro, Brazil, August 26, 2005; Tizuka Yamasaki, interview by author, tape recording, São Paulo, Brazil, August 21, 2005.

18. Tizuka Yamasaki, interview by author, tape recording, São Paulo, Brazil, August 21, 2005.

19. For a full account of the first years of Embrafilme's existence and the direction of its programs, see Johnson, *Film Industry*, 137–70.

20. These numbers are drawn from Hollanda, ed., *Quase catálogo*.

21. Ibid.

22. Ana Carolina, interview by author, tape recording, Rio de Janeiro, Brazil, August 26, 2005.

23. Hollanda, *Quase Catálogo*.

24. Johnson, *Film Industry*, 167–70.

25. Tereza Trautman, interview by author, tape recording, Rio de Janeiro, Brazil, November 29, 2001.

26. Ibid.

27. Ibid.

28. Ibid.

29. Ibid.

30. Although in a poor state of preservation, a copy of the film is available in the film archives of the FUNARTE in Rio de Janeiro.

31. Tereza Trautman, interview by author, tape recording, Rio de Janeiro, Brazil, November 29, 2001.

32. For a more nuanced discussion of the film industry at this time in Brazil, see Johnson, *Film Industry*, 142–63.

33. Eu, quando chego no cinema, os cineastas do Cinema Novo já estavam estabelecidos, consolidados. E já tinham criado uma estrategia de produção que a gente absorveu inteiramente. Este tipo de produção barata de muita gente no mesmo filme, muitas pessoas—você consegue a camera, depois você consegue o som, depois você consegue o laboratório. Não sei o quê. Um dá um dinheirinho. Outro dá um dinheirinho. Um dinheirinho. Isso ahi, eu assimilei completamente. A diferença é que quando eu chego na longametragem em 74 ou 75, a Embrafilme já está funcionando, já está existindo. E eu com o primeiro ficção, parto para fazer com a Embrafilme—que é uma mudança substancial do Cinema Novo. Eu sou fil-

hote do Cinema Novo. Eu não sou representante do Cinema Novo legítimo. Quando eu chego já estão crescidos. E os filhotes, os primeiros filhotes do Cinema Novo, que eu estou incluida, todos eles foram correndo para a Embrafilme. Ana Carolina Teixeira Soares, interview by author, tape recording, Rio de Janeiro, Brazil, August 26, 2005.

34. Tizuka Yamasaki, interview by author, tape recording, São Paulo, Brazil, August 21, 2005.

35. It is interesting to hear Yamasaki describe her experience as working *inside* and *outside* Embrafilme. Her comments reveal awareness that the film industry was developed such that there was an imagined structure where one could be positioned inside or outside the state-sponsored system of film financing.

36. Tizuka Yamasaki, interview by author, tape recording, São Paulo, Brazil, August 21, 2005.

37. Johnson notes that three films were not coproduced by Embrafilme. They are Nelson Pereira dos Santos's *Estrada da Vida* (Road of Life, 1980); Rui Guerra's *A Queda* (The Fall, 1978); and Arnaldo Jabor's *Eu Te Amo* (I Love You, 1981). Johnson, *Film Industry*, 150, 161.

38. Gustavo Dahl, "Embrafilme: Present Problems and Future Possibilities," in Johnson and Stam, *Brazilian Cinema*, 106.

39. Randal Johnson, "The Rise and Fall of Brazilian Cinema, 1960–1990," in Johnson and Stam, *Brazilian Cinema*, 369, 384n10.

40. Murat had broken into English. Lúcia Murat, interview by author, tape recording, Rio de Janeiro, Brazil, July 10, 2002.

41. Ibid.

42. "Eu brinco muito, eu falo assim, que demorou muito o Cinema Novo me aceitar, me dar carteirinha como cineasta. Eu fiz um filme mas isso não deu. Eu sou cria do Cinema Novo." Tizuka Yamasaki, interview by author, tape recording, São Paulo, Brazil, August 21, 2005.

43. "Eu não fui chamada pelo poder do cinema brasileiro, o que foi durante muitos anos, nas mãos do Cinema Novo. O Cinema Novo nunca me admitiu no grupo. [. . .] A gente nunca, nunca foi bem recebida. Durante muitos anos, a gente não, eu não fiz parte do poder do cinema brasileiro. A minha atividade sempre foi isolada, paralela, porque queria saber o que estava acontecendo." Ibid.

44. "Só tinha com a Embrafilme com o *Mar de Rosas*, que teve Embrafilme mais quatro produtores asociados, um com equipamento, outro com laboratório, tudo, como um grupo de gente." Ana Carolina Teixeira Soares, interview by author, tape recording, Rio de Janeiro, Brazil, August 26, 2006.

45. Acho que a Embrafilme foi uma criação extraordinária com um percentual de perversão muito grande. Porque ao mesmo tempo que ela vem para somar, para unir cineastas e dar guarita, ela vem com uma coisa muito perversa porque ela começa a eleger, 'Você sim, ele não. Você sim, ele não. Você sim, ele não.' Quál é o *darling* da Embrafilme? Ahí, você é o *darling* da Embrafilme e você tem o maldito

que está fora da Embrafilme. Não houve uma correção de rota na Embrafilme. Ela não precisava de ser demolida da maneira que foi. Ela foi demolida muito rápida e com muita raiva. Alguma coisa está estranho nisso. Ela passou a representar uma coisa madrastra, uma mãe perversa, que alimentava uns e matava outros. Isso é complicado. Isso foi a ausência total de política de cinema. Ibid.

46. Tata Amaral, interview by author, tape recording, São Paulo, Brazil, November 13, 2001.

47. *Ibid.*

48. Eunice Gutman, interview by author, tape recording, Rio de Janeiro, Brazil, August 28, 2005.

49. As with other compulsory exhibition programs, there were great tensions between exhibitors, producers, and the state such that the program was made unviable. See Johnson, "Rise and Fall," 376–78.

50. Eunice Gutman, interview by author, tape recording, Rio de Janeiro, Brazil, August 28, 2005.

51. Clearly this advantage was limited to those who lived and/or worked in the southern regions of the country.

52. A gente estava muito mais em contato do que hoje. A classe cinematográfica hoje está tudo dispersa. O grande golpe, um dos grandes golpes no cinema, foi o desaparecimento da Embrafilme. [. . .] Então a gente tinha uma vida muito ativa, a classe cinematográfica, porque a gente tinha uma representação nos congressos. Eu não estou dizendo que essa representação hoje não existe. Existe mas não da mesma forma. Eunice Gutman, interview by author, tape recording, Rio de Janeiro, Brazil, August 28, 2005.

53. Sandra Werneck, interview by author, tape recording, Rio de Janeiro, Brazil, July 16, 2002.

54. Ibid.

55. Ana Maria Magalhães states that she and other women she worked with wanted access to this form of communication, which had been dominated by men. Ana Maria Magalhães, interview by author, tape recording, Rio de Janeiro, Brazil, November 28, 2001.

56. Tizuka Yamasaki, interview by author, tape recording, São Paulo, Brazil, August 21, 2005.

57. Johnson, *Film Industry*, 161.

58. Johnson and Stam, *Brazilian Cinema*, 32–40, 47.

59. Eu tive na verdade o privilegio de ter dois, dois grandes cineastas na minha formação. Mas ao mesmo tempo essa convivência muito próxima aos dois me deixou muito frustrada, muito decepcionada. Os discursos do Cinema Novo eram maravilhosos, em termos de política, em termos de questões socias, em termos de pensar sobre o Brasil. Mas eles eram muito, muito machistas no cotidiano da vida deles. No trabalho não, mas é uma observação deles na familia, entre eles. Você pode ver o Cinema Novo. Não tem nenhuma mulher. Então isso foi uma observação. Nessa

época eu ainda não tinha muita noção das coisas. Mais tarde sim. Tizuka Yamasaki, interview by author, tape recording, São Paulo, Brazil, August 21, 2005.

60. Ismail Xavier, *Allegories of Underdevelopment*, 5.

61. Ana Carolina Teixeira Soares, interview by author, tape recording, Rio de Janeiro, Brazil, August 26, 2005.

62. Sandra Werneck also states that she proposes a cinema of emotion. I take up this issue again in chapter 3 in my discussion of the films by Yamasaki.

63. Tizuka Yamasaki, interview by author, tape recording, São Paulo, Brazil, August 21, 2005.

64. "Muitas vezes a gente vive no mundo de homens e esses valores são os conhecidos. AemoÇão de feminino não é conhecido publicamente. Ela não é posta na tela. Quando você faz uma coisa tão forte do ponto de vista do feminino, e põe isso na tela, é realmente supreendente para os homens também. É uma nova visão das coisas. É a revelaçã o de alguma coisa que estava lá—que nada de aquilo é novedade, mas que nunca foi visto." Tata Amaral, interview by author, tape recording, São Paolo, Brazil, November 13, 2001.

65. "Tive sempre experiências de censura. *Pantanal* foi. *Guerra do Paraguai* foi. *Getúlio* foi. *Mar de Rosas* foi. *Das Tripas* foi. Eu tive realmente anos e anos. *Sonho de Valsa* não foi. A Abertura já tinha chegado. Então a censura acabou com *Das Tripas*. Censura mesmo." Ana Carolina, interview by author, tape recording, Rio de Janeiro, Brazil, August 26, 2005.

66. Ibid.

67. Ibid.

68. Eu tive que assinar um termo de responsabilidade no *Das Tripas* e botar um letreiro antes. Eu achei ótimo. Eu falei, 'isso eu topo. Isso ahi, eu topo. Ou isso, nada.' [O letreiro falou] que era um filme delirante, que não tratava nenhuma realidade e que eu assumia totalmente a responsabilidade por aquela loucura. Eu falei ótimo. Eu achei legal porque é tão louco alguem fazer isso—uma pessoa fazer isso com a outra. Tão louco que eu falei que é bom que fique visível. Isso era o governo. Ahi, eu assinei. Botei esse texto na frente assinado por mim. Era como se eu me prometesse nunca mais falar bobagem. Como se tudo fosse uma loucura minha. Não existe, isso não existe. Era o governo militar. Eu achei, 'é claro que isso, como que isso não existe, cara!' Ibid.

69. Portugal, at the time of Ana Carolina's visit, had recently begun its own return to democracy after the protracted authoritarian, right-wing regime led by António de Oliveira Salazar (1932–74).

70. Johnson and Stam, *Brazilian Cinema*, 373–74.

71. Ibid.

72. Ana Carolina Teixeira Soares, interview by author, tape recording, Rio de Janeiro, Brazil, August 26, 2005.

73. Tereza Trautman, interview by author, tape recording, Rio de Janeiro, Brazil, November 29, 2001.

74. Ibid.

75. Ana Maria Magalhães, interview by author, tape recording, Rio de Janeiro, Brazil, November 28, 2001.

76. "[Nesse contexto] muitas injustiças são cometidas contra os artistas. Entre eles, entre si. Tem um artista com mais estatus. Tem outro com menos. Isso tudo é muito ligado ao poder econômico. [. . .] Tem uma censura econômica do poder aliada ápropria clase e isso é uma coisa muito triste." Ibid.

77. Ibid.

78. Ibid.

79. Sandra Werneck, interview by author, tape recording, Rio de Janeiro, Brazil July 16, 2002.

80. Lúcia Murat, interview by author, tape recording, Rio de Janeiro, Brazil, November 27, 2001.

81. Ibid.

82. Ana Carolina Teixeira Soares, interview by author, tape recording, Rio de Janeiro, Brazil, August 26, 2005. Os documentários já tem uma preocupação grande de "o que é isto aqui?" Mas com os documentários, eu ainda estava preocupada em ser uma intelectual que analisa as questões. Eu estava falível de grandes erros na condição de socióloga, que eu não sou. Mas quando eu parti para a ficção, abandonei completamente o salto alto e falei, "vou descrever a minha preocupação, o que estou sentindo na discussão da minha inserção á identidade brasileira, do meu mal-estar de ser ou não ser brasileiro."

83. In her interview Yamasaki thinks that, ironically, auteur filmmaking was likely subsidized by the success of *pornochanchadas*. Yamasaki, interview by author, tape recording, São Paulo, Brazil, August 21, 2005.

84. The filmmaker Sívlio Tendler addresses the importance of those films that are culturally and socially significant—and which may not be commercially viable—in his master's thesis "Cinema e Estado: Em Defesa do Miúra," (Pontífica Universidade Católica, Rio de Janeiro, 1982).

85. "O espaço da mulher era restrito. O espaço como produtora e como diretora, claro. Como técnica, a gente já tinha conseguido algumas vitórias. Não é isso. Mas quando chegar á área da produção e á direção era mais complicado." Eunice Gutman, interview by author, tape recording, Rio de Janeiro, Brazil, August 28, 2005).

86. "Nos anos 70, na é poca em que eu fiz esse filme, não era tão comum a mulher que estava dirigindo filmes. . . . Tinha umas pessoas fazendo filmes. Mas não era, assim, muito comum." Ana Maria Magalhães, interview by author, tape recording, Rio de Janeiro, Brazil, November 28, 2001.

87. " . . . já naquela época estavam começando a invadir o cinema pelo desempenho do equipe. Elas deixavam de ser só *script girl*—porque só tinha *script girl*—e elas começavam a deixar de fazer só isso para trabalhar um pouco em produção, assistente de direção, trabalhar um pouco aqui, um pouco ali. E isso foi formando uma geração de cineastas." Ibid.

88. Ibid.

89. Acho que a sociedade brasileira absorveu a liberação feminina e se manifestando dessa forma. Porque a forma do audiovisual, a forma de expressão do audiovisual era até então uma forma iminentemente masculina de expressão, com raras exceções. . . . A partir da liberação feminina e de uma produção grande, a cinematográfica no Brasil na época, nos anos 70, a produção é grande, juntou uma coisa com a outra e eu acho que a mulher começou a ocupar esse espaço na produção de filmes. Mais, equipes, em todas as áreas. E eu acho que essa é uma resposta das mulheres brasileiras. E das mulheres que sempre, em relação a essa liberação. Quer dizer, é uma resposta prática. Não foi uma coisa coordenada. Não foi uma coisa pensada. Não foi um movimento formal. Ibid.

90. Tata Amaral sees this not as a division that she engages with but rather as a gesture that film scholars take in order to critique films. Sandra Werneck asserts that women do not have any special talents. Tata Amaral, interview by author, tape recording, São Paulo, Brazil, November 13, 2001. Sandra Werneck, interviewed by author, tape recording, Rio de Janeiro, Brazil, July 16, 2002.

91. Ana Carolina Teixeira Soares, interview by author, tape recording, Rio de Janeiro, Brazil, August 26, 2005.

92. Tizuka Yamasaki, interview by author, tape recording, São Paulo, Brazil, August 21, 2005.

93. Eunice Gutman, interview by author, tape recording, Rio de Janeiro, Brazil, August 27, 2005.

94. My thanks to Zuzana Pick for pointing out this clarification.

95. "A linguagem cinematográfica é uma, que é uma técnica . . . como é que você usa um plano geral, como é que você usa uma *close*, como é que você usa um plano médio. Essa linguagem é única, é universal. Existe o filme de autor, existem várias tendências—mas dentro dessa linguagem. Agora, lógicamente, se você vai interpretar uma história, você vai interprear de acordo com a educação que você recebeu. Então tudo vem de ahi." Eunice Gutman, interview by author, tape recording, Rio de Janeiro, Brazil, August 27, 2005.

96. Ana Maria Magalhães, interview by author, tape recording, Rio de Janeiro, Brazil, November 28, 2001.

97. Tetê Moraes, interview by author, tape recording, Rio de Janeiro, Brazil, July 11, 2002.

98. Arquidiocese de São Paulo, *Brasil: Nunca Mais* (Petrópolis: Vozes, 1985).

99. Quase entrei na AP, a Ação Popular. Lutei. Rodopiei pelo partido comunista e detestei. Odiei as pessoas. Eu sai sempre muito mal disposta com as pessoas. E todos os, naquela época, o comportamento masculino e feminino era muito diferente do que é hoje. Os homens do partido comunista eram uma coisa horrorosa. Os companheiros. Os compaheiros—eles tinham uma discriminação [com] a mulher que, em fim. [. . .] Eles eram homens, melhores do que nós. Eles eram homens capazes. Nós éramos apenas mulheres. Nas reuniões eles saíram. Eles foram para outro lugar. Cineasta inclusive! Mandava eu sair para fazer reunião. Quase entrei

na Ação Popular. Não entrei. Eu participei de uma militância barra pesada da VPR, Vanguarda Popular Revolucionária. Logo sai porque em 1970 e 71 fui presa duas vezes. Então, falei, vou parar com esse negócio. Depois assisti a formação do PT (o Partido dos Trabalhadores). [. . .] Mas ahi, eu fiz filmes muito políticos mas eu não participei en nenhum partido político. [. . .] A minha militância foi no cinema. Nem foi no feminismo, nem foi nos partidos da esquerda. Foi no cinema. Foi a expressão cultural. Ana Carolina Teixeira Soares, interview by author, tape recording, Rio de Janeiro, Brazil, August 26, 2005.

100. Tizuka Yamasaki, interview by author, tape recording, São Paulo, Brazil, August 21, 2005.

101. Ibid.

102. Johnson, *Film Industry*, 171–97.

103. The extinction of Embrafilme meant that a total of three films were released in 1992, compared to an average of eighty during Embrafilme's existence. Many films that had been completed did not find distribution. Denise Costa Lopes, "Cinema Brasileiro pós-Collor," 31–32.

104. Susana Schild, "Um Gênero em transição," *Cinemais* 9 (1998): 124–25.

105. This percentage, intended to be used for illustrative purposes, is arrived at by consulting print published and online resources, noting the number of films directed or co-directed by a Brazilian woman and dividing by the total estimated number of films produced in Brazil during the defined time period. This number does not include films in preproduction or postproduction in 2009 and extends only to June of that year.

106. Tizuka Yamasaki, interview by author, tape recording, São Paulo, Brazil, August 21, 2005.

Chapter 2. Contesting the Boundaries of Belonging in the Films of Ana Carolina Teixeira Soares

1. Vivian Schelling, "Ana Carolina Teixeira: Audacity in the Cinema," *Index on Censorship* 14, no. 5 (1985): 60.

2. *Visible Nations O Estado de São Paulo* (November 6, 1994).

3. Flávio Cândido, "A trilogina de Ana Carolina em Niterói," *O Fluminense* September 29, 1989.

4. The DOI and the CODI were separate but related organizations within the military regime's repressive apparatus and answered to the SNI (Serviço Nacional de Informação [National Information Service]), which took on the responsibility of fighting "the enemy within." For further information on the DOI, the CODI, and other agencies cited as practitioners of torture in Brazil, see Maria Helena Moreira Alves, *State and Opposition in Military Brazil* (Austin: University of Texas Press, 1985), 119–31.

5. Marcos Napolitano, *Cultura e poder no Brasil contemporâneo (1977–1984)* (Curitiba: Juruá, 2003), 59.

6. By second-wave feminism, I refer to the rise in feminist activism in the 1960s. The second-wave contrasts with a period of first-wave feminism, taking place in the early years of the twentieth century. While the period of first-wave feminism sought to eliminate official obstacles to women's liberation (suffrage), the period of second-wave feminism generally sought to expand women's liberation, including increased access to education, healthcare, and greater career opportunities.

7. Florisa Verucci discusses the relationship between women and their defined civil, constitutional, and penal rights (or lack thereof) in her text *A Mulher e o direito* (São Paulo: Nobel, 1987), 39–97.

8. For a complete discussion of "crimes of passion," in which men kill their female partners, see Mariza Corrêa, *Os crimes da paixão* (São Paulo: Brasiliense, 1981). For a discussion of the "legitimate defense of *honra*" as justification for these violent crimes against women, see Danielle Ardaillon and Guita Grin Derbert, *Quando a vítima é mulher. Análise de julgamentos de crimes de estupro, espancamento e homicídios* (Brasília: CNDM, 1987) as well as Wânia Pasinato Izumino, *Justiça e violência contra a mulher: O papel do sistema judiciário na solução dos conflitos de gênero* (São Paulo: Annablume, FAPESP, 1998). For more information on the social importance of women's virginity, see Sueann Caulfield, *In Defense of Honor: Sexual Morality, Modernity, and Nation in Early-Twentieth-Century Brazil* (Durham: Duke University Press, 2000).

9. Alvarez, *Engendering Democracy*, 121.

10. Ibid., 96.

11. Ibid., 113–15.

12. It is interesting to note that a year prior to her role in Trautman's film, Glória was cast in the *pornochanchadas* (light-porn comedies) *A Viúva Virgem* (The Virgin Widow, directed by Pedro Carlos Rovai) and *Eu Transo, Ela Transa* (I Have Sex, She Has Sex, directed by Pedro Camargo).

13. Ismael Xavier, "The Humiliation of the Father: Melodrama and Cinema Novo's Critique of Conservative Modernization," in *Latin American Melodrama: Passion, Pathos, and Entertainment*, ed. Darlene J. Sadlier (Urbana: University of Illinois Press, 2009), 92.

14. Xavier, "Humiliation of the Father," 78.

15. Xavier, *Allegories of Underdevelopment*, 10, 18–21, 216, 219; see also Robert Stam, "On the Margins: Brazilian Avant-Garde Cinema," In Johnson and Stam, *Brazilian Cinema*, 306–27.

16. *Jornal da Tarde* São Paulo, September 25, 1978; Sérgio Habib, "Um filme incômodo," *Jornal de Brasília*, August 2, 1978: "Cinema"; Heloisa Buarque de Hollanda, "Leia o filme e veja," *Jornal do Brasil*, December 11, 1982, referring to the film *Das Tripas Coração*.

17. David Laderman, *Driving Visions: Exploring the Road Movie* (Austin: University of Texas Press, 2002), 1–2.

18. Keila Grinberg, *Código civil e cidadania* (Rio de Janeiro: Jorge Zahara, 2001), 77.

19. Ibid., 45.

20. For a comparative analysis of the struggle for legalizing divorce during military dictatorships, see Mala Htun, *Sex and the State: Abortion, Divorce, and the Family under Latin American Dictatorships and Democracies* (New York: Cambridge University Press, 2003), 78–112.

21. Xavier, *Allegories of Underdevelopment*, 16–28.

22. Ibid., 235–46.

23. Ibid., 4.

24. Ibid., 246–54.

25. Several plays and novels by Nelson Rodrigues have been adapted to film, including *O Beijo no Asfalto* (directed by Bruno Barreto, 1980), *Álbum de Família* (directed by Braz Chediak, 1981), and *Engraçadinha* (directed by Haroldo Marinho Barbosa, 1981).

26. Jill Scott, *Electra after Freud: Myth and Culture* (Cornell University Press, 2005), 8.

27. Catherine L. Benamou first notes the significance of the VW vehicle in her essay "Mar de Rosas," in *South American Cinema: A Critical Filmography, 1915–1994*, ed. Timothy Barnard and Peter Rist (Austin: University of Texas Press, 1998), 183–84.

28. Regarding the employ of ironic juxtapositions in Marginal Cinema, see Xavier, *Allegories of Underdevelopment*, 183–231.

29. Marilena Chauí, *Cultura e democracia: O discurso competente e outras falas* (São Paulo: Cortez, 2003), 3–7.

30. Ibid., 11–12.

31. See, for example, the discussion of psychosocial expression of national power in the *Doutrina básica* (Rio de Janeiro: Escola Superior de Guerra, 1979), 143–55, 185–95.

32. See, for example, E. Ann Kaplan, "The Realist Debate in the Feminist Film: A Historical Overview of Theories and Strategies in Realism and the Avant-Garde Theory Film (1971–81)," in E. Ann Kaplan, *Women and Film: Both Sides of the Camera* (New York: Methuen, 1983), 125–41.

33. Süssekind, *Literatura e vida literária*, 27.

34. Robin Wood, *Hollywood from Vietnam to Reagan*, 227–28.

35. For a discussion of how Brecht's theories have influenced cinema (including feminist film theory, women's cinema, and Latin American cinema), see, for example: Barton Byg, "Brecht, New Waves, and Political Modernism in Cinema," in *A Bertolt Brecht Reference Companion*, ed. Siegfried Mews, (Westport, Conn.: Greenwood Press, 1997), 220–37; Marc Silberman, "Brecht and Film," in Mews, *Brecht Reference Companion*, 197–219; Thomas Elsaesser, "From Anti-Illusionism to Hyper-Realism: Bertolt Brecht and Contemporary Film," in *Re-interpreting Brecht: His Influence on Contemporary Drama and Film*, eds. Pia Kleber and Colin Visser, (New York: Cambridge University Press, 1990), 170–85; Marina Pianca, "Brecht in Latin America: Theater Bearing Witness," in Mews, *Brecht Reference Companion*,

356–78; and Renate Möhrmann, "The Influence of Brecht on Women's Cinema in West Germany," in *Re-Interpreting Brecht*, 161–69.

36. See, for example, Ismail Xavier's discussion of estrangement effects in *Allegories of Underdevelopment*, 228–31.

37. Richard Grimm, "Alienation in Context: On the Theory and Practice of Brechtian Theater," in Mews, *Brecht Reference Companion*, 40–43.

38. Regarding this, see Stam, *Brazilian Cinema*, 310–11.

39. For more on this, see Xavier, *Allegories of Underdevelopment*, 254–60.

40. Noëlle McAfee, *Habermas, Kristeva and Citizenship* (Ithaca, N.Y.: Cornell University Press, 2000), 187.

41. Regarding this, see Ismail Xavier's argument regarding the teleology of Cinema Novo and Marginal Cinema's antiteleological position in *Allegories of Underdevelopment*, 192–200.

42. Laura Podaslky, "Fulfilling Fantasies, Diverting Pleasures: Ana Carolina and *Das Tripas Coração*," In *Visible Nations: Latin American Cinema and Video*, ed. Chon A. Noriega (Minneapolis: University of Minnesota Press, 2000), 115–29.

43. Stam, "On the Margins," in Johnson and Stam, *Brazilian Cinema*, 310–12.

44. Among many others, a few notable female artists whose work has been read as surrealist include Claude Cahun (France), Meret Oppenheim (Germany/Switzerland), Frida Kahlo (Mexico), Lenora Carrington (England), Kay Sage (USA), Remedio Varos (Spain), and Leila Ferraz (Brazil).

45. Raymond Spiteri and Donald LaCoss, eds., *Surrealism, Politics and Culture* (Burlington: Ashgate, 2003), 5.

46. Michael Richardson, *Surrealism and Cinema* (New York: BERG, 2006), 3–9.

47. Whitney Chadwick, ed. *Mirror Images: Women, Surrealism, and Self-Representation*. (Cambridge, Mass.: MIT Press, 1998), viii–ix.

48. Rosalind Krauss, *Bachelors* (Cambridge: MIT Press, 1990), 16–17.

49. Francine Masiello, "Women, State and Family in Latin American Literature of the 1920s," in *Women, Culture, and Politics in Latin America: Seminar on Feminism and Culture in Latin America*, compiled by the Seminar on Feminism and Culture in Latin America (Berkeley: University of California Press, 1990), 43.

50. Rudolf E. Kuenzli, "Surrealism and Misogyny," in *Surrealism and Women*, eds. Mary Ann Caws, Rudolf Kuenzli, and Gwen Raaberg (Cambridge: The MIT Press, 1993), 25.

51. Robert J. Belton, "Speaking with Forked Tongues: 'Male' Discourse in 'Female' Surrealism?" in Caws, Kuenzli, Raaberg, *Surrealism and Women*, 50–52.

52. "Alguma de vocês aqui conhece melhor da minha loucura do que eu mesmo? A loucura é a melhor maneira de se elogiar. Aqui hoje eu detono a minha loucura e vocês vão representá-la."

53. Whitney Chadwick notes that historical surrealist women embraced such antisocial behavior as a rejection of bourgeois values, (*Mirror Images*, 106–7).

54. Another important surrealist film that coincides here in a critique of religion,

repression of sexuality, and political authority is *La coquille et le clergyman* (The Seashell and the Clergyman, directed by Germaine Dulac, 1926).

55. Diane Richardson, "Heterosexuality and Social Theory," in *Theorising Heterosexuality: Telling it Straight*, ed. Diane Richardson (Buckingham/Philadelphia: Open University Press, 1996), 10–11.

56. David T. Evans, *Sexual Citizenship: The Material Construction of Sexualities* (London: Routledge, 1993), 9.

57. Silvia Oroz, *Melodrama: O cinema de lágrimas da América Latina* (Rio de Janeiro: FUNARTE, 1999), 46–47.

58. André Breton, "Exposition X . . ., Y . . .," in *Point du jour*, new revised and corrected edition (Paris: Gallimard, 1990), 58; André Breton, *What is Surrealism? Selected Writings*, ed. and intro. Franklin Rosemont (New York: Monad, 1978), 43, quoted in Johanna Malt, *Obscure Objects of Desire: Surrealism, Fetishism, and Politics* (Oxford: Oxford University Press, 2004), 23.

59. Malt, *Obscure Objects of Desire*, 21.

60. Whitney Chadwick, *Women Artists and the Surrealist Movement* (Boston: Little, Brown, 1985), 106.

61. It is noteworthy that the actress Cristina Pereira, who played Betinha in *Mar de Rosas* and the cleaning lady, Amindra, in *Das Tripas Coração* has a cameo appearance here in *Sonho de Valsa* during the party sequence.

62. This type of playful editing of images here is reminiscent of Méliés, whose celebration of the marvelous was in turn celebrated by the historical surrealists. Regarding this see Paul Hammond, ed. *The Shadow and its Shadow: Surrealist Writings on Cinema* (New York: Zoetrope, 1978).

63. The image of the black goat could also refer to a horned pagan deity celebrated in various cultural traditions and famously rendered in Francisco de Goya's painting *El sábado de las brujas* (Witches Sabbath, 1797–98).

Chapter 3. Rescreening the Past

1. Thomas Skidmore, *The Politics of Military Rule* (New York: Oxford University Press, 1988), 176–78, 183–88, 227–30.

2. Elizabeth Jelin, *State Repression and the Labors of Memory* (Minneapolis: University of Minnesota Press, 2003), xviii.

3. Ibid., 7.

4. Ibid., 1–2.

5. *Política Nacional de Cultura* (Brasil: MEC, 1975), 16.

6. Renato Ortiz, *Cultura Brasileira*, 90–95.

7. A few examples include books by Fernando Gabeira, Alfredo Sirkis, Gergório Bezerra, Mourão Filho, Hugo Abreo, Abelardo Jurema, and Reinaldo Guarany. Flora Süssekind, *Literatura e vida literária: Polêmicas, diários e retratos* (Rio de Janeiro: Jorge Zahar, 1985), 54.

8. Johnson, *Film Industry*, 117; Jean-Claude Bernardet notes that a special fund

was created in Embrafilme for historical films. See his essay "Qual é a história?" in *Anos 70: Ainda sob a tempestade*, ed. Aduato Novaes (Rio de Janeiro: SENAC Rio; Aeroplano, 2005), 327.

9. Robert Stam, João Luiz Viera, and Ismail Xavier, "The Shape of Brazilian Cinema in the Postmodern Age," in Johnson and Stam, *Brazilian Cinema*, 412–16.

10. Ibid.

11. Johnson, *Film Industry*, 159–60, 164.

12. Stam, Viera, and Xavier, "Shape of Brazilian Cinema," 412–15.

13. Randal Johnson, "The Romance-Reportagem and the Cinema: Babenco's *Lúcio Flávio* and *Pixote*" *Luso-Brazilian Review* 24, no. 2 (1987): 35–48.

14. For more on the history of state-sponsored censorship of films at this time, see Inimá Simões, *Roteiro da Intolerância: A censura cinematográfica no Brasil*. São Paulo: SENAC, 1999.

15. Ibid., 240–41. Prior to the censorship of this film, Tapajós's novel *Em câmera lenta* (1977), in which he discusses clandestine life as a member of armed resistance against the military regime, had been censored shortly after his release from prison.

16. Ana M. López, "Tears and Desire: Women and Melodrama in the 'Old' Mexican Cinema," in *Multiple Voices in Feminist Film Criticism*, eds. Diane Carson, Linda Dittmar, and Janice R. Welsch (Minneapolis: University of Minnesota Press, 1994), 258–59.

17. Cid Vasconcelos, "Women as Civilizers in 1940s Brazilian Cinema: Between Passion and the Nation," in *Latin American Melodrama: Passion, Pathos, and Entertainment*, ed. Darlene J. Sadlier (Urbana: University of Illinois Press, 2009), 64–76.

18. For more information on Cinema Novo and the use of allegory, see Xavier, *Allegories of Underdevelopment*.

19. See Hermann Herlinghaus, ed. *Narraciones anacrónicas de la modernidad: Melodrama e intermedialidad en América Latina* (Providencia, Santiago: Editorial Cuarto Propio, 2002).

20. Jesús Martín-Barbero, *Communication, Culture and Hegemony: From the Media to Mediation,* trans. Elizabeth Fox and Robert A. White (Newbury Park: SAGE, 1993), 225.

21. Simões, *Roteiro da Intolerância*, 230–36, 243–46.

22. Linda Williams "Melodrama Revisited," in *Refiguring American Film Genres: History and Theory*, ed. Nick Browne (Berkeley: University of California Press, 1998), 42–88.

23. See, for example, Ana M. López, "Tears and Desire," 147–63, and Sadlier, *Latin American Melodrama*, 1–15.

24. See, for example, Brooks, *The Melodramatic Imagination: Balzac, Henry James, Melodrama, and the Mode of Excess* (New Haven: Yale University Press, 1976); Brooks asserts that melodrama is a form that arises at the juncture of significant social upheaval where one finds breaks with previous systems of values.

25. Jelin, *State Repression*, 16.

26. Thanks to Catherine Benamou for sharing this observation.

27. Luis Trelles Plazaola, *Cine y mujer en América Latina: Directoras de largometrajes de ficción* (San Juan: Editorial de la Universidad de Puerto Rico, 1991), 275.

28. Darlene J. Sadlier, "Nelson Pereira dos Santos's *Cinema de lágrimas*," in *Latin American Melodrama: Passion, Pathos, and Entertainment* (Urbana: University of Illinois Press, 2009), 100.

29. Ibid., 108–9.

30. The Japanese government, interested in ridding itself of its poor, assisted in arranging for its citizens to work in the coffee plantations in the state of São Paulo in the early twentieth century. Regarding this history, see Jeffrey Lesser, *Negotiating National Identity: Immigrants, Minorities and the Struggle for Ethnicity in Brazil* (Durham, N.C.: Duke University Press, 1999).

31. My thanks to Zuzana Pick for offering this observation.

32. Jeffrey Lesser, "In Search of the Hyphen: Nikkei and the Struggle over Brazilian National Identity," in *New Worlds, New Lives: Globalization and People of Japanese Descent in the Americas and from Latin America in Japan*, eds. Lane Ryo Hirabayashi, Akemi Kikumura-Yano, and James A. Hirabayashi (Stanford: Stanford University Press, 2002), 37–58.

33. Regarding the participation of Japanese-Brazilians in the Brazilian film industry, see Jeffrey Lesser's "Beautiful Bodies and (Dis)appearing Identities: Contesting Images of Japanese-Brazilian Ethnicity, 1970–1980," in *Discontented Diaspora: Japanese Brazilians and the Meanings of Ethnic Militancy, 1960–1980* (Durham, N.C.: Duke University Press, 2007), 78–104.

34. During the first years of the military regime, a utopian vision of Brazil was promoted via a spectacular language (primarily on television), which was in turn subverted by the tropicalists who turned spectacular into a spectacle. See Süssekind, *Literatura e vida literária*, 14–15.

35. José Meirelles Passos, "A imigração vista por olhos puxados: Uma cineasta nissei filma a saga dos que fizeram esta América." *Isto É*, April 2, 1980: 62 (translated by the author).

36. Lesser, *Discontented Diaspora*, 66.

37. Ibid., 47–73.

38. Joan Ramón Resinas, "Introduction," in *Disremembering the Dictatorship: The Politics of Memory in the Spanish Transition to Democracy*, ed. Joan Ramón Resinas (Atlanta: Rodopi, 2000), 3.

39. Salvador Cardús i Ros, "Politics and the Invention of Memory: For a Sociology of the Transition to Democracy in Spain," in Resinas, *Disremembering the Dictatorship*, 23.

40. For a captivating history of Japanese and other immigrants to Brazil, see Lesser, *Negotiating National Identity*.

41. Maurice Halbwachs, *On Collective Memory* (Chicago: University of Chicago Press, 1992), 172, cited in Jelin, *State Repression*, 11.

42. Robert Stam, João Luiz Vieira, and Ismail Xavier, "The Shape of Brazilian Cinema in the Postmodern Age," in Johnson and Stam, *Brazilian Cinema*, 409–69.

43. Jeffrey Lesser, *Discontented Diaspora*, 67.

44. Ros, "Politics," 23.

45. Sadlier, "Introduction," 15.

46. "Eu sou cineasta. Dou á realidade uma interpretação poética, e conto as coisas do jeito que eu quiser. Você sai na rua e escolhe aquilo que quer ver. Eu saí na História do Brasil e escolhi uma ficção, mas uma ficção que me parece mais verdadeira que a de muitos livros de História." Tizuka Yamasaki quoted in Ney Gastal, "Para Tizuka, polêmica é a maior qualidade de 'Parahyba Mulher Macho,'" *Correio do Povo*, November 13, 1983. Especial, p. 9 (translated by the author).

47. Hayden White, *Tropics of Discourse: Essays in Cultural Criticism* (Baltimore: Johns Hopkins University Press, 1978), 85.

48. Jelin, *State Repression*, 59.

49. Stam, Vieira, and Xavier, "Shape of Brazilian Cinema," 423.

50. Wagner Pinheiro Pereira, "Guerra das imagens: Cinema e política nos governos de Adolf Hitler e Franklin Delano Roosevelt, 1933–1945" (master's thesis, Universidade de São Paulo, 2003), cited in Vasconcelos, "Women as Civilizers," in Sadlier, *Latin American Melodrama*, 65.

51. Ibid.

52. Similar to the *corrido* form in México, the *corrida* in Brazil is a popular musical ballad form that frequently treats themes of history, daily life of the poor, and legendary figures.

53. (Author's transcription and translation.)

> Pois, são essas pessoas
> que hoje estão conquistando
> a riqueza e o poder
> mas sem nunca jamais compreenderam
> os caminhos da história
> como são.
>
> Eles nunca entenderam a lição
> de quem sube
> nada contracorrente
> de que sempre arriscou
> um passa frente
> pisou sem ter medo do risco
> e empurrou na ladeira do futuro
> a carroça pesada do presente.

54. Pablo Pérez Rubio, *El cine melodramático* (Barcelona: Paidós, 2004), 40.

55. (Author's transcription and translation.)

Nos terremotos do drama
que abalava o pais
se enxergar a luz da chama
de Anayde Beiriz
pois da lições do passado
ficam exemplo guardado
fica rosto fica nome
é algo que permanece
que a memória não esquece.

56. Julianne Burton brings to light the intricate production process the crew of *Patriamada* undertook, adapting the fictional storyline to daily political developments in "Sing, the Beloved Country: An Interview with Tizuka Yamsaki on *Patriamada*," *Film Quarterly* 1, no. 41 (Fall 1982): 2–9. See also Burton's article "Transitional States: Creative Complicities with the Real in *Cabra Marcado Para Morrer: Vinte Anos Depois* [Man Marked to Die: Twenty Years Later] and *Patriamada* [Sing, the Beloved Country]," *Studies in Latin American Popular Culture* 7 (1988): 139–55.

57. For a history of TV Globo and its negotiations with the government, see Valério Cruz Brittos and César Ricardo Siqueira Bolaño, eds. *Rede Globo: 40 anos de poder e hegemonia*. São Paulo: Paulus, 2005.

58. Christine Gledhill, "The Melodramatic Field: An Investigation," in Christine Gledhill, *Home is Where the Heart Is: Studies in Melodrama and the Woman's Film* (London: British Film Institute, 1987), 30.

59. Mariana Baltar, "Weeping Reality: Melodramatic Imagination in Contemporary Brazilian Documentary," in Sadlier, *Latin American Melodrama*, 131.

60. Burton, "Transitional States," 140.

Chapter 4. Widening the Screen

1. For more on alternative media, its history and its politics, see Joshua D. Atkinson, *Alternative Media and Politics of Resistance* (New York: Peter Lang, 2010), Leah A. Lievrouw, *Alternative and Activist New Media* (Malden, Mass.: Polity, 2011), and Kate Coyer, Tony Dowmunt, and Alan Fountain, *The Alternative Media Handbook* (New York: Routledge, 2007).

2. Laura Mulvey, "Feminism, Film, and the Avant-Garde," *Framework* 10 (Spring 1979): 6–7.

3. See Luiz Fernando Santoro, *A imagem nas mãos: o vídeo popular no Brasil* (São Paulo: Summus, 1989).

4. For example, the Instituto Brasileiro do Audiovisual (Escola de Cinema Darcy Ribeiro) was established in 1998 and has since established partnerships with numerous NGOs in Rio de Janeiro to teach audiovisual production to disadvan-

taged youth. See http://www.escoladarcyribeiro.org.br/cgi/cgilua.exe/sys/start. htm?sid=64 (accessed June 15, 2011).

5. See, for example, Paloma Valdeavellano, "América Latina está construyendo su propria imagen," in *El vídeo en la educación popular*, ed. Paloma Valdeavellano (Lima, Peru: IPAL, 1989), 73–130; Rafael Roncagliolo, "The Growth of the Audiovisual Imagescape in Latin America," in *Video the Changing World*, ed. Nancy Thede and Alain Ambrosi (Cheektowaga, N.Y.: Black Rose, 1991), 26–27; and Ilene Goldman, "Latin American Women's Alternative Film and Video," in Noriega, *Visible Nations*, 241.

6. Claire Johnston, "Maeve," in *Films for Women*, ed. Charlotte Brunsdon (London: British Film Institute, 1986), 92.

7. Evaldo Vieira, "Brasil: Do Golpe de 1964 á Redemocratização," in *Viagem incompleta: A experiência Brasileira (1500–2000): A grande transação*, ed. Carlos Guilherme Mota (São Paulo: SENAC, 2000), 214.

8. Silvia Pimentel, *A Mulher e a Constituinte* (São Paulo: Cortez, EDUC, 1987), 11.

9. Ibid., 65–72.

10. According to Maria José Martins Duarte Osis, the program included the definition of reproductive health that was later adopted by the World Health Organization in 1988, expanded in Cairo in 1994 and in Beijing in 1995. See Osis's "PAISM: Um marco na abordagem da saúde reprodutiva no Brasil," *Cadernos saúde pública* 14, no.1 (1998): 25–32.

11. Ibid., 25.

12. Ibid., 31.

13. Alvarez, "(Trans)formation of Feminism(s) in Brazil," in *The Women's Movement in Latin America: Participation and Democracy*, ed. Jane S. Jaquette (Boulder: Westview, 1994), 49–50.

14. Eunice Gutman, interview with author, tape recording, August 28, 2005. Rio de Janeiro, Brazil.

15. Ibid.

16. Ibid.

17. The title of the film refers to a comment made by a seventy-seven-year-old woman who, having learned to read and realizing that there was so much to learn about the world, says: "O mundo é tão maior que a minha casa!" (The world is so much larger than my home!"). Ibid.

18. Leila de Andrade Linhares Barsted, "Legalização e descriminalização do aborto no Brasil: Dez anos de luta feminista," *Estudos Feministas* 0.0 (1992): 111.

19. Ibid., 117.

20. Ibid., 121.

21. With regard to the Brazilian context, the practice of female sterilization has been treated in the film *Ventre Livre* (Free Womb, 1994) by Ana Luiza Azevedo. The issue continues to be taken up by women filmmakers in Brazil as evidenced by the

2002 made-for-television documentary film *Born in Brazil* by American director Cara Biasucci. The issue is one that has affected women in other regions of Latin America. For example, the 1985 film *La Operación*, directed by Ana María García, focuses on the mass sterilization of women in Puerto Rico.

22. The story of Cícera and her daughter's legal fight became a book authored by Dando Prado, *Cícera, um destino de mulher* (São Paulo: Brasiliense, 1980).

23. Regarding the political push of neighborhood associations during the transition to democracy, see Robert Gay, "Neighborhood Associations and Political Change in Rio de Janeiro," *Latin American Research Review* 25, no.1 (1990): 102–18.

24. Eunice Gutman, interview by author, tape recording, Rio de Janeiro, August 28, 2005.

25. Thanks to Catherine Benamou for drawing out this point.

26. According to a woman interviewed in the documentary, there had been only two schools for more than two hundred thousand people living in Rocinha. They have continued to build a total of seven community schools without the assistance of the local, state, or federal government.

27. Ruth Corrêa Leite Cardoso discusses this briefly in "Popular Movements in the Context of the Consolidation of Democracy," in *The Making of Social Movements In Latin America*, ed. Arturo Escobar and Sonia E. Alvarez (Boulder: Westview, 1992), 300.

28. James Holston, *Insurgent Citizenship: Disjunctions of Democracy and Modernity in Brazil* (Princeton, N.J.: Princeton University Press, 2008), 3–18.

29. See Kaplan, *Women and Film*, 125–28.

30. As mentioned previously, regarding the realist debates in feminist film theory, see E. Ann Kaplan, "The Realist Debate in the Feminist Film: A Historical Overview of the Theories and Strategies in Realism and the Avant-Garde Theory Film (1971–81)," in Kaplan, *Women and Film*, 125–41.

31. Alberto Melucci, "Getting Involved: Identity and Mobilization in Social Movements," in *International Social Movement Research: From Structure to Action-Comparing Social Movements Research Across Cultures*, vol. 1, eds., Hansperter Kriesi, Sidney Tarrow, and Bert Klandermans (Philadelphia: Temple University Press, 1988), 342, quoted in Arturo Escobar, "Culture, Economics, and Politics in Latin American Social Movements Theory and Research," in *The Making of Social Movements in Latin America: Identity, Strategy, and Democracy*, ed. Arturo Escobar and Sonia E. Alvarez (Boulder, Colo.: Westview, 1992), 72.

32. Kaplan, *Women and Film*, 132.

33. Jacira de Melo, "Trabalho de formiga em terra de tamanduá: A Experiência feminista com vídeo" (master's thesis, Universidade de São Paulo, 1993), 77.

34. The Lilith Video Collective formed around the same time as the group Mulher Dá Vida, which was founded by a group of women studying social communication at the Instituto Metodista de Ensino Superior in São Paulo. Ibid., 75.

35. Goldman, "Alternative Film and Video," 240.

36. Lilith refers here to the historical figure of Lilith who refused to be subservient to Adam.

37. Goldman, "Alternative Film and Video," 241–44.

38. Julianne Burton and Julia Lesage, "Broadcast Feminism in Brazil: An Interview with the Lilith Video Collective," *Global Television*, ed. Cynthia Schneider and Brian Wallis (New York: Wedge Press; Cambridge, Mass.: MIT Press, 1988), 225–29.

39. Melo, "Trabalho de formiga," 77.

40. Burton and Lesage, "Broadcast Feminism," 225.

41. Melo, "Trabalho de formiga," 77.

42. Ibid.

43. Ibid., 65–66; Burton and Lesage, "Broadcast Feminism," 225; Maria Angélica Lemos, interview by author, tape recording, São Paulo, Brazil, October 12, 2001.

44. Melo, "Trabalho de formiga," 79.

45. Ibid.

46. Marcia Meireles, interview by author, tape recording, São Paulo, Brazil, October 16, 2001.

47. Silvana Afram, interview by author, tape recording, São Paulo, Brazil, October 15, 2001.

48. For additional information about this media organization, see http://www.patriciagalvao.org.br (accessed March 1, 2012).

49. For a videography of their works, including those made during the period of the Lilith Video Collective, consult the organization's website, http://comulher.sites.uol.com.br (accessed March 1, 2012).

50. Regarding the "rise and fall" of a united Brazilian women's movement, see Alvarez, *Engendering Democracy in Brazil*, 110–36.

51. Ibid., 134.

52. Ibid., 232–34.

53. Regarding the representation of AfroBrazilians in Brazilian media, see João Carlos Rodrigues, *O negro Brasileiro e o cinema* (Rio de Janeiro: Pallas, 2001) and Stam, *Brazilian Cinema*.

54. Cajado Filho is recognized as the first black Brazilian director with five feature-length fiction films to his credit, Rodrigues, *O negro Brasileiro e o cinema*, 135.

55. Based on my research, and at the time of this writing.

56. Other titles that address race and gender include, *Dandara Mulher Negra* (Fundação João Pinheiro, Rio de Janeiro, 1986), *De Olho no Preconceito* (Fúlvia Rosemberg, São Paulo, 1985), and *As Divas Negras do Cinema Brasileiro* (Enugbarijo Comunicações, Rio de Janeiro, 1989), Melo, "Trabalho de formiga," 59. Only *Mulheres Negras*, however, has distribution in the United States through Women Make Movies.

57. This is not the current situation. Adepts of *candomblé* have increased, *capoeira*

is widely practiced throughout Brazil, and a strong black movement has developed in Salvador, Bahia.

58. In her work on popular movements in Brazil, Ruth Cardoso observes that in the early 1980s, as part of *Abertura* politics, some sectors of the state apparatus instituted policies that promoted direct dialogue with popular movements. See Ruth Corrêa Leite Cardoso, "Popular Movements," 291–302.

59. Internal historical documents at SOS-Corpo indicate that the group's first financed project began in June of 1982. SOS-Corpo, *Relatório de atividades do período de Janeiro á Outubro de 1983* (Recife: SOS-Corpo, 1983), 4.

60. Internal institutional documents show that SOS-Corpo's relationships with NGOs began in the early 1980s but became solidified in the late 1980s. These organizations included international funding agencies such as the MacArthur Foundation, the Ford Foundation, the Pathfinder Fund, SACTES (Germany), Novib (Netherlands), and Oxfam (United Kingdom) as well as contacts established with Video Tiers Monde (Canada), International Planned Parenthood Foundation (IPPF), the Rede Alternativa dos Grupos de Saúde da Mulher, Centro de Información y Recursos para la Mujer (Bogotá, Colombia), OMM (Organização das Mulheres Moçambicanas), CIDHAL (México), FEMPRESS / ILET (Chile), Women's Reproductive Rights Information Center (London), ISIS International (Chile), Women's International Public Health Network (USA), and many women's groups throughout Brazil.

61. SOS-Corpo worked with a number of entities to help with its print and audiovisual projects, including the Casa Luiz Freire (Olinda, PE), Etapas video (Recife), ECOS (São Paulo), and Grupo Origem (Olinda).

62. SOS-Corpo. *Relatório de atividades do período Janeiro á Junho de 1984* (Recife: SOS-Corpo, 1984), 1.

63. SOS-Corpo. *Relatório de atividades 1983*, 12–14.

64. Ibid.

65. SOS-Corpo also established connections with the internationally active group Video Tiérs Monde (Montréal, Canada) but this relationship was not as key to their video work as that with TV VIVA.

66. Transas do Corpo is a difficult expression to render in English. The verb *transar* has two main meanings. The first means to plot or to scheme. The second meaning is common in colloquial speech and means to have sexual intercourse. Literally, the phrase could be translated as "Body Strategies."

67. SOS-Corpo, *Relatório de atividades do Período de Julho á Dezembro de 1986* (Recife: SOS-Corpo, Fevereiro, 1987), 7.

68. SOS-Corpo, *Relatório de atividades do Período de Julho á Dezembro de 1988* (Recife: SOS-Corpo, 1988), anexo I and anexo III.

69. Ibid.

70. SOS-Corpo, *Relatório de atividades 1988* (Recife: SOS-Corpo, 1989), 14; SOS-

Corpo, *Relatório de atividades do Período de Janeiro á Dezembro de 1991* (Recife: SOS-Corpo, 1992), 10–11.

71. Alvarez, *Engendering Democracy*, 180.

72. It is also important to note that none of the health clinics in Pernambuco screened for breast cancer. SOS-Corpo, *Atendimento Médico* (Recife: SOS-Corpo, 1986).

73. SOS-Corpo, "Prevenção do Câncer do Colo," (Recife: SOS-Corpo, 1986).

74. A case in point refers to the National Ministry of Health campaign against the spread of STDs and AIDS from 1994 to 1995. The campaign included posters and additional print materials in which an image appeared of an androgynous couple of European ancestry (light hair, fair skin, light-colored eyes). The result was that information in the campaign did not effectively reach the target audience. Tânia Cypriano's film *Odô Ya! Vida com AIDS* represents an important effort to address Afro-Brazilian communities.

75. The *Jornal da Rede*, a publication from the Rede Nacional Feminista de Saúde e Direitos Reprodutivos, published several articles since 1992 regarding women's reproductive rights and government-sponsored population control. Regarding the case mentioned here, see "Atendimento ao aborto legal é vetado na Câmara," *Jornal da Rede* 2, no.2 (1994): 6.

76. Here, the "T" refers to the word in Portuguese *tesão*, meaning sexual desire. The target audience for the video is adolescents and young adults.

77. SOS-Corpo, *Relatório de atividades do Perído de Janerio á Outubro de 1985* (Recife: SOS-Corpo, 1985), 17.

78. Ibid., 19.

79. The majority of these video segments include Ângela Freitas, a journalist by training who worked with SOS-Corpo for many years.

80. Lesage, "Women Make Media," 315–47.

81. Ibid., 342.

82. CEAS / SOS-Corpo, "Encontro de mulheres sobre a dupla jornada de trabalho" (Recife: SOS-Corpo, 1988), 13, 32.

Chapter 5. Developments under Democracy

1. Timothy J. Power, "Centering Democracy? Ideological Cleavages and Convergence in the Brazilian Political Class," in *Democratic Brazil Revisited*, ed. Peter R. Kingstone and Timothy J. Power (Pittsburgh: University of Pittsburgh Press, 2008), 84.

2. Kingstone and Power, *Democratic Brazil Revisited*, x.

3. Holston, *Insurgent Citizenship*, 3–18.

4. Janice Perlman, "Redemocratization Viewed from Below: Urban Poverty and Politics in Rio de Janeiro, 1968–2005," in Kingstone and Power, *Democratic Brazil Revisited*, 257–80.

5. Somers, "Citizenship," 587.

6. Nick Stevenson, *Culture and Citizenship* (Thousand Oaks, Calif.: SAGE, 2001), 2.

7. For an excellent discussion of the evolving relationship between civil society organizations and the Lula administration, see Kathryn Hochstetler, "Organized Civil Society in Lula's Brazil," in Kingstone and Power, *Democratic Brazil Revisited*, 33–53.

8. For example, Céli Regina Jardim Pinto reports that in 1989 Collor cut the budget for the Conselho Nacional dos Direitos da Mulher (CNDM, National Council on the Rights of Women), which led to the organization's losing the political position it had held from 1985 to 1989 during the drafting of a new constitution (in 1988). Céli Regina Jardim Pinto, *Uma história do feminismo no Brasil* (São Paulo: Editora Fundação Perseu Abramo, 2003), 71–72.

9. For analyses of ANCINE and recent history of Brazilan cinema, see Cacilda Rêgo, "Brazilian Cinema: Its Fall, Rise, and Renewal (1990–2003)," *New Cinemas: Journal of Contemporary Film* 3, no. 2 (2005): 85–100; and José Álvaro Moisés, "A New Policy for Brazilian Cinema," in *The New Brazilian Cinema*, ed. Lúcia Nagib (New York and London: Tauris; The Centre for Brazilian Studies, University of Oxford, 2003), 3–22.

10. Centro Cultural Banco do Brasil, *Cinema Brasileiro anos 90: 9 questões* (Rio de Janeiro: CCBB, 2001), 109–16.

11. In addition to the essays by Rêgo and Moisés cited above, see Luís Alberto Rocha Melo and Luiz Carlos Oliveira Jr., "1995–2005: Histórico de uma década," in *Cinema brasileiro 1995–2005: Revisão de uma década*, ed. Daniel Caetano (Rio de Janeiro: Azougue, 2005), 11–50; and Luís Alberto Rocha Melo, "Gêneros, produtores e autores—Linhas de produção no cinema brasileiro recente," in *Cinema brasileiro 1995–2005: Revisão de uma década*, ed. Daniel Caetano (Rio de Janeiro: Azougue Editorial, 2005): 67–78.

12. Luís Alberto Rocha Melo and Luiz Carlos Oliveira Jr., "1995–2005: Histórico de uma década," in *Cinema brasileiro 1995–2005: Revisão de uma década*, ed. Daniel Caetano (Rio de Janeiro: Azougue, 2005): 12.

13. Ibid., 38.

14. Susana Schild, "Um gênero em transição," 123.

15. Centro Cultural Banco do Brasil, *Cinema Brasileiro*, 109–16.

16. Cacilda Rêgo, "Mulheres de Retomada after the Retomada," paper presented at the Mulheres da Retomada Conference at Tulane University, New Orleans, Louisiana, February 16–18, 2011.

17. Moisés, "New Policy," 15.

18. Fernando Veríssimo, "Novos diretores: Uma geração em trânsito?" in Centro Cultural Banco do Brasil, *Cinema Brasileiro*, 42.

19. Melo and Oliveira, "1995–2005: Histórico de uma década," 28.

20. See Tamara Falicov, *The Cinematic Tango: Contemporary Argentine Film* (New York: Wallflower, 2007), 115–19.

21. David Bordwell and Kristin Thompson, *Film Art: An Introduction* (New York: McGraw Hill, 2003), 489.

22. Geoffrey Nowell-Smith advocated for studying thematic patterns in a director's work which, in his assessment, form "a structural hard core of basic and often recondite motifs." See his *[Luchino] Visconti* [1967] (Garden City, N.Y.: Doubleday, 1968), 10.

23. For an overview of approaches to authorship in cinema, see Janet Staiger, "Authorship Approaches," in *Authorship and Film*, eds. David A. Gerstner and Janet Staiger (New York: Routledge, 2003), 30–52.

24. Ibid., 49.

25. See for example, Judith Mayne, *The Woman at the Keyhole: Feminism and Women's Cinema* (Bloomington: Indiana University Press, 1990); Silverman, *Acoustic Mirror*; and Catherine Grant, "Secret Agents: Feminist Theories of Women's Film Authorship," *Feminist Theory* 2 (2001): 113–30.

26. Staiger, "Authorship Approaches," 30.

27. Regina Félix, "Her Laughter Contract: Image Demolition in *Carlota Joaquina, Princess of Brazil*," paper presented at Mulheres da Retomada Conference at Tulane University, New Orleans, Louisiana, February 16–18, 2011.

28. Available at http://www.cinetelabrasil.com.br (accessed March 1, 2012).

29. Geetha Ramanathan, *Feminist Auteurs: Reading Women's Films* (New York: Wallflower, 2006), 1–9.

30. Ann Braithwaite, "Politics and/of Backlash," *Journal of International Women's Studies* 5, no. 5 (2004): 27, quoted in Stéphanie Genz, *Postfemininities in Popular Culture* (New York: Palgrave Macmillan, 2009), 22.

31. See Laura Podalsky, "Out of Depth: The Politics of Disaffected Youth and Contemporary Latin American Cinema," in *Youth Culture in Global Cinema*, ed. Timothy Shary and Alexandra Seibel (Austin: University of Texas Press, 2007), 109–30; Hector Amaya and Laura Senio Blair, "Bridges between the Divide: The Female Body in *Y tu Mamá también* and *Machuca*," *Studies in Hispanic Cinemas* 4, no. 1 (2007): 47–62; and Deborah Shaw, "The Figure of the Absent Father in Recent Latin American Films," *Studies in Hispanic Cinemas* 1, no. 2 (2004): 85–101.

32. There have been important efforts to counter the criminalization of male youth as evident in documentaries such as *Justiça* (Maria Augusta Ramos, 2003), *Ônibus 174* (José Padilha and Felipe Lacerda, 2002) and *Falcão* (Central Único das Favelas, MV Bill, Celso Athayde, 2006). These works contest the representation of young males who have great life aspirations but whose lives are shaped by violence of narcotrafficking and limited life opportunities.

33. Beatriz Jaguaribe, "Cities without Maps: Favelas and the Aesthetics of Realism," in *Urban Imaginaries: Locating the Modern City*, ed. Alev Çinar and Thomas Bender (Minneapolis: University of Minnesota Press, 2007), 100–101.

34. Heilborn, Maria Luiza, Elaine Reis Brandão, and Cristiane da Silva Cabral,

"Teenage Pregnancy and Moral Panic in Brazil," *Culture, Health & Sexuality* 9, no. 4 (2007), 406–8.

35. Ibid., 403–14.

36. Interview with Sandra Werneck, *Meninas* (Rio de Janeiro: Videofilmes, 2005), DVD extras.

37. Sandra Werneck in Fernanda Ezabella, "Em 'Sonhos Roubados,' Sandra Werneck filma garotas de periferia' *Folha Online—Ilustrada* [journal on-line]; available at http://www1.folha.uol.com.br/folha/ilustrada/ult90u724722.shtml (accessed March 1, 2012).

38. Marta Peixoto, "Rio's Favelas in Recent Fiction and Film: Commonplaces of Urban Segregation," *PMLA* 122.1 (2007), 173.

39. Flora Süssekind, "Desterritorialização e forma literária: Literatura brasileira contemporânea e experiência urbana," *Literatura e Sociedade* 8 (2005): 62, cited in Marta Peixoto, "Rio's Favelas," 172.

40. Laura Susana Duque-Arrazola, "O Cotidiano Sexuado de Meninos e Meninas em Situação de Pobreza," in *Quem mandou nascer mulher? Estudos sobre crianças e adolescentes pobres no Brasil*, ed. Felícia Reicher Madeira (Rio de Janeiro: Record, Rosa dos Tempos, 1997), 351.

41. The documentary film *Vinte Dez* (2001), in which Amaral portrays hip-hop culture in the outskirts of São Paulo, served as an investigation of hip-hop culture and an influential point of departure, planting the seed for the future film *Antônia*.

42. Angela McRobbie and Jennie Garber, "Girls and Subcultures," in *Resistance through Rituals, Youth Subcultures in Postwar Britain*, ed. Stuart Hall and Tony Jefferson (London: Hutchinson, 1975), quoted in Anoop Nayak and Mary Jane Kehily, *Gender, Youth and Culture: Young Masculinities and Femininities* (New York: Palgrave Macmillan, 2008), 53–54.

43. See, for example, her short films *Mude Seu Dial* (1986) and *Queremos as Ondas do Ar!* (1986).

44. Pablo Goldbarg, "Paint It Black, Say It Loud: An Interview with Tata Amaral," *Cineaste* 33, no. 1 (2007) [journal on line]; available at http://www.cineaste.com/articles/an-interview-with-tata-amaral.htm (accessed March 1, 2012).

45. See the discussion on the Retomada-era representation of the favela in Ivana Bentes, "The *Sertão* and the *Favela* in Contemporary Brazilian Film," in *The New Brazilian Cinema*, ed. Lúcia Nagib (London: Tauris, 2003), 121–37.

Selected Filmography

Almeida, Neville de. *A Dama da Lotação*, 1978.

Amaral, Suzana. *A Hora da Estrela*, 1985.

Amaral, Tata. *Um Céu de Estrelas*, 1997.

———. *Vinte Dez*, 2001.

———. *Através da Janela*, 2000.

———. *Antônia*, 2006.

Azevedo, Ana Luiza. *Ventre Livre*. 1994.

Babenco, Hector. *Pixote*, 1980.

Barreto, Bruno. *Dona Flor e Seus Dois Maridos*, 1976.

———. *Última Parada: 174*, 2008.

Bengell, Norma. *Eternamente Pagú*, 1987.

Biasucci, Cara. *Born in Brazil*, 2002.

Bodanzky, Jorge, and Orlando Senna, *Iracema—Uma Transa Amazônica*, 1976.

Bressane, Julio. *Matou a Família e Foi ao Cinema*, 1969.

Camurati, Carla. *Carlota Joaquina, Princesa do Brazil*, 1995.

Central Única das Favelas, MV Bill, Celso Athayde. *Falcão*, 2006.

Cypriano, Tânia. *Odô Ya! Vida Com Aids*, 1997.

De Paula, Betse. *O Casamento de Louise*, 2001.

———. *Celeste & Estrela*, 2005.

Diegues, Carlos. *Xica da Silva*, 1976.

Do Rosario, Maria. *As Pequenas Taras*, 1980.

Fonseca, Eliana. *Coisa de Mulher*, 2005.

Gallo, Carla. *O Aborto dos Outros*, 2009.

García, Ana María. *La Operación*, 1985.

Garcia, Denise. *Sou Feia Mas Tô Na Moda*, 2005.

Gutman, Eunice. *E o Mundo Era Muito Maior Que a Minha Casa*, 1976.

———. *Só No Carnaval*, 1982.

———. *Vida de Mãe É Assim Mesmo?* 1983.

———. *A Rocinha Tem Histórias*, 1985

———. *Duas Vezes Mulher*, 1985.

———. *Amores da Rua*, 1994.

———. *Feminino Sagrado*, 1995.

———. *Segredos de Amor*, 1998.

———. *O Outro Lado do Amor*, 2000.

———. *Nos Caminhos do Lixo*, 2008.

ISER, *Acorda Raimundo! Acorda!* IBASE Vídeo and ISER Vídeo, 1990.

Jabor, Arnaldo. *Toda Nudez Será Castigada*, 1973.

———. *O Casamento*, 1976.

———. *Tudo Bem*, 1978.

Jessouroun, Thereza. *Fim do Silêncio*, 2009.

Lilith Video Collective. *Mulheres Negras*, 1986.

Lund, Kátia. *Notícias de uma Guerra Particular*, 1999.

——— and Fernando Meirelles, *Cidade de Deus*, 2002

Magalhães, Ana Maria. *Mulheres de Cinema*, 1978.

———. *Lara*, 2002.

Moraes, Tetê. *Terra para Rose*, 1987.

———. *O Sonho de Rose—Dez Anos Depois*, 1997.

———. *O Sol—Caminhando Contra o Vento*, 2006.

Morelli, Paulo. *Cidade dos Homens*, 2007.

Mourão, Mara. *Avassaladoras*, 2002.

Muylaert, Anna. *Durval Discos*, 2002.

———. *É Proibido Fumar*, 2009.

Murat, Lúcia, *Que Bom Te Ver Viva*, 1989.

———. *Doces Poderes*, 1997.

———. *Brava Gente Brasileira,* 2000.

———. *Quase Dois Irmãos*, 2004.

———. *Olhar Estrangeiro*, 2006.

———. *Maré—Nossa História de Amor*, 2007.

Padilha, José. *Tropa de Élite*, 2007.

——— and Felipe Lacerda. *Ônibus 174*, 2002.

Priscilla, Claudia, *Leite e Ferro*, 2009.

Ramos, Maria Augusta, *Justiça*, 2003.

———. *Juízo*, 2008.

Rocha, Glauber. *Deus e o Diabo na Terra do Sol*, 1964.

———. *A Idade da Terra*, 1980.

Soares, Ana Carolina Teixeira. *Getúlio,* 1974.

———. *Mar de Rosas*, 1978.

———. *Das Tripas Coração*, 1982.

————. *Sonho de Valsa*, 1986.

————. *Amélia*, 2000.

————. *Gregório de Mattos*, 2003.

Solberg, Helena. *A Entrevista*, 1966.

————. *Carmen Miranda: Bananas is My Business*, 1995.

————. *Vida de Menina*, 2003.

————. *Palabra (En)cantada*, 2008.

SOS-Corpo. *Transas do Corpo*, 1985.

————. *Denise*, 1988.

————. *Dupla Jornada*, 1989.

————. *Almerinda*, 1991.

————. *Em Busca da Saúde*, 1993.

————. *Sertanejas*, 1995.

————. *Aborto: Desafio da Legalidade*, 1995.

————. *Quem Faz Sexo, Faz Prevenção*, 1995/1996.

Svartman, Rosane, *Como Ser Solteiro*, 1998.

————. *Mais uma Vez Amor*, 2005.

Tapajós, Renato. *Em Nome da Segurança Nacional*, 1983.

Tonacci, Andrea. *Bang, Bang*, 1970.

Trautman, Tereza. *Os Homens Que Eu Tive*, 1973.

————. *Sonhos de Menina Moça*, 1988.

Werneck, Sandra. *Damas da Noite*, 1979.

————. *Ritos de Passagem*, 1979.

————. *Pena Prisão*, 1983.

————. *Pequeno Diccionário Amoroso*, 1997.

————. *Amores Possíveis*, 2001.

————. *Meninas*, 2003.

————. *Cazuza—O Tempo Não Pára*, 2004.

————. *Sonhos Roubados*, 2009.

Yamasaki, Tizuka. *Gaijin: Os Caminhos da Liberdade*, 1980

————. *Parahyba, Mulher Macho*, 1983.

————. *Patriamada*, 1984.

————. *Gaijin: Ame-me Como Sou*, 2005.

Bibliography

Primary Sources: Recorded Interviews

Afram, Silvana. Interview by author, October 15, 2001, São Paulo, Brazil.

Amaral, Suzana. Interview by author, November 14, 2001, São Paulo, Brazil.

Amaral, Tata. Interview by author, November 13, 2001, São Paulo, Brazil.

Freitas, Angela. Interview by author, June 21, 2002, Rio de Janeiro, Brazil.

Gutman, Eunice. Interviews by author, August 27 and 28, 2005, Rio de Janeiro, Brazil.

Homem, Eduardo. Interview by author, May 18, 2002, Olinda, Brazil.

Lemos, Maria Angélica. Interview by author, October 12, 2001, São Paulo, Brazil.

Magalhães, Ana Maria. Interview by author, November 28, 2001, Rio de Janeiro, Brazil.

Meireles, Marcia. Interview by author, October 16, 2001, São Paulo, Brazil.

Moraes, Tetê. Interview by author, July 11, 2002, Rio de Janeiro, Brazil.

Murat, Lúcia. Interviews by author, November 27, 2001, and July 10, 2002, Rio de Janeiro, Brazil.

Portella, Tarciana. Interview by author, May 10, 2002, Recife, Brazil.

Santos, Luciana. Interview by author, May 15, 2002, Olinda, Brazil.

Soares, Ana Carolina Teixeira. Interview by author, August 26, 2005, Rio de Janeiro, Brazil.

Solberg, Helena. Interview by author, November 27, 2001, Rio de Janeiro, Brazil.

Trautman, Tereza. Interview by author, November 29, 2001, Rio de Janeiro, Brazil.

Werneck, Sandra. Interview by author, July 16, 2002, Rio de Janeiro, Brazil.

Yamasaki, Tizuka. Interview by author, August 21, 2005, São Paulo, Brazil.

Secondary Sources

Alvarez, Sonia E. *Engendering Democracy in Brazil: Women's Movements in Transition Politics*. Princeton, N.J.: Princeton University Press, 1990.

———. "(Trans)formation of Feminism(s) in Brazil." In *The Women's Movement in Latin America: Participation and Democracy*, edited by Jane S. Jaquette, 13–63. Boulder, Colo.: Westview, 1994.

Alvarez, Sonia, Evelina Dagnino, and Arturo Escobar, eds. *Culture of Politics, Politics of Culture: Re-Visioning Latin American Social Movements*. Boulder, Colo.: Westview, 1998.

Alves, Maria Helena Moreira. *State and Opposition in Military Brazil*. Austin: University of Texas Press, 1985.

Amaya, Hector, and Laura Senio Blair. "Bridges between the Divide: The Female Body in *Y tu mamá también* and *Machuca*." *Studies in Hispanic Cinemas* 4, no.1 (2007): 47–62.

Archdiocese of São Paulo. *Nunca Mais: Um relato para a história*. 9th ed. Petrópolis: Vozes, 1985.

Ardaillon, Danielle, and Guita Grin Derbert. *Quando a vítima émulher: Análise de julgamentos de crimes de estupro, espancamento e homicídios*. Brasília: CNDM, 1987.

"Atendimento ao aborto legal é vetado na Câmara." *Jornal da Rede* 2, no. 2 (1994): 6.

Aufderheide, Patricia. "Grassroots Video in Latin America." In Noriega, *Visible Nations*, 219–38.

Baltar, Mariana. "Weeping Reality: Melodramatic Imagination in Contemporary Brazilian Documentary." In Sadlier, *Latin American Melodrama*, 130–38.

Barbalho, Alexandre. "O Estado pós-64: Intervenção planejada na cultura." *Política e Trabalho* 15 (1999): 63–78.

Barsted, Leila de Andrade Linhares. "Legalização e descriminalização de aborto no Brasil: Dez anos de luta feminista." *Estudos Feministas* (1992): 104–30.

Belton, Robert J. "Speaking with Forked Tongues: 'Male' Discourse in 'Female' Surrealism?" In Caws, Kuenzli, and Raaberg, *Surrealism and Women*, 50–62.

Benamou, Catherine L. "Mar de Rosas." In *South American Cinema: A Critical Filmography, 1915–1994*, edited by Timothy Barnard and Peter Rist, 183–84. Austin: University of Texas Press, 1998.

Bentes, Ivana. "The *sertão* and the *favela* in Contemporary Brazilian Film." In Nagib, *New Brazilian Cinema*, 121–37.

Bernardet, Jean-Claude. "Qual é a história?" In Novaes, *Anos 70*, 325–33.

Bordwell, David, and Kristin Thompson. *Film Art: An Introduction*. New York: McGraw Hill, 2003.

Breton, André, *What is Surrealism? Selected Writings*. Edited and introduced by Franklin Rosemont. New York: Monad, 1978.

Brittos, Valério Cruz, and César Ricardo Siqueira Bolaño, eds. *Rede Globo: 40 anos de poder e hegemonia*. São Paulo: Paulus, 2005.

Brooks, Peter. *The Melodramatic Imagination*. New Haven, Conn.: Yale University Press, 1976.

Buckingham, Susan, and Geraldine Lievesley, eds. *In the Hands of Women: Paradigms of Citizenship*. Manchester: Manchester University Press, 2006.

Burton, Julianne. "Transitional States: Creative Complicities with the Real in *Cabra Marcado Para Morrer: Vinte Anos Depois* [Man Marked to Die: Twenty Years Later] and *Patriamada* [Sing, the Beloved Country]." *Studies in Latin American Popular Culture* 7 (1988): 139–55

———. "Sing, the Beloved Country: An Interview with Tizuka Yamasaki on *Patriamada*." *Film Quarterly* 41, no. 1 (Fall 1982): 2–9.

Burton, Julianne, and Julia Lesage. "Broadcast Feminism in Brazil: An Interview with the Lilith Video Collective." In *Global Television*, edited by Cynthia Schneider and Brian Wallis, 225–29. New York: Wedge; Cambridge, Mass.: MIT Press, 1988.

Byg, Barton. "Brecht, New Waves, and Political Modernism in Cinema." In Mews, *Bertolt Brecht Reference Companion*, 220–37.

Caetano, Daniel, ed. *Cinema brasileiro 1995–2005: Revisão de uma década*. Rio de Janeiro: Azougue, 2005.

Caldeira, Teresa do Rio Pires. *City of Walls: Crime, Segregation, and Citizenship in São Paulo*. Berkeley: University of California Press, 2000.

Cândido, Flávio, "A trilogina de Ana Carolina em Niterói." *O Fluminense* 29 (September 1989): n.p.

Canning, Kathleen. *Gender History in Practice: Historical Perspectives on Bodies, Class and Citizenship*. Ithaca, N.Y.: Cornell University Press, 2006.

Cappellin, Paula. "As mulheres e o acesso á cidadania no Rio de Janeiro: Anotaçoes sobre a pesquisa 'Lei, justiça e cidadania.'" In Pandolfi, *Cidadania, justiça e violência*, 205–28.

Cardoso, Ruth Corrêa Leite. "Popular Movements in the Context of the Consolidation of Democracy in Brazil." In Escobar and Alvarez, *Making of Social Movements*, 291–302.

Carson, Diane, Linda Dittmar, and Janice R. Welsch, eds. *Multiple Voices in Feminist Film Criticism*. Minneapolis: University of Minnesota Press, 1994.

Caulfield, Sueann. *In Defense of Honor: Sexual Morality, Modernity, and Nation in Early-Twentieth-Century Brazil*. Durham, N.C.: Duke University Press, 2000.

Caws, Mary Ann, Rudolf Kuenzli, and Gwen Raaberg, eds. *Surrealism and Women*. Cambridge, Mass.: MIT Press, 1993.

Centro Cultural Banco do Brasil. *Cinema Brasileiro anos 90: 9 questões*. Rio de Janeiro: CCBB, 2001.

Chadwick, Whitney. *Women Artists and the Surrealist Movement*. Boston: Little, Brown, 1985.

———, ed. *Mirror Images: Women, Surrealism, and Self-Representation*. Cambridge, Mass.: MIT Press, 1998.

Chauí, Marilene. *Cultura e democracia: O discurso competente e outras falas.* São Paulo: Cortez, 2003.

Cine Tela Brasil. http://www.cinetelabrasil.com.br (accessed February 12, 2012).

Cohn, Amélia. "A questão social no Brasil: A difícil construção da cidadania." In Mota, *Viagem incompleta,* 385–403.

Cohn, Gabriel. "A concepção oficial da política cultural nos anos 70." In *Estado e Cultura no Brasil,* edited by Sérgio Miceli, 85–96. São Paulo: DIFEL, 1984.

Corrêa, Mariza. *Os crimes da paixão.* São Paulo: Brasiliense, 1981.

Cossman, Brenda. *Sexual Citizens: The Legal and Cultural Regulation of Sex and Belonging.* Palo Alto, Calif.: Stanford University Press, 2007.

Cruz, Consuelo. "Latin American Citizenship: Civic Microfoundations in Historical Perspective." In Hite and Cesarini, *Authoritarian Legacies,* 305–21.

Dagnino, Evelina. "Culture, Citizenship and Democracy: Changing Discourses and Practices of the Latin American Left." In Alvarez, Dagnino, and Escobar, *Culture of Politics,* 33–63.

Dahl, Gustavo. "Embrafilme: Present Problems and Future Possibilities." In Johnson and Stam, *Brazilian Cinema,* 104–8.

Dietz, Mary G. "Context Is All: Feminism and Theories of Citizenship." In Phillips, *Feminism and Politics,* 378–400.

Doane, Mary Ann. "Woman's Stake: Filming the Female Body." In Kaplan, *Feminism and Film,* 86–99.

Dunn, Christopher. *Brutality Garden: Tropicália and the Emergence of a Brazilian Counterculture.* Chapel Hill: University of North Carolina Press, 2001.

Duque-Arrazola, Laura Susana. "O cotidiano sexuado de meninos e meninas em situações de pobreza." In *Quem mandou nascer mulher? Estudos sobre crianças e adolescentes no Brasil,* edited by Felícia Reicher Madeira, 343–402. Rio de Janeiro: Record, Rosa dos Tempos, 1997.

Elsaesser, Thomas. "From Anti-Illusionism to Hyper-Realism: Bertolt Brecht and Contemporary Film." In Kleber and Visser, *Re-interpreting Brecht,* 170–85.

Escobar, Arturo, and Sonia Alvarez, eds. *The Making of Social Movements in Latin America.* Boulder, Colo.: Westview, 1992.

Escola Superior de Guerra. *Fundamentos da Doutrina.* Rio de Janeiro: ESG, 1981.

———. *Doutrina Básica.* Rio de Janeiro: ESG, 1979.

Esslin, Martin. "Some Reflections on Brecht and Acting." In Kleber and Visser, *Re-interpreting Brecht,* 135–46.

Evans, David T. *Sexual Citizenship: The Material Construction of Sexualities.* London: Routledge, 1993.

Ezabella, Fernanda. "Em 'Sonhos Roubados,' Sandra Werneck filma garotas de periferia." *Folha Online—Ilustrada,* http://www1.folha.uol.com.br/folha/ilustrada/ult90u724722.shtml (accessed February 12, 2012).

Falicov, Tamara. *The Cinematic Tango: Contemporary Argentine Film.* New York: Wallflower, 2007.

Félix, Regina. "Her Laughter Contract: Image Demolition in *Carlota Joaquina, Princess of Brazil*." Paper presented at Mulheres da Retomada Conference at Tulane University, New Orleans, February 16–18, 2011.

Fico, Carlos. *Reinventando o otimismo: Ditadura, propaganda e imaginário social no Brasil*. Rio de Janeiro: Fundação Getúlio Vargas, 1997.

———. "A pluralidade das censuras e das propagandas da ditadura." In *1964–2004: 40 anos do golpe: Ditadura militar e resistência no Brasil*, Seminário 40 Anos do Golpe de 1964 (2004: Niterói e Rio de Janeiro), 71–79. Rio de Janeiro: 7 Letras, 2004.

Gaspari, Elio, Heloisa Buarque de Hollanda, and Zuenir Ventura, eds. *Cultura em trânsito: Da repressão à Abertura*. Rio de Janeiro: Aeroplano, 2000.

Gastal, Ney. "Para Tizuka, polêmica é a maior qualidade de 'Parahyba Mulher Macho.'" *Correio do Povo*. November 13, 1983. Especial, 9.

Gatti, André Piero. *Cinema Brasileiro em Ritmo de Indústria*. São Paulo: Núcleo de Cinema e Vídeo do Centro Cultural de São Paulo, Divisão de Pesquisas—ETP Cinema, 1999.

Gay, Robert. "Neighborhood Associations and Political Change in Rio de Janeiro." *Latin American Research Review* 25.1 (1990): 102–18.

Genz, Stéphanie. *Postfemininities in Popular Culture*. New York: Palgrave Macmillan, 2009.

Gerstner, David A., and Janet Staiger, eds. *Authorship and Film*. New York: Routledge, 2003.

Gill, Rosalind. *Gender and the Media*. Malden, Mass.: Polity, 2007.

Gledhill, Christine. *Home is Where the Heart Is: Studies in Melodrama and the Woman's Film*. London: British Film Institute, 1987.

———. "Image and Voice: Approaches to Marxist Feminism." In Carson, Dittmar, and Welsch, *Multiple Voices*, 109–23. Minneapolis: University of Minnesota Press, 1994.

Goldbarg, Pablo. "Paint It Black, Say It Loud: An Interview with Tata Amaral." *Cineaste* 33, no. 1 (2007): available at http://www.cineaste.com/articles/an-interview-with-tata-amaral.htm (accessed February 12, 2012).

Goldman, Ilene. "Latin American Women's Alternative Film and Video." In Noriega, *Visible Nations*, 239–62.

Grant, Catherine. "Secret Agents: Feminist Theories of Women's Film Authorship." *Feminist Theory* 2 (2001): 113–30.

Grimm, Richard. "Alienation in Context: On the Theory and Practice of Brechtian Theater." In Mews, *Bertolt Brecht Reference Companion*, 35–46.

Grinberg, Keila. *Código civil e cidadania*. Rio de Janeiro: Jorge Zahara, 2001.

Habib, Sérgio, "Um filme incômodo," *Jornal de Brasília*, August 2, 1978: n.p.

Halbwachs, Maurice. *On Collective Memory*. Chicago: University of Chicago Press, 1992.

Hammond, Paul, ed. *The Shadow and Its Shadow: Surrealist Writings on Cinema*. New York: Zoetrope, 1978.

Heilborn, Maria Luiza, Eliane Reis Brandão, and Cristiane da Silva Cabral. "Teenage Pregnancy and Moral Panic in Brazil." *Culture, Health & Sexuality* 9, no. 4 (2007): 403–14.

Herlinghaus, Hermann. *Narraciones anacrónicas de la modernidad: Melodrama e intermedialidad en América Latina.* Providencia, Santiago: Cuarto Propio, 2002.

Hite, Katherine, and Paola Cesarini, eds. *Authoritarian Legacies and Democracy in Latin America and Southern Europe.* Notre Dame, Ind.: University of Notre Dame Press, 2004.

Hochstetler, Kathryn. "Organized Civil Society in Lula's Brazil." In Kingstone and Power, *Democratic Brazil Revisited*, 33–53.

Hollanda, Heloisa Buarque de. "Leia o filme e veja," *Jornal do Brasil*. December 11, 1982, n.p.

———, ed. *Quase catálogo: Realizadoras de cinema no Brasil (1930/1988).* Rio de Janeiro: CIEC, 1987.

Hollanda, Heloisa Buarque de, and Marcos Augusto Gonçalves, "A ficção da realidade brasileira." In Novaes, *Anos 70*, 97–159.

Holston, James. *Insurgent Citizenship: Disjunctions of Democracy and Modernity in Brazil.* Princeton, N.J.: Princeton University Press, 2008.

Htun, Mala. *Sex and the State: Abortion, Divorce, and the Family under Latin American Dictatorships and Democracies.* New York: Cambridge University Press, 2003.

Isin, Engin K., and Patricia K. Wood, eds. *Citizenship and Identity.* Thousand Oaks, Calif.: SAGE, 1999.

Izumino, Wânia Pasinato. *Justiça e violência contra a mulher: O papel do sistema judicírio na solução dos conflitos de gênero.* São Paulo: Annablume; FAPESP, 1998.

Jaguaribe, Beatriz. "Cities without Maps: Favelas and the Aesthetics of Realism." In *Urban Imaginaries: Locating the Modern City*, edited by Alev Çinar and Thomas Bender, 100–120. Minneapolis: University of Minnesota Press, 2007.

Jelin, Elizabeth. *State Repression and the Labors of Memory.* Minneapolis: University of Minnesota Press, 2003.

Johnson, Randal. *The Film Industry in Brazil: Culture and the State.* Pittsburgh: University of Pittsburgh Press, 1987.

———. "The Rise and Fall of Brazilian Cinema, 1960–1990." In Johnson and Stam, *Brazilian Cinema*, 362–86.

Johnson, Randal, and Robert Stam, eds. *Brazilian Cinema.* Expanded Edition. New York: Columbia University Press, 1995.

———. "The Shape of Brazilian Film History." In Johnson and Stam, *Brazilian Cinema*, 17–51.

———. "The Romance-Reportagem and the Cinema: Babenco's *Lúcio Flávio* and *Pixote*." *Luso-Brazilian Review* 24, no. 2 (1987): 35–48.

Johnston, Clarie. "Maeve." In *Films for Women*, edited by Charlotte Brunsdon, 91–98. London: British Film Institute, 1986.

———. "Women's Cinema as Counter Cinema." In Kaplan, *Feminism and Film*, 22–33.

Juhasz, Alexandra. *Women of Vision: Histories of Feminist Film and Video*. Minneapolis: University of Minnesota Press, 2001.

Kaplan, E. Ann, ed. *Feminism and Film*. New York: Oxford University Press, 2000.

———. *Women and Film: Both Sides of the Camera*. New York: Methuen, 1983.

———. "Women, Film, Resistance: Changing Paradigms." In *Women Filmmakers: Refocusing*, edited by Jacqueline Levitin, Judith Plessis, and Valerie Raoul, 15–28. New York: Routledge, 2003.

Kingstone, Peter R., and Timothy J. Power, eds. *Democratic Brazil Revisited*. Pittsburgh: University of Pittsburgh Press, 2008.

Kleber, Pia, and Colin Visser, eds. *Re-interpreting Brecht: His Influence on Contemporary Drama and Film*. New York: Cambridge University Press, 1990.

Krauss, Rosalind. *Bachelors*. Cambridge, Mass.: MIT Press, 1990.

Kruks, Sonia. *Retrieving Experience: Subjectivity and Recognition in Feminist Politics*. Ithaca, N.Y.: Cornell University Press, 2001.

Kuenzli, Rudolf E. "Surrealism and Misogyny." In Caws, Kuenzli, and Raaberg, *Surrealism and Women*, 17–26.

Laderman, David. *Driving Visions: Exploring the Road Movie*. Austin: University of Texas Press, 2002.

Landes, Joan B. *Feminism, the Public and the Private*. New York: Oxford University Press, 1998.

Lauretis, Teresa de. *Technologies of Gender: Essays on Theory, Film, and Fiction*. Bloomington: Indiana University Press, 1987.

———. "Rethinking Women's Cinema: Aesthetics and Feminist Theory." In Carson, Dittmar, and Welsch, *Multiple Voices*, 140–61. Minneapolis: University of Minnesota Press, 1994.

Lesage, Julia. "Women Make Media: Three Modes of Production." In *The Social Documentary in Latin America*, edited by Julianne Burton, 315–47. Pittsburgh: University of Pittsburgh Press, 1990.

Lesser, Jeffrey. *Negotiating National Identity: Immigrants, Minorities, and the Struggle for Ethnicity in Brazil*. Durham, N.C.: Duke University Press, 1999.

———. *Discontented Diaspora: Japanese Brazilians and the Meanings of Ethnic Militancy, 1960–1980*. Durham: Duke University Press, 2007.

———. "In Search of the Hyphen: Nikkei and the Struggle over Brazilian National Identity." In *New Worlds, New Lives: Globalization and People of Japanese Descent in the Americas and from Latin America in Japan*, edited by Lane Ryo Hirabayashi, Akemi Kikumura-Yano, and James A. Hirabayashi, 37–58. Palo Alto, Calif.: Stanford University Press, 2002.

Lievesley, Geraldine. "Women and the Experience of Citizenship." In Buckingham and Lievesley, *In the Hands of Women*, 6–32.

Lister, Ruth. "Dilemmas in Engendering Citizenship." In *Gender and Citizenship in Transition*, edited by Barbara Hobson, 33–83. New York: Routledge, 2000.

Lopes, Denise Costa. "O Cinema Pós-Collor." M.A. thesis. Universidade Federal Fluminense, 2001.

López, Ana. "The Melodrama in Latin America: Films, Telenovelas, and the Currency of a Popular Form." In *Imitations of Life: A Reader on Film & Television Melodrama*, edited by Marcia Landy, 596–606. Detroit: Wayne State University Press, 1991.

———. "Tears and Desire: Women and Melodrama in the 'Old' Mexican Cinema." In Carson, Dittmar, and Welsch, *Multiple Voices*, 254–70.

"The Making of Social Movements in Latin America: Identity, Strategy, and Democracy: Identity and Mobilization in Social Movements." In *International Social Movement Research: From Structure to Action; Comparing Social Movements Research across Cultures*, vol. 1, edited by Bert Klandermans, Hanspeter Kriesi, and Sidney G. Tarrow. Philadelphia: Temple University Press, 1988; quoted in Arturo Escobar, "Culture, Economics, and Politics in Latin American Social Movements Theory and Research." In Escobar and Alvarez, *Making of Social Movements*, 72.

Malt, Johanna. *Obscure Objects of Desire: Surrealism, Fetishism, and Politics*. Oxford: Oxford University Press, 2004.

Marshall, T. H. *Citizenship and Social Class*. Cambridge: Cambridge University Press, 1950.

Martín-Barbero, Jesús. *Communication, Culture and Hegemony: From the Media to Mediation*. Translated by Elizabeth Fox and Robert A. White. Newbury Park, Calif.: SAGE, 1993.

Masiello, Francine. "Women, State and Family in Latin American Literature of the 1920s." In *Women, Culture, and Politics in Latin America: Seminar on Feminism and Culture in Latin America*, compiled by the Seminar on Feminism and Culture in Latin America, 27–47. Berkeley; University of California Press, 1990.

Mayne, Judith. *Woman at the Keyhole: Feminism and Women's Cinema*. Bloomington: Indiana University Press, 1988.

McAfee, Noëlle. *Habermas, Kristeva, and Citizenship*. Ithaca, N.Y.: Cornell University Press, 2000.

Melo, Luís Alberto Rocha. "Gêneros, produtores e autores—Linhas de produção no cinema brasileiro recente." In Caetano, *Cinema brasileiro 1995–2005*, 67–78.

Melo, Jacira de. "Trabalho de formiga em terra de tamanduá: A experiência feminista com vídeo." M.A. thesis, Universidade de São Paulo, 1993.

Melo, Luís Alberto Rocha, and Luiz Carlos Oliveira Jr. "1995–2005: Histórico de uma década." In Caetano, *Cinema brasileiro 1995–2005*.

Mews, Siegfied, ed. *A Bertolt Brecht Reference Companion*. Westport, Conn.: Greenwood, 1997.

Miller, Toby. *Cultural Citizenship: Cosmopolitanism, Consumerism, and Television in a Neoliberal Age*. Philadelphia: Temple University Press, 2007.

Möhrmann, Renate. "The Influence of Brecht on Women's Cinema in West Germany." In Kleber and Visser, *Re-interpreting Brecht*, 161–69.

Moisés, José Álvaro. "A New Policy for Brazilian Cinema." In Nagib, *New Brazilian Cinema*, 3–22.

Mota, Carlos Guilherme, ed. *Viagem incompleta: A experiência brasileira: 1500–2000*. São Paulo: SENAC, 2000.

Mulvey, Laura. "Feminism, Film, and the Avant-Garde." *Framework* 10 (Spring 1979): 3–10.

Munerato, Elice, and Maria Helena Darcy de Oliveira. "When Women Film." In Johnson and Stam, *Brazilian Cinema*, 340–50.

Nagib, Lúcia, ed. *The New Brazilian Cinema*. London: Tauris, 2003.

Napolitano, Marcos. *Cultura e Poder no Brasil Contemporâneo (1977–1984)*. Curitiba: Juruá, 2003.

Nayak, Anoop, and Mary Jane Kehily, eds. *Gender, Youth and Culture: Young Masculinities and Femininities*. New York: Palgrave Macmillan, 2008.

Noriega, Chon, ed. *Visible Nations: Latin American Film and Video*. Minneapolis: University of Minnesota Press, 2000.

Novaes, Aduato, ed. *Anos 70: Ainda sob a tempestade*. Rio de Janeiro: SENAC; Aeroplano, 2005.

Nowell-Smith, Geoffrey. *Luchino Visconti*. Garden City, N.Y.: Doubleday, 1968.

Oroz, Silvia. *Melodrama: O cinema de lágrimas da América Latina*. Rio de Janeiro: FUNARTE, 1999.

Ortiz, Renato. *Cultura Brasileira e identidade nacional*. São Paulo: Brasiliense, 1985.

Osis, Maria José Martins Duarte. "PAISM: Um marco na abordagem da saúde reprodutiva no Brasil." *Cadernos Saúde Pública* 14, no. 1 (1998): 25–32.

Pandolfi, Dulce Chaves, ed. *Cidadania, justiça e violência*. Rio de Janeiro: Fundação Getúlio Vargas, 1999.

Paoli, Maria Selia, and Vera da Siva Telles. "Social Rights: Conflicts and Negotiations in Contemporary Brazil." In Alvarez, Dagnino, and Escobar, *Cultures of Politics*, 64–92.

Passos, José Meirelles. "A imigração vista por olhos puxados: Uma cineasta nissei filma a saga dos que fizeram esta América." *Isto É*. April 2, 1980: 62.

Peixoto, Marta. "Rio's Favelas in Recent Fiction and Film: Commonplaces of Urban Segregation." *PMLA* 122, no. 1 (2007): 170–78.

Perlman, Janice. "Redemocratization Viewed from Below: Urban Poverty and Politics in Rio de Janeiro, 1968–2005." In Kingstone and Power, *Democratic Brazil Revisited*, 257–80.

———. *Favela: Four Decades of Living on the Edge in Rio de Janeiro*. New York: Oxford University Press, 2010.

Pessoa, Ana. *Carmen Santos: O cinema do anos 20*. Rio de Janeiro: Aeroplano, 2002.

Phillips, Anne, ed. *Feminism and Politics*. New York: Oxford University Press, 1998.

Pianca, Marina. "Brecht in Latin America: Theater Bearing Witness." In Mews, *Bertolt Brecht Reference Companion*, 356–78.

Pimentel, Silvia. *A mulher e a Constituinte: Uma contribuçã ao debate*. São Paulo: Cortez, EDUC, 1987.

Pinto, Célia Regina Jardim. *Uma história do feminismo no Brasil*. São Paulo: Fundação Perseu Abramo, 2003.

Plazaola, Luis Trelles. *Cine y mujer en América Latina: Directoras de largometrajes de ficción*. San Juan: Editorial de la Universidad de Puerto Rico, 1991.

Podalsky, Laura. "Fulfilling Fantasies, Diverting Pleasures: Ana Carolina and *Das Tripas Coração*," In Noriega, *Visible Nations*, 115–29.

———. "Out of Depth: The Politics of Disaffected Youth and Contemporary Latin American Cinema." In *Youth Culture in Global Cinema*, edited by Timothy Shary and Alexandra Seibel, 109–30. Austin: University of Texas Press, 2007.

Pool, Ithiel de Sola. *Technologies of Freedom*. Cambridge, Mass.: Belknap, 1983.

Power, Timothy J. "Centering Democracy? Ideological Cleavages and Convergence in the Brazilian Political Class." In Kingstone and Power, *Democratic Brazil Revisited*, 81–106.

Ramanathan, Geetha. *Feminist Auteurs: Reading Women's Films*. New York: Wallflower, 2006.

Ramos, José Mário Ortiz. *Cinema, estado e lutas culturais*. Rio de Janeiro: Paz e Terra, 1983.

Rêgo, Cacilda. "Brazilian Cinema: Its Fall, Rise, and Renewal (1990–2003)." *New Cinemas: Journal of Contemporary Film* 3, no. 2 (2005): 85–100.

———. "Mulheres da Retomada after the Retomada." Paper presented at the Mulheres da Retomada Conference at Tulane University, New Orleans, February 16–18, 2011.

Resinas, Joan Ramón, ed. *Disremembering the Dictatorship: The Politics of Memory in the Spanish Transition to Democracy*. Atlanta: Rodopi, 2000.

Richardson, Diane. "Heterosexuality and Social Theory." In *Theorising Heterosexuality: Telling it Straight*, edited by Diane Richardson, 1–20. Philadelphia: Open University Press, 1996.

———. "Extending Citizenship: Cultural Citizenship and Sexuality." In Stevenson, *Culture and Citizenship*, 153–66.

Richardson, Michael. *Surrealism and Cinema*. New York: BERG, 2006.

Roberts, Marion. "A Place for Citizenship? Women, Urban Design, and Neighbourhood Planning." In Buckingham and Lievesley, *In the Hands of Women*, 95–126.

Robin, Diana, and Ira Jaffe, eds. *Re-Directing the Gaze: Gender, Theory, and Cinema in the Third World*. Albany: State University of New York, 1999.

Rodrigues, João Carlos. *O Negro Brasileiro e o Cinema*. Rio de Janeiro: Pallas, 2001.

Roncagliolo, Rafael. "The Growth of the Audiovisual Imagescape in Latin America." In *Video the Changing World*, edited by Nancy Thede and Alain Ambrosi, 22–30. Cheektowaga, N.Y.: Black Rose, 1991.

Ros, Salvador Cardús i. "Politics and the Invention of Memory: For a Sociology of the Transition to Democracy in Spain." In *Disremembering the Dictatorship: The Politics of Memory in the Spanish Transition to Democracy*, edited by Joan Ramon Resina, 17–28. Atlanta: Rodopi, 2000.

Rubio, Pablo Pérez. *El cine melodramático*. Barcelona: Paidós, 2004.

Sadlier, Darlene J., ed. *Latin American Melodrama: Passion, Pathos, and Entertainment*. Urbana: University of Illinois Press, 2009.

———. "Nelson Pereira dos Santos's *Cinema de lágrimas*." In Sadlier, *Latin American Melodrama*, 96–109.

Santoro, Luiz Fernando. *A imagem nas mãos: O vídeo popular no Brasil*. São Paulo: Summus, 1989.

Santos, Hamilton dos. "Projeto cultural de Collor é moderno, diz Rouanet." *O Estado de São Paulo* 2 (March 15 1991): 18; quoted in Denise Costa Lopes, "O Cinema Pós-Collor," 42. M.A. thesis, Universidade Federal Fluminense, 2001.

Sarti, Cynthia. "The Panorama of Feminism in Brazil." *New Left Review* 173 (1989): 75–90.

Schelling, Vivian. "Ana Carolina Teixeira Soares: Audacity in the Cinema." *Index on Censorship* 14, no. 5 (1985): 58–60.

Schild, Susana. "Um gênero em transição." *Cinemais* 9 (1998): 123–28.

Schild, Verónica. "New Subjects of Rights? Women's Movements and the Construction of Citizenship in the 'New Democracies.'" In Alvarez, Dagnino, and Escobar, *Culture of Politics*, 93–117.

Scott, Jill. *Electra after Freud: Myth and Culture*. Ithaca, N.Y.: Cornell University Press, 2005.

Shaw, Deborah. "The Figure of the Absent Father in Recent Latin American Films." *Studies in Hispanic Cinemas* 1, no. 2 (2004): 85–101.

Silberman, Marc. "Brecht and Film." In Mews, *Bertolt Brecht Reference Companion*, 197–219.

Silva, Deonísio da. *Nos bastidores da censura: Sexualidade, literatura e repressão póós-64*. São Paulo: Estação Liberdade, 1989.

Silverman, Kaja. *The Acoustic Mirror: The Female Voice in Psychoanalysis and Cinema*. Bloomington: Indiana University Press, 1988.

Simis, Anita. *Estado e cinema no Brasil*. São Paulo: ANNABLUME, 1996.

Simões, Inimá. *Roteiro da intolerância: A censura cinematográfica no Brasil*. São Paulo: SENAC, 1999.

Simões, Solange de Deus. *Deus, patria e família: As mulheres no golpe de 1964*. Petrópolis: Vozes, 1985.

Skidmore, Thomas. *The Politics of Military Rule in Brazil, 1964–1985*. New York: Oxford University Press, 1988.

Sodré, Muniz. *O monopólio da fala*. Petrópolis: Vozes, 1981.

Somers, Margaret. "Citizenship and the Place of the Public Sphere: Law, Community, and Political Culture in the Transition to Democracy." *American Sociological Review* 58, no. 5 (1993): 587–620.

SOS-Corpo. *Atendimento médico*. Recife: SOS-Corpo, 1986.

———. *Prevenção do câncer do colo*. Recife: SOS-Corpo, 1986.

———. *Relatório de atividades do periódo de Janeiro á Outubro de 1983*. SOS-Corpo: Recife, 1983.

———. *Relatório de atividades do periódo de Janeiro á Junho de 1984*. SOS-Corpo: Recife, 1984.

———. *Relatório de atividades do periódo de Janeiro á Outubro de 1985*. SOS-Corpo: Recife, 1985.

———. *Relatório de atividades do periódo de Julho á Dezembro de 1986*. SOS-Corpo: Recife, 1987.

———. *Relatório de atividades do periódo de Julho á Dezembro de 1988*. SOS-Corpo: Recife, 1989.

———. *Relatório de atividades do periódo de Janeiro á Dezembro do 1991*. SOS-Corpo: Recife, 1992.

Spiteri, Raymond, and Donald LaCoss, eds. *Surrealism, Politics, and Culture*. Burlington, Vt.: Ashgate, 2003.

Stam, Robert. "On the Margins: Brazilian Avant-Garde Cinema." In Johnson and Stam, *Brazilian Cinema*, 306–27.

Stam, Robert, João Luiz Vieira, and Ismail Xavier, "The Shape of Brazilian Cinema in the Postmodern Age." In Johnson and Stam, *Brazilian Cinema*, 389–472.

Stam, Robert, and Ismail Xavier. "Recent Brazilian Cinema: Allegory/Metacinema/ Carnival." *Film Quarterly* 3, no. 4 (Spring 1988): 15–30.

Stevenson, Nick, ed. *Culture and Citizenship*. Thousand Oaks, Calif.: SAGE, 2001.

Suleiman, Susan Rubin. "Dialogue and Double Allegiance: Some Contemporary Women Artists and the Historical Avant-Garde." In Chadwick, *Mirror Images*, 125–54.

Süssekind, Flora. *Tal Brasil, qual romance? Uma ideologia e sua história: o naturalismo*. Rio de Janeiro: Achiamé, 1984.

———. *Literatura e vida literária: Polêmicas, diários & retratos*. Rio de Janeiro: Jorge Zahar, 1985.

Tendler, Sílvio. "Em defesa do miúra." M.A. thesis, Pontífica Universidad Católica, Rio de Janeiro, 1982.

Thompson, Paul. *The Voice of the Past*. New York: Oxford University Press, 2000.

Trindade, Eliane. *As meninas da esquina: Diários dos sonhos, dores e aventuras de seis adolescentes do Brasil*. Rio de Janeiro: Record, 2005.

UNESCO, *Many Voices, One World: Towards a New, More Just, and More Efficient World Information and Communication Order*. New York: Unipub, 1980.

Valdevellano, Paloma. "América Latina está construyendo su propria imagen." In Paloma Valdevellano, *El vídeo en la educación popular*. Lima, Peru: IPAL, 1989.

Vasconcellos, Cid. "Women as Civilizers in 1940s Brazilian Cinema: Between Passion and the Nation." In Sadlier, *Latin American Melodrama*, 64–76.

Ventura, Zuenir. "O Vazio Cultural." In Gaspari, Hollanda, and Ventura, *Cultura em trânsito*, 40–51.

———. "A Falta do Ar." In Gaspari, Hollanda, and Ventura, *Cultura em trânsito*, 52–85.

Veríssimo, Fernando. "Novos diretores: Uma geração em trânsito?" In *Cinema brasileiro Anos 90: 9 questões*, 41–42. Rio de Janeiro: Centro Cultural Banco do Brasil, 2001.

Verucci, Florisa. *A mulher e o direito*. São Paulo: Nobel, 1987.

Vieira, Evaldo. "Brasil: Do golpe de 1964 á redemocratização." In Mota, *Viagem incompleta*, 185–217.

White, Hayden. *Tropics of Discourse: Essays in Cultural Criticism*. Baltimore: Johns Hopkins University Press, 1978.

Williams, Linda. "Melodrama Revisited." In *Refiguring American Film Genres: History and Theory*, edited by Nick Browne, 42–82. Berkeley: University of California Press, 1998.

Wood, Robin. *Hollywood from Vietnam to Reagan*. New York: Columbia University Press, 1986.

Xavier, Ismail. *Allegories of Underdevelopment: Aesthetics and Politics in Modern Brazilian Cinema*. Minneapolis: University of Minnesota Press, 1995.

———. "The Humiliation of the Father: Melodrama and Cinema Novo's Critique of Conservative Modernization." In Sadlier, *Latin American Melodrama*. 77–95.

Yashar, Deborah. "Citizenship Regimes: The State and Ethnic Cleavages." In Deborah Yashar, *Contesting Citizenship in Latin America: The Rise of Indigenous Movements and the Postliberal Challenge*, 31–53. Cambridge: Cambridge University Press, 2005.

Young, Iris Marion. "Polity and Group Difference: A Critique of the Ideal of Universal Citizenship." In Phillips, *Feminism and Politics*, 401–29.

Yuval-Davis, Nira. "Women, Citizenship and Difference." *Feminist Review* 57 (1997): 4–27.

Index

LESLIE MARSH is an assistant professor
of Spanish at Georgia State University.

The University of Illinois Press
is a founding member of the
Association of American University Presses.

Composed in 10.5/13 Chaparral
with Scala Sans display
by Jim Proefrock
at the University of Illinois Press
Manufactured by Thomson-Shore, Inc.

University of Illinois Press
1325 South Oak Street
Champaign, IL 61820-6903
www.press.uillinois.edu